OpenGL Development Cookbook

Over 40 recipes to help you learn, understand, and implement modern OpenGL in your applications

Muhammad Mobeen Movania

PUBLISHING

BIRMINGHAM - MUMBAI

OpenGL Development Cookbook

First published: June 2013

Production Reference: 1180613

Published by Packt Publishing Ltd.
Livery Place
35 Livery Street
Birmingham B3 2PB, UK.

ISBN 978-1-84969-504-6

www.packtpub.com

Cover Image by Duraid Fatouhi (duraidfatouhi@yahoo.com)

Credits

Author

Muhammad Mobeen Movania

Reviewers

Bastien Berthe

Dimitrios Christopoulos

Oscar Ripolles Mateu

Acquisition Editor

Erol Staveley

Commisioning Editor

Shreerang Deshpande

Lead Technical Editor

Madhuja Chaudhari

Technical Editors

Jeeten Handu

Sharvari H. Baet

Ankita R. Meshram

Priyanka Kalekar

Project Coordinator

Rahul Dixit

Proofreaders

Stephen Silk

Lauren Tobon

Indexer

Tejal R. Soni

Graphics

Abhinash Sahu

Production Coordinator

Aparna Bhagat

Cover Work

Aparna Bhagat

About the Author

Muhammad Mobeen Movania received his PhD degree in Advance Computer Graphics and Visualization from Nanyang Technological Unviversity (NTU), Singapore. He completed his Bachelors of Science Honors (BCS(H)) in Computer Sciences from Iqra University, Karachi with majors in Computer Graphics and Multimedia. Before joining NTU, he was a junior graphics programmer at Data Communication and Control (DCC) Pvt. Ltd., Karachi, Pakistan. He was working on DirectX and OpenGL API for producing real-time interactive tactical simulators and dynamic integrated training simulators. His research interests include GPU-based volumetric rendering techniques, GPU technologies, real-time soft body physics, real-time dynamic shadows, real-time collision detection and response, and hierarchical geometric data structures. He authored a book chapter in a recent OpenGL book (OpenGL Insights: AK Peters/CRC Press). He is also the author of the OpenCloth project (`http://code.google.com/p/opencloth`), which implements various cloth simulation algorithms in OpenGL. His blog (`http://mmmovania.blogspot.com`) lists a lot of useful graphics tips and tricks. When not involved with computer graphics, he composes music and is an avid squash player. He is currently working at a research institute in Singapore.

I would like to thank my family: my parents (Mr. and Mrs. Abdul Aziz Movania), my wife (Tanveer Taji), my brothers and sisters (Mr. Muhammad Khalid Movania, Mrs. Azra Saleem, Mrs. Sajida Shakir, and Mr. Abdul Majid Movania), my nephews/nieces, and my new born baby daughter (Muntaha Movania).

About the Reviewers

Bastien Berthe is a young and passionate 3D programmer. Always attracted by 3D and video games, after a few years of studying in France, he went to the Sherbrooke University in Canada and received a postgraduate degree in Computer Science, specializing in real-time systems, 3D visualization, and video games development.

He is now working as a 3D Graphics Specialist Consultant at CAE (Montreal, QC) since 2012 and, more precisely, he is working on a new generation simulator's visualization system using mainly OpenSceneGraph and OpenGL.

CAE (`http://www.cae.com`) is a global leader in modeling, simulation, and training for civil aviation, defence, healthcare, and mining.

Dimitrios Christopoulos studied Computer Engineering and informatics at the University of Patras, Greece and holds a Master of Science (MSc) in Virtual Reality and Computer Graphics from the University of Hull in Great Britain. He started game programming in the '80s, and has been using OpenGL since 1997 for games, demos, European Union research projects, museum exhibits, and virtual reality productions. His research interests include virtual reality, human computer interaction, computer graphics, and games, with numerous publications in relevant conferences and journals. He coauthored the book *More OpenGL Game Programming, Cengage Learning PTR* and has also contributed to *OpenGL Game Programming*. He currently works as a virtual reality and 3D graphics software engineer producing games, educational applications, and cultural heritage productions for virtual reality installations.

Oscar Ripolles received his degree in Computer Engineering in 2004 and his Ph.D. in 2009 at the Universitat Jaume I in Castellon, Spain. He has also been a researcher at the Université de Limoges, France and at the Universidad Politecnica de Valencia, Spain. He is currently working in neuroimaging at Neuroelectrics in Barcelona, Spain. His research interests include multiresolution modeling, geometry optimization, hardware programming, and medical imaging.

www.PacktPub.com

Support files, eBooks, discount offers and more

You might want to visit www.PacktPub.com for support files and downloads related to your book.

Did you know that Packt offers eBook versions of every book published, with PDF and ePub files available? You can upgrade to the eBook version at www.PacktPub.com and as a print book customer, you are entitled to a discount on the eBook copy. Get in touch with us at service@packtpub.com for more details.

At www.PacktPub.com, you can also read a collection of free technical articles, sign up for a range of free newsletters and receive exclusive discounts and offers on Packt books and eBooks.

http://PacktLib.PacktPub.com

Do you need instant solutions to your IT questions? PacktLib is Packt's online digital book library. Here, you can access, read and search across Packt's entire library of books.

Why Subscribe?

- ▶ Fully searchable across every book published by Packt
- ▶ Copy and paste, print and bookmark content
- ▶ On demand and accessible via web browser

Free Access for Packt account holders

If you have an account with Packt at www.PacktPub.com, you can use this to access PacktLib today and view nine entirely free books. Simply use your login credentials for immediate access.

Table of Contents

Preface

This book is based on modern OpenGL v3.3 and above. It covers a myriad of topics of interest ranging from basic camera models and view frustum culling to advanced topics, such as dual quaternion skinning and GPU based simulation techniques. The book follows the cookbook format whereby a number of steps are detailed showing how to accomplish a specific task and are later dissected to show how the whole technique works.

The book starts with a gentle introduction to modern OpenGL. It then elaborates how to set up a basic shader application. Following this discussion, all shader stages are introduced using practical examples so that readers may understand how the different stages of the modern GPU pipeline work. Following the introductory chapter, a vector-based camera viewing model is presented with two camera types: target and free camera. In addition, we also detail how to carry out picking in modern OpenGL using depth buffer, color buffer, and scene intersection queries.

In simulation applications and games in particular, skybox is a very useful object. We will detail its implementation in a simple manner. For reflective objects, such as mirrors and dynamic reflections, render-to-texture functionality using FBO and dynamic cube mapping are detailed. In addition to graphics, image processing techniques are also presented to implement digital convolution filters using the fragment shader, and basic transformation, such as twirl is also detailed. Moreover, effects such as glow are also covered to enable rendering of glowing geometry.

Seldom do we find a graphics application without light. Lights play an important role in portraying the mood of a scene. We will cover point, directional, and spot lights with attenuation and both per-vertex and per-fragment approaches. In addition, shadow mapping techniques are also covered including support of percentage closer filtering (PCF) and variance shadow mapping.

In typical applications, more complex mesh models are used which are stored in external model files modeled in a 3D modeling package. We elaborate two techniques for loading such models by using separate and interleaved buffer objects. Concrete examples are given by parsing 3DS and OBJ model formats. These model loaders provide support for most attributes, including materials. Skeletal characters are introduced by a new skeletal animation format (the EZMesh format). We will see how to load such models with animation using both matrix palette skinning and dual quaternion skinning. Wherever possible, the recipes also detail pointers to external libraries and web addresses for more information. Fuzzy objects, such as smoke are often used to add special effects. Such objects are typically handled using a particle system. We introduce a stateless and a state-preserving particle system in detail.

When a scene with a high depth complexity is presented, normal alpha blending techniques fail miserably. Hence, approaches such as depth peeling are used to render the geometry in the correct depth order with correct blending. We will take a look at the implementation of both the conventional front-to-back depth peeling as well as the more recent dual depth peeling approach. All steps needed in the process are detailed.

With computer graphics, we are always pushing the limits of hardware to get a true life-like rendering. Lighting is one thing that can convincingly represent such a depiction. Unfortunately however, normal everyday lighting is impossible to simulate in real-time. The computer graphics community has developed various approximation methods for modeling of such lighting. These are grouped under global illumination techniques. The recipes elaborate two common approaches, spherical harmonics and screen space ambient occlusion, on the modern GPU. Finally, we present two additional methods for rendering scenes, namely, ray tracing and path tracing. Both of these methods have been detailed and implemented on the modern GPU.

Computer graphics have influenced several different fields ranging from visual effects in movies to biomedical and engineering simulations. In the latter domain in particular, computer graphics and visualization methods have been widely adopted. Modern GPUs have tremendous horsepower, which can be utilized for advanced visualization methods, and volume rendering is one of them. We will take a look at several algorithms for volume rendering, namely view-aligned 3D texture slicing, single-pass GPU ray casting, pseudo-isosurface rendering, splatting, polygonal isosurface extraction using the Marching Tetrahedra algorithm, and half-angle slicing method for volumetric lighting.

Physically-based simulations are an important class of algorithms that enable us to predict the motion of objects through approximations of the physical models. We harness the new transform feedback mechanism to carry out two physically-based simulations entirely on the GPU. We first present a model for cloth simulation (with collision detection and response) and then a model for particle system simulation on the modern GPU.

In summary, this book contains a wealth of information from a wide array of topics. I had a lot of fun writing this book and I learned a lot of techniques on the way. I do hope that this book serves as a useful resource for others in the years to come.

What this book covers

Chapter 1, Introduction to Modern OpenGL, details how to set up a modern OpenGL v3.3 core profile application on Visual Studio 2010 professional version.

Chapter 2, 3D Viewing and Object Picking, discusses how to implement a vector-based camera model for a viewing system. Two camera types are explained along with view frustum culling. Finally, object picking methods are also detailed.

Chapter 3, Offscreen Rendering and Environment Mapping, explains how to use the framebuffer object (FBO) for offscreen rendering. Mirror and dynamic cube mapping are implemented. In addition, image processing using digital convolution and environment mapping using static cube mapping are also elaborated.

Chapter 4, Lights and Shadows, discusses how to implement point, spot, and directional lights with attenuation. Moreover, methods of rendering dynamic shadows, such as shadow mapping, percentage close filtered (PCF) shadow maps, and variance shadow mapping are also covered in detail.

Chapter 5, Mesh Model Formats and Particle Systems, shows how to parse standard model formats, such as 3DS and OBJ models using separate and interleaved buffer object formats. Skeletal animation format using the EZMesh model format is also detailed along with the simple particle system.

Chapter 6, GPU-based Alpha Blending and Global Illumination, explains how to implement order-independent transparency with front-to-back and dual depth peeling. It also covers screen space ambient occlusion (SSAO) and the spherical harmonics method for image-based lighting and global illumination. Finally, alternate methods to render geometry, that is, GPU ray tracing and GPU path tracing are presented.

Chapter 7, GPU-based Volume Rendering Techniques, discusses how to implement several volume rendering algorithms in modern OpenGL including view-aligned 3D texture slicing, single-pass GPU ray casting, splatting, pseudo-isosurface as well as polygonal isosurface rendering using Marching Tetrahedra algorithm. Volume classification and volume lighting using the half-angle slicing technique are also detailed.

Chapter 8, Skeletal and Physically-based Simulation on the GPU, describes how to implement skeletal animation using matrix palette skinning and dual quaternion skinning on the modern GPU. In addition, it details how to use the transform feedback mode of the modern GPU for implementing a cloth simulation system with collision detection and response as well as particle systems entirely on the GPU.

What you need for this book

The book assumes that the reader has basic knowledge of using the OpenGL API. The example code distributed with this book contains Visual Studio 2010 Professional version project files. In order to build the source code, you will need freeglut, GLEW, GLM, and SOIL libraries. The code has been tested on a Windows 7 platform with an NVIDIA graphics card and the following versions of libraries:

- freeglut v2.8.0 (latest version available from: `http://freeglut.sourceforge.net`)
- GLEW v1.9.0 (latest version available from: `http://glew.sourceforge.net`)
- GLM v0.9.4.0 (latest version available from: `http://glm.g-truc.net`)
- SOIL (latest version available from: `http://www.lonesock.net/soil.html`)

We recommend using the latest version of these libraries. The code should compile and build fine with the latest libraries.

Who this book is for

This book is for intermediate graphics programmers who have working experience of any graphics API, but experience of OpenGL will be a definite plus. Introductory knowledge of GPU and graphics shaders will be an added advantage. The book and the accompanying code have been written with simplicity in mind. We have tried to keep it simple to understand. A wide array of topics are covered and step-by-step instructions are given on how to implement each technique. Detailed explanations are given that helps in comprehending the content of the book.

Conventions

In this book, you will find a number of styles of text that distinguish between different kinds of information. Here are some examples of these styles, and an explanation of their meaning.

Code words in text are shown as follows: "The maximum number of color attachments supported on any GPU can be queried using the `GL_MAX_COLOR_ATTACHMENTS` field."

A block of code is set as follows:

```
for(int i=0;i<16;i++) {
  float indexA = (random(vec4(gl_FragCoord.xyx, i))*0.25);
  float indexB = (random(vec4(gl_FragCoord.yxy, i))*0.25);
  sum += textureProj(shadowMap, vShadowCoords +
        vec4(indexA, indexB, 0, 0));
}
```

When we wish to draw your attention to a particular part of a code block, the relevant lines or items are set in bold:

```
void main()
{
  vEyeSpacePosition = (MV*vec4(vVertex,1)).xyz;
  vEyeSpaceNormal   = N*vNormal;
  vShadowCoords     = S*(M*vec4(vVertex,1));
  gl_Position       = MVP*vec4(vVertex,1);
}
```

New terms and **important words** are shown in bold. Words that you see on the screen, in menus or dialog boxes for example, appear in the text like this: "by going to the **Properties** menu item in the **Project** menu".

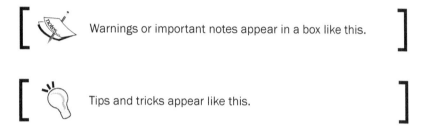

Warnings or important notes appear in a box like this.

Tips and tricks appear like this.

Reader feedback

Feedback from our readers is always welcome. Let us know what you think about this book—what you liked or may have disliked. Reader feedback is important for us to develop titles that you really get the most out of.

To send us general feedback, simply send an e-mail to feedback@packtpub.com, and mention the book title via the subject of your message.

If there is a topic that you have expertise in and you are interested in either writing or contributing to a book, see our author guide on www.packtpub.com/authors.

Customer support

Now that you are the proud owner of a Packt book, we have a number of things to help you to get the most from your purchase.

Downloading the example code

You can download the example code files for all Packt books you have purchased from your account at http://www.packtpub.com. If you purchased this book elsewhere, you can visit http://www.packtpub.com/support and register to have the files e-mailed directly to you.

Downloading the color images of this book

We also provide you a PDF file that has color images of the screenshots/diagrams used in this book. The color images will help you better understand the changes in the output. You can download this file from http://www.packtpub.com/sites/default/files/downloads/5046OT_ColoredImages.pdf.

Errata

Although we have taken every care to ensure the accuracy of our content, mistakes do happen. If you find a mistake in one of our books—maybe a mistake in the text or the code—we would be grateful if you would report this to us. By doing so, you can save other readers from frustration and help us improve subsequent versions of this book. If you find any errata, please report them by visiting http://www.packtpub.com/submit-errata, selecting your book, clicking on the **errata submission form** link, and entering the details of your errata. Once your errata are verified, your submission will be accepted and the errata will be uploaded on our website, or added to any list of existing errata, under the Errata section of that title. Any existing errata can be viewed by selecting your title from http://www.packtpub.com/support.

Piracy

Piracy of copyright material on the Internet is an ongoing problem across all media. At Packt, we take the protection of our copyright and licenses very seriously. If you come across any illegal copies of our works, in any form, on the Internet, please provide us with the location address or website name immediately so that we can pursue a remedy.

Please contact us at copyright@packtpub.com with a link to the suspected pirated material.

We appreciate your help in protecting our authors, and our ability to bring you valuable content.

Questions

You can contact us at questions@packtpub.com if you are having a problem with any aspect of the book, and we will do our best to address it.

1
Introduction to Modern OpenGL

In this chapter, we will cover:

- ▶ Setting up the OpenGL v3.3 core profile on Visual Studio 2010 using the GLEW and freeglut libraries
- ▶ Designing a GLSL shader class
- ▶ Rendering a simple colored triangle using shaders
- ▶ Doing a ripple mesh deformer using the vertex shader
- ▶ Dynamically subdividing a plane using the geometry shader
- ▶ Dynamically subdividing a plane using the geometry shader with instanced rendering
- ▶ Drawing a 2D image in a window using the fragment shader and SOIL image loading library

Introduction

The OpenGL API has seen various changes since its creation in 1992. With every new version, new features were added and additional functionality was exposed on supporting hardware through extensions. Until OpenGL v2.0 (which was introduced in 2004), the functionality in the graphics pipeline was fixed, that is, there were fixed set of operations hardwired in the graphics hardware and it was impossible to modify the graphics pipeline. With OpenGL v2.0, the shader objects were introduced for the first time. That enabled programmers to modify the graphics pipeline through special programs called shaders, which were written in a special language called OpenGL shading language (GLSL).

After OpenGL v2.0, the next major version was v3.0. This version introduced two profiles for working with OpenGL; the core profile and the compatibility profile. The core profile basically contains all of the non-deprecated functionality whereas the compatibility profile retains deprecated functionality for backwards compatibility. As of 2012, the latest version of OpenGL available is OpenGL v4.3. Beyond OpenGL v3.0, the changes introduced in the application code are not as drastic as compared to those required for moving from OpenGL v2.0 to OpenGL v3.0 and above.

In this chapter, we will introduce the three shader stages accessible in the OpenGL v3.3 core profile, that is, vertex, geometry, and fragment shaders. Note that OpenGL v4.0 introduced two additional shader stages that is tessellation control and tessellation evaluation shaders between the vertex and geometry shader.

Setting up the OpenGL v3.3 core profile on Visual Studio 2010 using the GLEW and freeglut libraries

We will start with a very basic example in which we will set up the modern OpenGL v3.3 core profile. This example will simply create a blank window and clear the window with red color.

OpenGL or any other graphics API for that matter requires a window to display graphics in. This is carried out through platform specific codes. Previously, the GLUT library was invented to provide windowing functionality in a platform independent manner. However, this library was not maintained with each new OpenGL release. Fortunately, another independent project, freeglut, followed in the GLUT footsteps by providing similar (and in some cases better) windowing support in a platform independent way. In addition, it also helps with the creation of the OpenGL core/compatibility profile contexts. The latest version of freeglut may be downloaded from `http://freeglut.sourceforge.net`. The version used in the source code accompanying this book is v2.8.0. After downloading the freeglut library, you will have to compile it to generate the libs/dlls.

The extension mechanism provided by OpenGL still exists. To aid with getting the appropriate function pointers, the GLEW library is used. The latest version can be downloaded from `http://glew.sourceforge.net`. The version of GLEW used in the source code accompanying this book is v1.9.0. If the source release is downloaded, you will have to build GLEW first to generate the libs and dlls on your platform. You may also download the pre-built binaries.

Prior to OpenGL v3.0, the OpenGL API provided support for matrices by providing specific matrix stacks such as the modelview, projection, and texture matrix stacks. In addition, transformation functions such as translate, rotate, and scale, as well as projection functions were also provided. Moreover, immediate mode rendering was supported, allowing application programmers to directly push the vertex information to the hardware.

In OpenGL v3.0 and above, all of these functionalities are removed from the core profile, whereas for backward compatibility they are retained in the compatibility profile. If we use the core profile (which is the recommended approach), it is our responsibility to implement all of these functionalities including all matrix handling and transformations. Fortunately, a library called `glm` exists that provides math related classes such as vectors and matrices. It also provides additional convenience functions and classes. For all of the demos in this book, we will use the `glm` library. Since this is a headers only library, there are no linker libraries for `glm`. The latest version of `glm` can be downloaded from `http://glm.g-truc.net`. The version used for the source code in this book is v0.9.4.0.

There are several image formats available. It is not a trivial task to write an image loader for such a large number of image formats. Fortunately, there are several image loading libraries that make image loading a trivial task. In addition, they provide support for both loading as well as saving of images into various formats. One such library is the `SOIL` image loading library. The latest version of `SOIL` can be downloaded from `http://www.lonesock.net/soil.html`.

Once we have downloaded the `SOIL` library, we extract the file to a location on the hard disk. Next, we set up the include and library paths in the Visual Studio environment. The include path on my development machine is `D:\Libraries\soil\Simple OpenGL Image Library\src` whereas, the library path is set to `D:\Libraries\soil\Simple OpenGL Image Library\lib\VC10_Debug`. Of course, the path for your system will be different than mine but these are the folders that the directories should point to.

These steps will help us to set up our development environment. For all of the recipes in this book, Visual Studio 2010 Professional version is used. Readers may also use the free express edition or any other version of Visual Studio (for example, Ultimate/Enterprise). Since there are a myriad of development environments, to make it easier for users on other platforms, we have provided premake script files as well.

The code for this recipe is in the `Chapter1/GettingStarted` directory.

Downloading the example code

You can download the example code files for all Packt books you have purchased from your account at `http://www.packtpub.com`. If you purchased this book elsewhere, you can visit `http://www.packtpub.com/support` and register to have the files e-mailed directly to you.

How to do it...

Let us setup the development environment using the following steps:

1. After downloading the required libraries, we set up the Visual Studio 2010 environment settings.

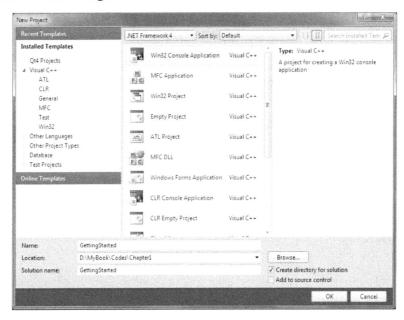

2. We first create a new **Win32 Console Application** project as shown in the preceding screenshot. We set up an empty Win32 project as shown in the following screenshot:

3. Next, we set up the include and library paths for the project by going into the **Project** menu and selecting project **Properties**. This opens a new dialog box. In the left pane, click on the **Configuration Properties** option and then on **VC++ Directories**.

4. In the right pane, in the **Include Directories** field, add the GLEW and freeglut subfolder paths.

5. Similarly, in the **Library Directories**, add the path to the lib subfolder of GLEW and freeglut libraries as shown in the following screenshot:

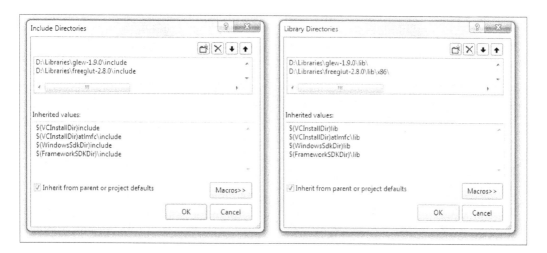

6. Next, we add a new `.cpp` file to the project and name it `main.cpp`. This is the main source file of our project. You may also browse through `Chapter1/ GettingStarted/GettingStarted/main.cpp` which does all this setup already.

7. Let us skim through the `Chapter1/ GettingStarted/GettingStarted/main. cpp` file piece by piece.

```
#include <GL/glew.h>
#include <GL/freeglut.h>
#include <iostream>
```

These lines are the include files that we will add to all of our projects. The first is the GLEW header, the second is the freeglut header, and the final include is the standard input/output header.

8. In Visual Studio, we can add the required linker libraries in two ways. The first way is through the Visual Studio environment (by going to the **Properties** menu item in the **Project** menu). This opens the project's property pages. In the configuration properties tree, we collapse the **Linker** subtree and click on the **Input** item. The first field in the right pane is `Additional Dependencies`. We can add the linker library in this field as shown in the following screenshot:

9. The second way is to add the `glew32.lib` file to the linker settings programmatically. This can be achieved by adding the following `pragma`:

```
#pragma comment(lib, "glew32.lib")
```

10. The next line is the using directive to enable access to the functions in the std namespace. This is not mandatory but we include this here so that we do not have to prefix `std::` to any standard library function from the iostream header file.

```
using namespace std;
```

11. The next lines define the width and height constants which will be the screen resolution for the window. After these declarations, there are five function definitions . The `OnInit()` function is used for initializing any OpenGL state or object, `OnShutdown()` is used to delete an OpenGL object, `OnResize()` is used to handle the resize event, `OnRender()` helps to handle the paint event, and `main()` is the entry point of the application. We start with the definition of the `main()` function.

```
const int WIDTH  = 1280;
const int HEIGHT = 960;
```

```
int main(int argc, char** argv) {
    glutInit(&argc, argv);
    glutInitDisplayMode(GLUT_DEPTH | GLUT_DOUBLE |
    GLUT_RGBA);
    glutInitContextVersion (3, 3);
    glutInitContextFlags (GLUT_CORE_PROFILE | GLUT_DEBUG);
    glutInitContextProfile(GLUT_FORWARD_COMPATIBLE);
    glutInitWindowSize(WIDTH, HEIGHT);
```

12. The first line `glutInit` initializes the GLUT environment. We pass the command line arguments to this function from our entry point. Next, we set up the display mode for our application. In this case, we request the GLUT framework to provide support for a depth buffer, double buffering (that is a front and a back buffer for smooth, flicker-free rendering), and the format of the frame buffer to be RGBA (that is with red, green, blue, and alpha channels). Next, we set the required OpenGL context version we desire by using the `glutInitContextVersion`. The first parameter is the major version of OpenGL and the second parameter is the minor version of OpenGL. For example, if we want to create an OpenGL v4.3 context, we will call `glutInitContextVersion (4, 3)`. Next, the context flags are specified:

    ```
    glutInitContextFlags (GLUT_CORE_PROFILE | GLUT_DEBUG);
    glutInitContextProfile(GLUT_FORWARD_COMPATIBLE);
    ```

> In OpenGL v4.3, we can register a callback when any OpenGL related error occurs. Passing `GLUT_DEBUG` to the `glutInitContextFlags` functions creates the OpenGL context in debug mode which is needed for the debug message callback.

13. For any version of OpenGL including OpenGL v3.3 and above, there are two profiles available: the core profile (which is a pure shader based profile without support for OpenGL fixed functionality) and the compatibility profile (which supports the OpenGL fixed functionality). All of the matrix stack functionality `glMatrixMode(*)`, `glTranslate*`, `glRotate*`, `glScale*`, and so on, and immediate mode calls such as `glVertex*`, `glTexCoord*`, and `glNormal*` of legacy OpenGL, are retained in the compatibility profile. However, they are removed from the core profile. In our case, we will request a forward compatible core profile which means that we will not have any fixed function OpenGL functionality available.

14. Next, we set the screen size and create the window:

    ```
    glutInitWindowSize(WIDTH, HEIGHT);
    glutCreateWindow("Getting started with OpenGL 3.3");
    ```

15. Next, we initialize the GLEW library. It is important to initialize the GLEW library after the OpenGL context has been created. If the function returns `GLEW_OK` the function succeeds, otherwise the GLEW initialization fails.

```
glewExperimental = GL_TRUE;
GLenum err = glewInit();
if (GLEW_OK != err){
    cerr<<"Error: "<<glewGetErrorString(err)<<endl;
} else {
    if (GLEW_VERSION_3_3)
    {
        cout<<"Driver supports OpenGL 3.3\nDetails:"<<endl;
    }
}
cout<<"\tUsing glew "<<glewGetString(GLEW_VERSION)<<endl;
cout<<"\tVendor: "<<glGetString (GL_VENDOR)<<endl;
cout<<"\tRenderer: "<<glGetString (GL_RENDERER)<<endl;
cout<<"\tVersion: "<<glGetString (GL_VERSION)<<endl;
cout<<"\tGLSL:
"<<glGetString(GL_SHADING_LANGUAGE_VERSION)<<endl;
```

The `glewExperimental` global switch allows the GLEW library to report an extension if it is supported by the hardware but is unsupported by the experimental or pre-release drivers. After the function is initialized, the GLEW diagnostic information such as the GLEW version, the graphics vendor, the OpenGL renderer, and the shader language version are printed to the standard output.

16. Finally, we call our initialization function `OnInit()` and then attach our uninitialization function `OnShutdown()` as the `glutCloseFunc` method—the close callback function which will be called when the window is about to close. Next, we attach our display and reshape function to their corresponding callbacks. The main function is terminated with a call to the `glutMainLoop()` function which starts the application's main loop.

```
    OnInit();
    glutCloseFunc(OnShutdown);
    glutDisplayFunc(OnRender);
    glutReshapeFunc(OnResize);
    glutMainLoop();
    return 0;
}
```

There's more...

The remaining functions are defined as follows:

```
void OnInit() {
    glClearColor(1,0,0,0);
```

```
        cout<<"Initialization successfull"<<endl;
}
void OnShutdown() {
        cout<<"Shutdown successfull"<<endl;
}
void OnResize(int nw, int nh) {
}
void OnRender() {
        glClear(GL_COLOR_BUFFER_BIT|GL_DEPTH_BUFFER_BIT);
        glutSwapBuffers();
}
```

For this simple example, we set the clear color to red (R:1, G:0, B:0, A:0). The first three are the red, green, and blue channels and the last is the alpha channel which is used in alpha blending. The only other function defined in this simple example is the `OnRender()` function, which is our display callback function that is called on the paint event. This function first clears the color and depth buffers to the clear color and clear depth values respectively.

 Similar to the color buffer, there is another buffer called the depth buffer. Its clear value can be set using the `glClearDepth` function. It is used for hardware based hidden surface removal. It simply stores the depth of the nearest fragment encountered so far. The incoming fragment's depth value overwrites the depth buffer value based on the depth clear function specified for the depth test using the `glDepthFunc` function. By default the depth value gets overwritten if the current fragment's depth is lower than the existing depth in the depth buffer.

The `glutSwapBuffers` function is then called to set the current back buffer as the current front buffer that is shown on screen. This call is required in a double buffered OpenGL application. Running the code gives us the output shown in the following screenshot.

Designing a GLSL shader class

We will now have a look at how to set up shaders. Shaders are special programs that are run on the GPU. There are different shaders for controlling different stages of the programmable graphics pipeline. In the modern GPU, these include the **vertex shader** (which is responsible for calculating the clip-space position of a vertex), the **tessellation control shader** (which is responsible for determining the amount of tessellation of a given patch), the **tessellation evaluation shader** (which computes the interpolated positions and other attributes on the tessellation result), the **geometry shader** (which processes primitives and can add additional primitives and vertices if needed), and the **fragment shader** (which converts a rasterized fragment into a colored pixel and a depth). The modern GPU pipeline highlighting the different shader stages is shown in the following figure.

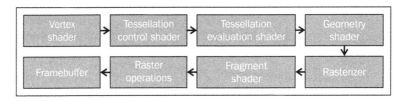

Note that the tessellation control/evaluation shaders are only available in the hardware supporting OpenGL v4.0 and above. Since the steps involved in shader handling as well as compiling and attaching shaders for use in OpenGL applications are similar, we wrap these steps in a simple class we call GLSLShader.

Getting ready

The GLSLShader class is defined in the GLSLShader.[h/cpp] files. We first declare the constructor and destructor which initialize the member variables. The next three functions, LoadFromString, LoadFromFile, and CreateAndLinkProgram handle the shader compilation, linking, and program creation. The next two functions, Use and UnUse functions bind and unbind the program. Two std::map datastructures are used. They store the attribute's/uniform's name as the key and its location as the value. This is done to remove the redundant call to get the attribute's/uniform's location each frame or when the location is required to access the attribute/uniform. The next two functions, AddAttribute and AddUniform add the locations of the attribute and uniforms into their respective std::map (_attributeList and _uniformLocationList).

```
class GLSLShader
{
public:
  GLSLShader(void);
  ~GLSLShader(void);
```

```
    void LoadFromString(GLenum whichShader, const string& source);
    void LoadFromFile(GLenum whichShader, const string& filename);
    void CreateAndLinkProgram();
    void Use();
    void UnUse();
    void AddAttribute(const string& attribute);
    void AddUniform(const string& uniform);
    GLuint operator[](const string& attribute);
    GLuint operator()(const string& uniform);
    void DeleteShaderProgram();

private:
    enum ShaderType{VERTEX_SHADER,FRAGMENT_SHADER,GEOMETRY_SHADER};
    GLuint  _program;
    int _totalShaders;
    GLuint _shaders[3];
    map<string,GLuint> _attributeList;
    map<string,GLuint> _uniformLocationList;
};
```

To make it convenient to access the attribute and uniform locations from their maps , we declare the two indexers. For attributes, we overload the square brackets ([]) whereas for uniforms, we overload the parenthesis operation (). Finally, we define a function `DeleteShaderProgram` for deletion of the shader program object. Following the function declarations are the member fields.

How to do it...

In a typical shader application, the usage of the `GLSLShader` object is as follows:

1. Create the `GLSLShader` object either on stack (for example, `GLSLShader shader;`) or on the heap (for example, `GLSLShader* shader=new GLSLShader();`)

2. Call `LoadFromFile` on the `GLSLShader` object reference

3. Call `CreateAndLinkProgram` on the `GLSLShader` object reference

4. Call `Use` on the `GLSLShader` object reference to bind the shader object

5. Call `AddAttribute/AddUniform` to store locations of all of the shader's attributes and uniforms respectively

6. Call `UnUse` on the `GLSLShader` object reference to unbind the shader object

Note that the above steps are required at initialization only. We can set the values of the uniforms that remain constant throughout the execution of the application in the `Use/UnUse` block given above.

At the rendering step, we access uniform(s), if we have uniforms that change each frame (for example, the modelview matrices). We first bind the shader by calling the `GLSLShader::Use` function. We then set the uniform by calling the `glUniform{*}` function, invoke the rendering by calling the `glDraw{*}` function, and then unbind the shader (`GLSLShader::UnUse`). Note that the `glDraw{*}` call passes the attributes to the GPU.

How it works...

In a typical OpenGL shader application, the shader specific functions and their sequence of execution are as follows:

```
glCreateShader
glShaderSource
glCompileShader
glGetShaderInfoLog
```

Execution of the above four functions creates a shader object. After the shader object is created, a shader program object is created using the following set of functions in the following sequence:

```
glCreateProgram
glAttachShader
glLinkProgram
glGetProgramInfoLog
```

> Note that after the shader program has been linked, we can safely delete the shader object.

There's more...

In the `GLSLShader` class, the first four steps are handled in the `LoadFromString` function and the later four steps are handled by the `CreateAndLinkProgram` member function. After the shader program object has been created, we can set the program for execution on the GPU. This process is called **shader binding**. This is carried out by the `glUseProgram` function which is called through the `Use/UnUse` functions in the `GLSLShader` class.

To enable communication between the application and the shader, there are two different kinds of fields available in the shader. The first are the attributes which may change during shader execution across different shader stages. All per-vertex attributes fall in this category. The second are the uniforms which remain constant throughout the shader execution. Typical examples include the modelview matrix and the texture samplers.

In order to communicate with the shader program, the application must obtain the location of an attribute/uniform after the shader program is bound. The location identifies the attribute/uniform. In the GLSLShader class, for convenience, we store the locations of attributes and uniforms in two separate std::map objects.

For accessing any attribute/uniform location, we provide an indexer in the GLSLShader class. In cases where there is an error in the compilation or linking stage, the shader log is printed to the console. Say for example, our GLSLshader object is called shader and our shader contains a uniform called MVP. We can first add it to the map of GLSLShader by calling shader.AddUniform("MVP"). This function adds the uniform's location to the map. Then when we want to access the uniform, we directly call shader("MVP") and it returns the location of our uniform.

Rendering a simple colored triangle using shaders

We will now put the GLSLShader class to use by implementing an application to render a simple colored triangle on screen.

Getting ready

For this recipe, we assume that the reader has created a new empty Win32 project with OpenGL 3.3 core profile as shown in the first recipe. The code for this recipe is in the Chapter1/SimpleTriangle directory.

In all of the code samples in this book, you will see a macro GL_CHECK_ERRORS dispersed throughout. This macro checks the current error bit for any error which might be raised by passing invalid arguments to an OpenGL function, or when there is some problem with the OpenGL state machine. For any such error, this macro traps it and generates a debug assertion signifying that the OpenGL state machine has some error. In normal cases, no assertion should be raised, so adding this macro helps to identify errors. Since this macro calls glGetError inside a debug assert, it is stripped in the release build.

Now we will look at the different transformation stages through which a vertex goes, before it is finally rendered on screen. Initially, the vertex position is specified in what is called the object space. This space is the one in which the vertex location is specified for an object. We apply modeling transformation to the object space vertex position by multiplying it with an affine matrix (for example, a matrix for scaling, rotating, translating, and so on). This brings the object space vertex position into world space. Next, the world space positions are multiplied by the camera/viewing matrix which brings the position into view/eye/camera space. OpenGL stores the modeling and viewing transformations in a single (modelview) matrix.

The view space positions are then projected by using a projection transformation which brings the position into clip space. The clip space positions are then normalized to get the normalized device coordinates which have a canonical viewing volume (coordinates are [-1,-1,0] to [1,1,1] in x, y, and z coordinates respectively). Finally, the viewport transformation is applied which brings the vertex into window/screen space.

How to do it...

Let us start this recipe using the following steps:

1. Define a vertex shader (`shaders/shader.vert`) to transform the object space vertex position to clip space.

    ```
    #version 330 core
    layout(location = 0) in vec3 vVertex;
    layout(location = 1) in vec3 vColor;
    smooth out vec4 vSmoothColor;
    uniform mat4 MVP;
    void main()
    {
        vSmoothColor = vec4(vColor,1);
        gl_Position = MVP*vec4(vVertex,1);
    }
    ```

2. Define a fragment shader (`shaders/shader.frag`) to output a smoothly interpolated color from the vertex shader to the frame buffer.

    ```
    #version 330 core
    smooth in vec4 vSmoothColor;
    layout(location=0) out vec4 vFragColor;
    void main()
    {
        vFragColor = vSmoothColor;
    }
    ```

3. Load the two shaders using the `GLSLShader` class in the `OnInit()` function.

    ```
    shader.LoadFromFile(GL_VERTEX_SHADER,
    "shaders/shader.vert");
    shader.LoadFromFile(GL_FRAGMENT_SHADER, "shaders/shader.frag
    ");
    shader.CreateAndLinkProgram();
    shader.Use();
        shader.AddAttribute("vVertex");
         shader.AddAttribute("vColor");
         shader.AddUniform("MVP");
    shader.UnUse();
    ```

4. Create the geometry and topology. We will store the attributes together in an interleaved vertex format, that is, we will store the vertex attributes in a struct containing two attributes, position and color.

```
vertices[0].color=glm::vec3(1,0,0);
vertices[1].color=glm::vec3(0,1,0);
vertices[2].color=glm::vec3(0,0,1);

vertices[0].position=glm::vec3(-1,-1,0);
vertices[1].position=glm::vec3(0,1,0);
vertices[2].position=glm::vec3(1,-1,0);

indices[0]  = 0;
indices[1]  = 1;
indices[2]  = 2;
```

5. Store the geometry and topology in the buffer object(s). The stride parameter controls the number of bytes to jump to reach the next element of the same attribute. For the interleaved format, it is typically the size of our vertex struct in bytes, that is, `sizeof(Vertex)`.

```
glGenVertexArrays(1, &vaoID);
glGenBuffers(1, &vboVerticesID);
glGenBuffers(1, &vboIndicesID);
glBindVertexArray(vaoID);
glBindBuffer (GL_ARRAY_BUFFER, vboVerticesID);
glBufferData (GL_ARRAY_BUFFER, sizeof(vertices),
&vertices[0],                  GL_STATIC_DRAW);
glEnableVertexAttribArray(shader["vVertex"]);
glVertexAttribPointer(shader["vVertex"], 3, GL_FLOAT,
GL_FALSE,stride,0);
glEnableVertexAttribArray(shader["vColor"]);
glVertexAttribPointer(shader["vColor"], 3, GL_FLOAT,
GL_FALSE,stride, (const GLvoid*)offsetof(Vertex, color));

glBindBuffer(GL_ELEMENT_ARRAY_BUFFER, vboIndicesID);
glBufferData(GL_ELEMENT_ARRAY_BUFFER, sizeof(indices),
&indices[0], GL_STATIC_DRAW);
```

6. Set up the resize handler to set up the viewport and projection matrix.

```
void OnResize(int w, int h) {
    glViewport (0, 0, (GLsizei) w, (GLsizei) h);
    P = glm::ortho(-1,1,-1,1);
}
```

7. Set up the rendering code to bind the `GLSLShader` shader, pass the uniforms, and then draw the geometry.

```
void OnRender() {
    glClear(GL_COLOR_BUFFER_BIT|GL_DEPTH_BUFFER_BIT);
    shader.Use();
    glUniformMatrix4fv(shader("MVP"), 1, GL_FALSE,
    glm::value_ptr(P*MV));
    glDrawElements(GL_TRIANGLES, 3, GL_UNSIGNED_SHORT,
    0);
    shader.UnUse();
    glutSwapBuffers();
}
```

8. Delete the shader and other OpenGL objects.

```
void OnShutdown() {
    shader.DeleteShaderProgram();
    glDeleteBuffers(1, &vboVerticesID);
    glDeleteBuffers(1, &vboIndicesID);
    glDeleteVertexArrays(1, &vaoID);
}
```

How it works...

For this simple example, we will only use a vertex shader (`shaders/shader.vert`) and a fragment shader (`shaders/shader.frag`). The first line in the shader signifies the GLSL version of the shader. Starting from OpenGL v3.0, the version specifiers correspond to the OpenGL version used. So for OpenGL v3.3, the GLSL version is 330. In addition, since we are interested in the core profile, we add another keyword following the version number to signify that we have a core profile shader.

Another important thing to note is the layout qualifier. This is used to bind a specific integral attribute index to a given per-vertex attribute. While we can give the attribute locations in any order, for all of the recipes in this book the attribute locations are specified starting from 0 for position, 1 for normals, 2 for texture coordinates, and so on. The layout location qualifier makes the `glBindAttribLocation` call redundant as the location index specified in the shader overrides any `glBindAttribLocation` call.

The vertex shader simply outputs the input per-vertex color to the output (vSmoothColor). Such attributes that are interpolated across shader stages are called **varying attributes**. It also calculates the clip space position by multiplying the per-vertex position (vVertex) with the combined modelview projection (MVP) matrix.

```
vSmoothColor = vec4(vColor,1);
gl_Position = MVP*vec4(vVertex,1);
```

By prefixing `smooth` to the output attribute, we tell the GLSL shader to do smooth perspective-correct interpolation for the attribute to the next stage of the pipeline. The other qualifiers usable are `flat` and `noperspective`. When no qualifier is specified the default interpolation qualifier is `smooth`.

The fragment shader writes the input color (vSmoothColor) to the frame buffer output (vFragColor).

```
vFragColor = vSmoothColor;
```

There's more...

In the simple triangle demo application code, we store the GLSLShader object reference in the global scope so that we can access it in any function we desire. We modify the OnInit() function by adding the following lines:

```
shader.LoadFromFile(GL_VERTEX_SHADER, "shaders/shader.vert");
shader.LoadFromFile(GL_FRAGMENT_SHADER,"shaders/shader.frag");
shader.CreateAndLinkProgram();
shader.Use();
    shader.AddAttribute("vVertex");
    shader.AddAttribute("vColor");
    shader.AddUniform("MVP");
shader.UnUse();
```

The first two lines create the GLSL shader of the given type by reading the contents of the file with the given filename. In all of the recipes in this book, the vertex shader files are stored with a .vert extension, the geometry shader files with a .geom extension, and the fragment shader files with a .frag extension. Next, the GLSLShader::CreateAndLinkProgram function is called to create the shader program from the shader object. Next, the program is bound and then the locations of attributes and uniforms are stored.

We pass two attributes per-vertex, that is vertex position and vertex color. In order to facilitate the data transfer to the GPU, we create a simple Vertex struct as follows:

```
struct Vertex {
    glm::vec3 position;
    glm::vec3 color;
};
Vertex vertices[3];
GLushort indices[3];
```

Next, we create an array of three vertices in the global scope. In addition, we store the triangle's vertex indices in the indices global array. Later we initialize these two arrays in the OnInit() function. The first vertex is assigned the red color, the second vertex is assigned the green color, and the third vertex is assigned the blue color.

```
vertices[0].color=glm::vec3(1,0,0);
vertices[1].color=glm::vec3(0,1,0);
vertices[2].color=glm::vec3(0,0,1);

vertices[0].position=glm::vec3(-1,-1,0);
vertices[1].position=glm::vec3(0,1,0);
vertices[2].position=glm::vec3(1,-1,0);

indices[0] = 0;
indices[1] = 1;
indices[2] = 2;
```

Next, the vertex positions are given. The first vertex is assigned an object space position of (-1,-1, 0), the second vertex is assigned (0,1,0), and the third vertex is assigned (1,-1,0). For this simple demo, we use an orthographic projection for a view volume of (-1,1,-1,1). Finally, the three indices are given in a linear order.

In OpenGL v3.3 and above, we typically store the geometry information in buffer objects, which is a linear array of memory managed by the GPU. In order to facilitate the handling of buffer object(s) during rendering, we use a **vertex array object** (**VAO**). This object stores references to buffer objects that are bound after the VAO is bound. The advantage we get from using a VAO is that after the VAO is bound, we do not have to bind the buffer object(s).

In this demo, we declare three variables in global scope; vaoID for VAO handling, and vboVerticesID and vboIndicesID for buffer object handling. The VAO object is created by calling the glGenVertexArrays function. The buffer objects are generated using the glGenBuffers function. The first parameter for both of these functions is the total number of objects required, and the second parameter is the reference to where the object handle is stored. These functions are called in the OnInit() function.

```
glGenVertexArrays(1, &vaoID);
glGenBuffers(1, &vboVerticesID);
glGenBuffers(1, &vboIndicesID);
glBindVertexArray(vaoID);
```

After the VAO object is generated, we bind it to the current OpenGL context so that all successive calls affect the attached VAO object. After the VAO binding, we bind the buffer object storing vertices (vboVerticesID) using the glBindBuffer function to the GL_ARRAY_BUFFER binding. Next, we pass the data to the buffer object by using the glBufferData function. This function also needs the binding point, which is again GL_ARRAY_BUFFER. The second parameter is the size of the vertex array we will push to the GPU memory. The third parameter is the pointer to the start of the CPU memory. We pass the address of the vertices global array. The last parameter is the usage hint which tells the GPU that we are not going to modify the data often.

```
glBindBuffer (GL_ARRAY_BUFFER, vboVerticesID);
glBufferData (GL_ARRAY_BUFFER, sizeof(vertices), &vertices[0],
GL_STATIC_DRAW);
```

The usage hints have two parts; the first part tells how frequently the data in the buffer object is modified. These can be STATIC (modified once only), DYNAMIC (modified occasionally), or STREAM (modified at every use). The second part is the way this data will be used. The possible values are DRAW (the data will be written but not read), READ (the data will be read only), and COPY (the data will be neither read nor written). Based on the two hints a qualifier is generated. For example, GL_STATIC_DRAW if the data will never be modified and GL_DYNAMIC_DRAW if the data will be modified occasionally. These hints allow the GPU and the driver to optimize the read/write access to this memory.

In the next few calls, we enable the vertex attributes. This function needs the location of the attribute, which we obtain by the GLSLShader::operator[], passing it the name of the attribute whose location we require. We then call glVertexAttributePointer to tell the GPU how many elements there are and what is their type, whether the attribute is normalized, the stride (which means the total number of bytes to skip to reach the next element; for our case since the attributes are stored in a Vertex struct, the next element's stride is the size of our Vertex struct), and finally, the pointer to the attribute in the given array. The last parameter requires explanation in case we have interleaved attributes (as we have). The offsetof operator returns the offset in bytes, to the attribute in the given struct. Hence, the GPU knows how many bytes it needs to skip in order to access the next attribute of the given type. For the vVertex attribute, the last parameter is 0 since the next element is accessed immediately after the stride. For the second attribute vColor, it needs to hop 12 bytes before the next vColor attribute is obtained from the given vertices array.

```
glEnableVertexAttribArray(shader["vVertex"]);
glVertexAttribPointer(shader["vVertex"], 3, GL_FLOAT,
GL_FALSE,stride,0);
glEnableVertexAttribArray(shader["vColor"]);
glVertexAttribPointer(shader["vColor"], 3, GL_FLOAT,
GL_FALSE,stride, (const GLvoid*)offsetof(Vertex, color));
```

The indices are pushed similarly using `glBindBuffer` and `glBufferData` but to a different binding point, that is, `GL_ELEMENT_ARRAY_BUFFER`. Apart from this change, the rest of the parameters are exactly the same as for the vertices data. The only difference being the buffer object, which for this case is `vboIndicesID`. In addition, the passed array to the `glBufferData` function is the indices array.

```
glBindBuffer(GL_ELEMENT_ARRAY_BUFFER, vboIndicesID);
glBufferData(GL_ELEMENT_ARRAY_BUFFER, sizeof(indices),
&indices[0], GL_STATIC_DRAW);
```

To complement the object generation in the `OnInit()` function, we must provide the object deletion code. This is handled in the `OnShutdown()` function. We first delete the shader program by calling the `GLSLShader::DeleteShaderProgram` function. Next, we delete the two buffer objects (`vboVerticesID` and `vboIndicesID`) and finally we delete the vertex array object (`vaoID`).

```
void OnShutdown() {
    shader.DeleteShaderProgram();
    glDeleteBuffers(1, &vboVerticesID);
    glDeleteBuffers(1, &vboIndicesID);
    glDeleteVertexArrays(1, &vaoID);
}
```

 We do a deletion of the shader program because our `GLSLShader` object is allocated globally and the destructor of this object will be called after the main function exits. Therefore, if we do not delete the object in this function, the shader program will not be deleted and we will have a graphics memory leak.

The rendering code of the simple triangle demo is as follows:

```
void OnRender() {
    glClear(GL_COLOR_BUFFER_BIT|GL_DEPTH_BUFFER_BIT);
    shader.Use();
      glUniformMatrix4fv(shader("MVP"), 1, GL_FALSE,
      glm::value_ptr(P*MV));
      glDrawElements(GL_TRIANGLES, 3, GL_UNSIGNED_SHORT, 0);
    shader.UnUse();
    glutSwapBuffers();
}
```

The rendering code first clears the color and depth buffer and binds the shader program by calling the GLSLShader::Use() function. It then passes the combined modelview and projection matrix to the GPU by invoking the glUniformMatrix4fv function. The first parameter is the location of the uniform which we obtain from the GLSLShader::operator() function, by passing it the name of the uniform whose location we need. The second parameter is the total number of matrices we wish to pass. The third parameter is a Boolean signifying if the matrix needs to be transposed, and the final parameter is the float pointer to the matrix object. Here we use the glm::value_ptr function to get the float pointer from the matrix object. Note that the OpenGL matrices are concatenated right to left since it follows a right handed coordinate system in a column major layout. Hence we keep the projection matrix on the left and the modelview matrix on the right. For this simple example, the modelview matrix (MV) is set as the identity matrix.

After this function, the glDrawElements call is made. Since we have left our VAO object (vaoID) bound, we pass 0 to the final parameter of this function. This tells the GPU to use the references of the GL_ELEMENT_ARRAY_BUFFER and GL_ARRAY_BUFFER binding points of the bound VAO. Thus we do not need to explicitly bind the vboVerticesID and vboIndicesID buffer objects again. After this call, we unbind the shader program by calling the GLSLShader::UnUse() function. Finally, we call the glutSwapBuffer function to show the back buffer on screen. After compiling and running, we get the output as shown in the following figure:

See also

Learn modern 3D graphics programming by Jason L. McKesson at http://www.arcsynthesis.org/gltut/Basics/Basics.html.

Doing a ripple mesh deformer using the vertex shader

In this recipe, we will deform a planar mesh using the vertex shader. We know that the vertex shader is responsible for outputting the clip space position of the given object space vertex. In between this conversion, we can apply the modeling transformation to transform the given object space vertex to **world space position**.

Getting ready

For this recipe, we assume that the reader knows how to set up a simple triangle on screen using a vertex and fragment shader as detailed in the previous recipe. The code for this recipe is in the `Chapter1\RippleDeformer` directory.

How to do it...

We can implement a ripple shader using the following steps:

1. Define the vertex shader that deforms the object space vertex position.

    ```
    #version 330 core
    layout(location=0) in vec3 vVertex;
    uniform mat4 MVP;
    uniform float time;
    const float amplitude = 0.125;
    const float frequency = 4;
    const float PI = 3.14159;
    void main()
    {
      float distance = length(vVertex);
      float y = amplitude*sin(-PI*distance*frequency+time);
      gl_Position = MVP*vec4(vVertex.x, y, vVertex.z,1);
    }
    ```

2. Define a fragment shader that simply outputs a constant color.

    ```
    #version 330 core
    layout(location=0) out vec4 vFragColor;
    void main()
    {
      vFragColor = vec4(1,1,1,1);
    }
    ```

Chapter 1

3. Load the two shaders using the GLSLShader class in the OnInit() function.

```
shader.LoadFromFile(GL_VERTEX_SHADER, "shaders/shader.vert");
shader.LoadFromFile(GL_FRAGMENT_SHADER, "shaders/shader.frag");
shader.CreateAndLinkProgram();
shader.Use();
   shader.AddAttribute("vVertex");
   shader.AddUniform("MVP");
   shader.AddUniform("time");
shader.UnUse();
```

4. Create the geometry and topology.

```
int count = 0;
int i=0, j=0;
for( j=0;j<=NUM_Z;j++) {
   for( i=0;i<=NUM_X;i++) {
      vertices[count++] = glm::vec3(
      ((float(i)/(NUM_X-1)) *2-1)* HALF_SIZE_X, 0,
      ((float(j)/(NUM_Z-1))*2-1)*HALF_SIZE_Z);
   }
}
GLushort* id=&indices[0];
for (i = 0; i < NUM_Z; i++) {
   for (j = 0; j < NUM_X; j++) {
      int i0 = i * (NUM_X+1) + j;
      int i1 = i0 + 1;
      int i2 = i0 + (NUM_X+1);
      int i3 = i2 + 1;
      if ((j+i)%2) {
         *id++ = i0; *id++ = i2; *id++ = i1;
         *id++ = i1; *id++ = i2; *id++ = i3;
      } else {
         *id++ = i0; *id++ = i2; *id++ = i3;
         *id++ = i0; *id++ = i3; *id++ = i1;
      }
   }
}
```

5. Store the geometry and topology in the buffer object(s).

```
glGenVertexArrays(1, &vaoID);
glGenBuffers(1, &vboVerticesID);
glGenBuffers(1, &vboIndicesID);
glBindVertexArray(vaoID);
glBindBuffer (GL_ARRAY_BUFFER, vboVerticesID);
```

29

```
glBufferData (GL_ARRAY_BUFFER, sizeof(vertices),
&vertices[0], GL_STATIC_DRAW);
glEnableVertexAttribArray(shader["vVertex"]);
glVertexAttribPointer(shader["vVertex"], 3, GL_FLOAT,
GL_FALSE,0,0);
glBindBuffer(GL_ELEMENT_ARRAY_BUFFER, vboIndicesID);
glBufferData(GL_ELEMENT_ARRAY_BUFFER, sizeof(indices),
&indices[0], GL_STATIC_DRAW);
```

6. Set up the perspective projection matrix in the resize handler.

```
P = glm::perspective(45.0f, (GLfloat)w/h, 1.f, 1000.f);
```

7. Set up the rendering code to bind the `GLSLShader` shader, pass the uniforms and then draw the geometry.

```
void OnRender() {
  time = glutGet(GLUT_ELAPSED_TIME)/1000.0f * SPEED;
  glm::mat4 T=glm::translate(glm::mat4(1.0f),
  glm::vec3(0.0f, 0.0f, dist));
  glm::mat4 Rx= glm::rotate(T,  rX, glm::vec3(1.0f, 0.0f,
  0.0f));
  glm::mat4 MV= glm::rotate(Rx, rY, glm::vec3(0.0f, 1.0f,
  0.0f));
  glm::mat4 MVP= P*MV;
  shader.Use();
    glUniformMatrix4fv(shader("MVP"), 1, GL_FALSE,
    glm::value_ptr(MVP));
    glUniform1f(shader("time"), time);
    glDrawElements(GL_TRIANGLES,TOTAL_INDICES,
    GL_UNSIGNED_SHORT,0);
  shader.UnUse();
  glutSwapBuffers();
}
```

8. Delete the shader and other OpenGL objects.

```
void OnShutdown() {
  shader.DeleteShaderProgram();
  glDeleteBuffers(1, &vboVerticesID);
  glDeleteBuffers(1, &vboIndicesID);
  glDeleteVertexArrays(1, &vaoID);
}
```

How it works...

In this recipe, the only attribute passed in is the per-vertex position (vVertex). There are two uniforms: the combined modelview projection matrix (MVP) and the current time (time). We will use the time uniform to allow progression of the deformer so we can observe the ripple movement. After these declarations are three constants, namely amplitude (which controls how much the ripple moves up and down from the zero base line), frequency (which controls the total number of waves), and PI (a constant used in the wave formula). Note that we could have replaced the constants with uniforms and had them modified from the application code.

Now the real work is carried out in the main function. We first find the distance of the given vertex from the origin. Here we use the length built-in GLSL function. We then create a simple sinusoid. We know that a general sine wave can be given using the following function:

$$y = A.\sin(2\pi ft + \varphi)$$

Here, A is the wave amplitude, f is the frequency, t is the time, and φ is the phase. In order to get our ripple to start from the origin, we modify the function to the following:

$$d(x,y,z) = \sqrt{x^2 + y^2 + z^2}$$
$$F(x,y,x) = A.\sin(-\pi f d(x,y,z) + \varphi)$$

In our formula, we first find the distance (d) of the vertex from the origin by using the Euclidean distance formula. This is given to us by the length built-in GLSL function. Next, we input the distance into the sin function multiplying the distance by the frequency (f) and (π). In our vertex shader, we replace the phase (φ) with time.

```
#version 330 core
layout(location=0) in vec3 vVertex;
uniform mat4 MVP;
uniform float time;
const float amplitude = 0.125;
const float frequency = 4;
const float PI = 3.14159;
void main()
{
  float distance = length(vVertex);
  float y = amplitude*sin(-PI*distance*frequency+time);
  gl_Position = MVP*vec4(vVertex.x, y, vVertex.z,1);
}
```

After calculating the new y value, we multiply the new vertex position with the combined modelview projection matrix (MVP). The fragment shader simply outputs a constant color (in this case white color, vec4(1,1,1,1)).

```
#version 330 core
layout(location=0) out vec4 vFragColor;
void main()
{
    vFragColor = vec4(1,1,1,1);
}
```

There's more

Similar to the previous recipe, we declare the GLSLShader object in the global scope to allow maximum visibility. Next, we initialize the GLSLShader object in the OnInit() function.

```
shader.LoadFromFile(GL_VERTEX_SHADER, "shaders/shader.vert");
shader.LoadFromFile(GL_FRAGMENT_SHADER,"shaders/shader.frag");
shader.CreateAndLinkProgram();
shader.Use();
  shader.AddAttribute("vVertex");
  shader.AddUniform("MVP");
  shader.AddUniform("time");
shader.UnUse();
```

The only difference in this recipe is the addition of an additional uniform (time).

We generate a simple 3D planar grid in the XZ plane. The geometry is stored in the vertices global array. The total number of vertices on the X axis is stored in a global constant NUM_X, whereas the total number of vertices on the Z axis is stored in another global constant NUM_Z. The size of the planar grid in world space is stored in two global constants, SIZE_X and SIZE_Z, and half of these values are stored in the HALF_SIZE_X and HALF_SIZE_Z global constants. Using these constants, we can change the mesh resolution and world space size.

The loop simply iterates (NUM_X+1) * (NUM_Z+1) times and remaps the current vertex index first into the 0 to 1 range and then into the -1 to 1 range, and finally multiplies it by the HALF_SIZE_X and HALF_SIZE_Z constants to get the range from –HALF_SIZE_X to HALF_SIZE_X and –HALF_SIZE_Z to HALF_SIZE_Z.

The topology of the mesh is stored in the indices global array. While there are several ways to generate the mesh topology, we will look at two common ways. The first method keeps the same triangulation for all of the mesh quads as shown in the following screenshot:

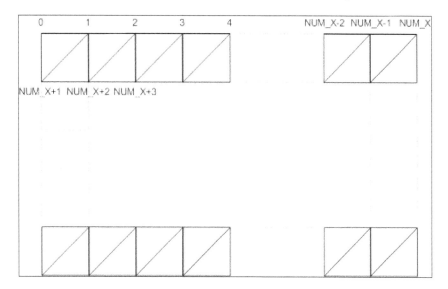

This sort of topology can be generated using the following code:

```
GLushort* id=&indices[0];
for (i = 0; i < NUM_Z; i++) {
  for (j = 0; j < NUM_X; j++) {
    int i0 = i * (NUM_X+1) + j;
    int i1 = i0 + 1;
    int i2 = i0 + (NUM_X+1);
    int i3 = i2 + 1;
    *id++ = i0; *id++ = i2; *id++ = i1;
    *id++ = i1; *id++ = i2; *id++ = i3;
  }
}
```

The second method alternates the triangulation at even and odd iterations resulting in a better looking mesh as shown in the following screenshot:

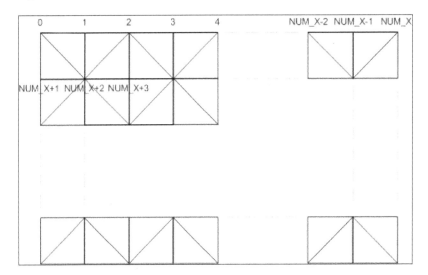

In order to alternate the triangle directions and maintain their winding order, we take two different combinations, one for an even iteration and second for an odd iteration. This can be achieved using the following code:

```
GLushort* id=&indices[0];
for (i = 0; i < NUM_Z; i++) {
   for (j = 0; j < NUM_X; j++) {
      int i0 = i * (NUM_X+1) + j;
      int i1 = i0 + 1;
      int i2 = i0 + (NUM_X+1);
      int i3 = i2 + 1;
      if ((j+i)%2) {
         *id++ = i0; *id++ = i2; *id++ = i1;
         *id++ = i1; *id++ = i2; *id++ = i3;
      } else {
         *id++ = i0; *id++ = i2; *id++ = i3;
         *id++ = i0; *id++ = i3; *id++ = i1;
      }
   }
 }
}
```

After filling the vertices and indices arrays, we push this data to the GPU memory. We first create a vertex array object (vaoID) and two buffer objects, the GL_ARRAY_BUFFER binding for vertices and the GL_ELEMENT_ARRAY_BUFFER binding for the indices array. These calls are exactly the same as in the previous recipe. The only difference is that now we only have a single per-vertex attribute, that is, the vertex position (vVertex). The OnShutdown() function is also unchanged as in the previous recipe.

The rendering code is slightly changed. We first get the current elapsed time from freeglut so that we can move the ripple deformer in time. Next, we clear the color and depth buffers. After this, we set up the modelview matrix. This is carried out by using the matrix transformation functions provided by the glm library.

```
glm::mat4 T=glm::translate(glm::mat4(1.0f),
glm::vec3(0.0f, 0.0f, dist));
glm::mat4 Rx= glm::rotate(T,  rX, glm::vec3(1.0f, 0.0f, 0.0f));
glm::mat4 MV= glm::rotate(Rx, rY, glm::vec3(0.0f, 1.0f,  0.0f));
glm::mat4 MVP= P*MV;
```

Note that the matrix multiplication in glm follows from right to left. So the order in which we generate the transformations will be applied in the reverse order. In our case the combined modelview matrix will be calculated as MV = (T*(Rx*Ry)). The translation amount, dist, and the rotation values, rX and rY, are calculated in the mouse input functions based on the user's input.

After calculating the modelview matrix, the combined modelview projection matrix (MVP) is calculated. The projection matrix (P) is calculated in the OnResize() handler. In this case, the perspective projection matrix is used with four parameters, the vertical fov, the aspect ratio, and the near and far clip plane distances. The GLSLShader object is bound and then the two uniforms, MVP and time are passed to the shader program. The attributes are then transferred using the glDrawElements call as we saw in the previous recipe. The GLSLShader object is then unbound and finally, the back buffer is swapped.

In the ripple deformer main function, we attach two new callbacks; glutMouseFunc handled by the OnMouseDown function and glutMotionFunc handled by the OnMouseMove function. These functions are defined as follows:

```
void OnMouseDown(int button, int s, int x, int y) {
  if (s == GLUT_DOWN)  {
    oldX = x;
    oldY = y;
  }
  if(button == GLUT_MIDDLE_BUTTON)
  state = 0;
  else
  state = 1;
}
```

This function is called whenever the mouse is clicked in our application window. The first parameter is for the button which was pressed (GLUT_LEFT_BUTTON for the left mouse button, GLUT_MIDDLE_BUTTON for the middle mouse button, and GLUT_RIGHT_BUTTON for the right mouse button). The second parameter is the state which can be either GLUT_DOWN or GLUT_UP. The last two parameters are the x and y screen location of the mouse click. In this simple example, we store the mouse click location and then set a state variable when the middle mouse button is pressed.

The OnMouseMove function is defined as follows:

```
void OnMouseMove(int x, int y) {
  if (state == 0)
    dist *= (1 + (y - oldY)/60.0f);
  else {
    rY += (x - oldX)/5.0f;
    rX += (y - oldY)/5.0f;
  }
  oldX = x; oldY = y;
  glutPostRedisplay();
}
```

The OnMouseMove function has only two parameters, the x and y screen location where the mouse currently is. The mouse move event is raised whenever the mouse enters and moves in the application window. Based on the state set in the OnMouseDown function, we calculate the zoom amount (dist) if the middle mouse button is pressed. Otherwise, we calculate the two rotation amounts (rX and rY). Next, we update the oldX and oldY positions for the next event. Finally we request the freeglut framework to repaint our application window by calling glutPostRedisplay() function. This call sends the repaint event which re-renders our scene.

In order to make it easy for us to see the deformation, we enable wireframe rendering by calling the glPolygonMode(GL_FRONT_AND_BACK, GL_LINE) function in the OnInit() function.

There are two things to be careful about with the glPolygonMode function. Firstly, the first parameter can only be GL_FRONT_AND_BACK in the core profile. Secondly, make sure that the second parameter is named GL_LINE instead of GL_LINES which is used with the glDraw* functions. To disable the wireframe rendering and return to the default fill rendering, change the second parameter from GL_LINE to GL_FILL.

Running the demo code shows a ripple deformer propagating the deformation in a mesh grid as shown in the following screenshot. Hopefully, this recipe should have cleared how to use vertex shaders, especially for doing per-vertex transformations.

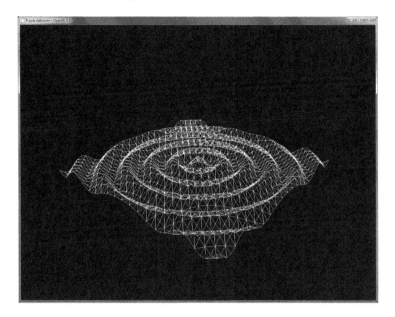

Dynamically subdividing a plane using the geometry shader

After the vertex shader, the next programmable stage in the OpenGL v3.3 graphics pipeline is the geometry shader. This shader contains inputs from the vertex shader stage. We can either feed these unmodified to the next shader stage or we can add/omit/modify vertices and primitives as desired. One thing that the vertex shaders lack is the availability of the other vertices of the primitive. Geometry shaders have information of all on the vertices of a single primitive.

The advantage with geometry shaders is that we can add/remove primitives on the fly. Moreover it is easier to get all vertices of a single primitive, unlike in the vertex shader, which has information on a single vertex only. The main drawback of geometry shaders is the limit on the number of new vertices we can generate, which is dependent on the hardware. Another disadvantage is the limited availability of the surrounding primitives.

In this recipe, we will dynamically subdivide a planar mesh using the geometry shader.

Getting ready

This recipe assumes that the reader knows how to render a simple triangle using vertex and fragment shaders using the OpenGL v3.3 core profile. We render four planar meshes in this recipe which are placed next to each other to create a bigger planar mesh. Each of these meshes is subdivided using the same geometry shader. The code for this recipe is located in the `Chapter1\SubdivisionGeometryShader` directory.

How to do it...

We can implement the geometry shader using the following steps:

1. Define a vertex shader (`shaders/shader.vert`) which outputs object space vertex positions directly.

```
#version 330 core
  layout(location=0) in vec3 vVertex;
  void main() {
    gl_Position =  vec4(vVertex, 1);
}
```

2. Define a geometry shader (`shaders/shader.geom`) which performs the subdivision of the quad. The shader is explained in the next section.

```
#version 330 core
layout (triangles) in;
layout (triangle_strip, max_vertices=256) out;
uniform int sub_divisions;
uniform mat4 MVP;
void main() {
  vec4 v0 = gl_in[0].gl_Position;
  vec4 v1 = gl_in[1].gl_Position;
  vec4 v2 = gl_in[2].gl_Position;
  float dx = abs(v0.x-v2.x)/sub_divisions;
  float dz = abs(v0.z-v1.z)/sub_divisions;
  float x=v0.x;
  float z=v0.z;
  for(int j=0;j<sub_divisions*sub_divisions;j++) {
    gl_Position =  MVP * vec4(x,0,z,1);
    EmitVertex();
    gl_Position =  MVP * vec4(x,0,z+dz,1);
    EmitVertex();
    gl_Position =  MVP * vec4(x+dx,0,z,1);
    EmitVertex();
    gl_Position =  MVP * vec4(x+dx,0,z+dz,1);
```

```
      EmitVertex();
      EndPrimitive();
      x+=dx;
      if((j+1) %sub_divisions == 0) {
        x=v0.x;
        z+=dz;
      }
    }
  }
```

3. Define a fragment shader (shaders/shader.frag) that simply outputs a constant color.

```
#version 330 core
layout(location=0) out vec4 vFragColor;
void main() {
  vFragColor = vec4(1,1,1,1);
}
```

4. Load the shaders using the GLSLShader class in the OnInit() function.

```
shader.LoadFromFile(GL_VERTEX_SHADER,
"shaders/shader.vert");
shader.LoadFromFile(GL_GEOMETRY_SHADER,"shaders/shader.
geom");
shader.LoadFromFile(GL_FRAGMENT_SHADER,"shaders/shader.
frag");
shader.CreateAndLinkProgram();
shader.Use();
  shader.AddAttribute("vVertex");
  shader.AddUniform("MVP");
  shader.AddUniform("sub_divisions");
  glUniform1i(shader("sub_divisions"), sub_divisions);
shader.UnUse();
```

5. Create the geometry and topology.

```
vertices[0] = glm::vec3(-5,0,-5);
vertices[1] = glm::vec3(-5,0,5);
vertices[2] = glm::vec3(5,0,5);
vertices[3] = glm::vec3(5,0,-5);
GLushort* id=&indices[0];

*id++ = 0;
*id++ = 1;
*id++ = 2;
*id++ = 0;
*id++ = 2;
*id++ = 3;
```

6. Store the geometry and topology in the buffer object(s). Also enable the line display mode.

```
glGenVertexArrays(1, &vaoID);
glGenBuffers(1, &vboVerticesID);
glGenBuffers(1, &vboIndicesID);
glBindVertexArray(vaoID);
glBindBuffer (GL_ARRAY_BUFFER, vboVerticesID);
glBufferData (GL_ARRAY_BUFFER, sizeof(vertices),
&vertices[0], GL_STATIC_DRAW);
glEnableVertexAttribArray(shader["vVertex"]);
glVertexAttribPointer(shader["vVertex"], 3, GL_FLOAT,
GL_FALSE,0,0);
glBindBuffer(GL_ELEMENT_ARRAY_BUFFER, vboIndicesID);
glBufferData(GL_ELEMENT_ARRAY_BUFFER, sizeof(indices),
&indices[0], GL_STATIC_DRAW);
glPolygonMode(GL_FRONT_AND_BACK, GL_LINE);
```

7. Set up the rendering code to bind the GLSLShader shader, pass the uniforms and then draw the geometry.

```
void OnRender() {
  glClear(GL_COLOR_BUFFER_BIT|GL_DEPTH_BUFFER_BIT);
  glm::mat4 T = glm::translate( glm::mat4(1.0f),
  glm::vec3(0.0f,0.0f, dist));
  glm::mat4 Rx=glm::rotate(T,rX,glm::vec3(1.0f, 0.0f,
  0.0f));
  glm::mat4 MV=glm::rotate(Rx,rY,
  glm::vec3(0.0f,1.0f,0.0f));
  MV=glm::translate(MV, glm::vec3(-5,0,-5));
  shader.Use();
    glUniform1i(shader("sub_divisions"), sub_divisions);
    glUniformMatrix4fv(shader("MVP"), 1, GL_FALSE,
    glm::value_ptr(P*MV));
    glDrawElements(GL_TRIANGLES, 6, GL_UNSIGNED_SHORT,
    0);

    MV=glm::translate(MV, glm::vec3(10,0,0));
    glUniformMatrix4fv(shader("MVP"), 1, GL_FALSE,
    glm::value_ptr(P*MV));
    glDrawElements(GL_TRIANGLES, 6, GL_UNSIGNED_SHORT,
    0);

    MV=glm::translate(MV, glm::vec3(0,0,10));
    glUniformMatrix4fv(shader("MVP"), 1, GL_FALSE,
    glm::value_ptr(P*MV));
    glDrawElements(GL_TRIANGLES, 6, GL_UNSIGNED_SHORT,
    0);
```

```
      MV=glm::translate(MV, glm::vec3(-10,0,0));
      glUniformMatrix4fv(shader("MVP"), 1, GL_FALSE,
      glm::value_ptr(P*MV));
      glDrawElements(GL_TRIANGLES, 6, GL_UNSIGNED_SHORT,
      0);
    shader.UnUse();
    glutSwapBuffers();
  }
```

8. Delete the shader and other OpenGL objects.

```
void OnShutdown() {
  shader.DeleteShaderProgram();
  glDeleteBuffers(1, &vboVerticesID);
  glDeleteBuffers(1, &vboIndicesID);
  glDeleteVertexArrays(1, &vaoID);
  cout<<"Shutdown successfull"<<endl;
}
```

How it works...

Let's dissect the geometry shader.

```
#version 330 core
layout (triangles) in;
layout (triangle_strip, max_vertices=256) out;
```

The first line signifies the GLSL version of the shader. The next two lines are important as they tell the shader processor about the input and output primitives of our geometry shader. In this case, the input will be `triangles` and the output will be a `triangle_strip`.

In addition, we also need to give the maximum number of output vertices from this geometry shader. This is a hardware specific number. For the hardware used in this development, the `max_vertices` value is found to be `256`. This information can be obtained by querying the `GL_MAX_GEOMETRY_OUTPUT_VERTICES` field and it is dependent on the primitive type used and the number of attributes stored per-vertex.

```
uniform int sub_divisions;
uniform mat4 MVP;
```

Next, we declare two uniforms, the total number of subdivisions desired (`sub_divisions`) and the combined modelview projection matrix (`MVP`).

```
void main() {
  vec4 v0 = gl_in[0].gl_Position;
  vec4 v1 = gl_in[1].gl_Position;
  vec4 v2 = gl_in[2].gl_Position;
```

The bulk of the work takes place in the main entry point function. For each triangle pushed from the application, the geometry shader is run once. Thus, for each triangle, the positions of its vertices are obtained from the `gl_Position` attribute which is stored in the built-in `gl_in` array. All other attributes are input as an array in the geometry shader. We store the input positions in local variable `v0`, `v1`, and `v2`.

Next, we calculate the size of the smallest quad for the given subdivision based on the size of the given base triangle and the total number of subdivisions required.

```
float dx = abs(v0.x-v2.x)/sub_divisions;
float dz = abs(v0.z-v1.z)/sub_divisions;
float x=v0.x;
float z=v0.z;
for(int j=0;j<sub_divisions*sub_divisions;j++) {
  gl_Position =  MVP * vec4(x,    0,    z,1);  EmitVertex();
  gl_Position =  MVP * vec4(x,    0,z+dz,1);  EmitVertex();
  gl_Position =  MVP * vec4(x+dx,0,    z,1);  EmitVertex();
  gl_Position =  MVP * vec4(x+dx,0,z+dz,1);  EmitVertex();
  EndPrimitive();
  x+=dx;
  if((j+1) % sub_divisions == 0) {
    x=v0.x;
    z+=dz;
  }
}
```

We start from the first vertex. We store the x and z values of this vertex in local variables. Next, we iterate `N*N` times, where `N` is the total number of subdivisions required. For example, if we need to subdivide the mesh three times on both axes, the loop will run nine times, which is the total number of quads. After calculating the positions of the four vertices, they are emitted by calling `EmitVertex()`. This function emits the current values of output variables to the current output primitive on the primitive stream. Next, the `EndPrimitive()` call is issued to signify that we have emitted the four vertices of `triangle_strip`.

After these calculations, the local variable x is incremented by dx amount. If we are at an iteration that is a multiple of `sub_divisions`, we reset variable x to the x value of the first vertex while incrementing the local variable z.

The fragment shader outputs a constant color (white: `vec4(1,1,1,1)`).

There's more...

The application code is similar to the last recipes. We have an additional shader (`shaders/shader.geom`), which is our geometry shader that is loaded from file.

```
shader.LoadFromFile(GL_VERTEX_SHADER, "shaders/shader.vert");
shader.LoadFromFile(GL_GEOMETRY_SHADER,"shaders/shader.geom");
shader.LoadFromFile(GL_FRAGMENT_SHADER,"shaders/shader.frag");
shader.CreateAndLinkProgram();
shader.Use();
    shader.AddAttribute("vVertex");
    shader.AddUniform("MVP");
    shader.AddUniform("sub_divisions");
    glUniform1i(shader("sub_divisions"), sub_divisions);
shader.UnUse();
```

The notable additions are highlighted, which include the new geometry shader and an additional uniform for the total subdivisions desired (`sub_divisions`). We initialize this uniform at initialization. The buffer object handling is similar to the simple triangle recipe. The other difference is in the rendering function where there are some additional modeling transformations (translations) after the viewing transformation.

The `OnRender()` function starts by clearing the color and depth buffers. It then calculates the viewing transformation as in the previous recipe.

```
void OnRender() {
  glClear(GL_COLOR_BUFFER_BIT|GL_DEPTH_BUFFER_BIT);
  glm::mat4 T = glm::translate( glm::mat4(1.0f),
  glm::vec3(0.0f,0.0f, dist));
  glm::mat4 Rx=glm::rotate(T,rX,glm::vec3(1.0f, 0.0f, 0.0f));
  glm::mat4 MV=glm::rotate(Rx,rY, glm::vec3(0.0f,1.0f,0.0f));
  MV=glm::translate(MV, glm::vec3(-5,0,-5));
```

Since our planer mesh geometry is positioned at origin going from -5 to 5 on the X and Z axes, we have to place them in the appropriate place by translating them, otherwise they would overlay each other.

Next, we first bind the shader program. Then we pass the shader uniforms which include the `sub_divisions` uniform and the combined modelview projection matrix (`MVP`) uniform. Then we pass the attributes by issuing a call to the `glDrawElements` function. We then add the relative translation for each instance to get a new modelview matrix for the next draw call. This is repeated three times to get all four planar meshes placed properly in the world space.

In this recipe, we handle keyboard input to allow the user to change the subdivision level dynamically. We first attach our keyboard event handler (OnKey) to glutKeyboardFunc. The keyboard event handler is defined as follows:

```
void OnKey(unsigned char key, int x, int y) {
  switch(key) {
    case ',':  sub_divisions--; break;
    case '.':  sub_divisions++; break;
  }
  sub_divisions = max(1,min(8, sub_divisions));
  glutPostRedisplay();
}
```

We can change the subdivision levels by pressing the , and . keys. We then check to make sure that the subdivisions are within the allowed limit. Finally, we request the freeglut function, glutPostRedisplay(), to repaint the window to show the new mesh. Compiling and running the demo code displays four planar meshes. Pressing the , key decreases the subdivision level and the . key increases the subdivision level. The output from the subdivision geometry shader showing multiple subdivision levels is displayed in the following screenshot:

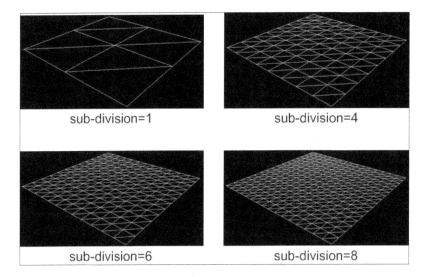

We can change the subdivision levels by pressing the , and . keys.

See also

You can view the Geometry shader tutorial part 1 and 2 at Geeks3D:

http://www.geeks3d.com/20111111/simple-introduction-to-geometry-shaders-glsl-opengl-tutorial-part1/

http://www.geeks3d.com/20111117/simple-introduction-to-geometry-shader-in-glsl-part-2/

Dynamically subdividing a plane using the geometry shader with instanced rendering

In order to avoid pushing the same data multiple times, we can exploit the instanced rendering functions. We will now see how we can omit the multiple `glDrawElements` calls in the previous recipe with a single `glDrawElementsInstanced` call.

Getting ready

Before doing this, we assume that the reader knows how to use the geometry shader in the OpenGL 3.3 core profile. The code for this recipe is in the `Chapter1\SubdivisionGeometryShader_Instanced` directory.

How to do it...

Converting the previous recipe to use instanced rendering requires the following steps:

1. Change the vertex shader to handle the instance modeling matrix and output world space positions (`shaders/shader.vert`).

```
#version 330 core
layout(location=0) in vec3 vVertex;
uniform mat4 M[4];
void main()
{
   gl_Position =  M[gl_InstanceID]*vec4(vVertex, 1);
}
```

2. Change the geometry shader to replace the MVP matrix with the PV matrix (`shaders/shader.geom`).

```
#version 330 core
layout (triangles) in;
layout (triangle_strip, max_vertices=256) out;
uniform int sub_divisions;
uniform mat4 PV;

void main()
{
  vec4 v0 = gl_in[0].gl_Position;
  vec4 v1 = gl_in[1].gl_Position;
  vec4 v2 = gl_in[2].gl_Position;
  float dx = abs(v0.x-v2.x)/sub_divisions;
  float dz = abs(v0.z-v1.z)/sub_divisions;
```

```
    float x=v0.x;
    float z=v0.z;
    for(int j=0;j<sub_divisions*sub_divisions;j++) {
      gl_Position =  PV * vec4(x,0,z,1);        EmitVertex();
      gl_Position =  PV * vec4(x,0,z+dz,1);     EmitVertex();
      gl_Position =  PV * vec4(x+dx,0,z,1);     EmitVertex();
      gl_Position =  PV * vec4(x+dx,0,z+dz,1);  EmitVertex();
      EndPrimitive();
      x+=dx;
      if((j+1) %sub_divisions == 0) {
        x=v0.x;
        z+=dz;
      }
    }
  }
}
```

3. Initialize the per-instance model matrices (M).

```
void OnInit() {
  //set the instance modeling matrix
  M[0] = glm::translate(glm::mat4(1), glm::vec3(-5,0,-5));
  M[1] = glm::translate(M[0], glm::vec3(10,0,0));
  M[2] = glm::translate(M[1], glm::vec3(0,0,10));
  M[3] = glm::translate(M[2], glm::vec3(-10,0,0));
  ..
  shader.Use();
    shader.AddAttribute("vVertex");
    shader.AddUniform("PV");
    shader.AddUniform("M");
    shader.AddUniform("sub_divisions");
    glUniform1i(shader("sub_divisions"), sub_divisions);
    glUniformMatrix4fv(shader("M"), 4, GL_FALSE,
    glm::value_ptr(M[0]));
  shader.UnUse();
```

4. Render instances using the glDrawElementInstanced call.

```
void OnRender() {
  glClear(GL_COLOR_BUFFER_BIT|GL_DEPTH_BUFFER_BIT);
  glm::mat4 T =glm::translate(glm::mat4(1.0f),
  glm::vec3(0.0f, 0.0f, dist));
  glm::mat4 Rx=glm::rotate(T,rX,glm::vec3(1.0f, 0.0f,
  0.0f));
  glm::mat4 V =glm::rotate(Rx,rY,glm::vec3(0.0f,
  1.0f,0.0f));
  glm::mat4 PV = P*V;
```

```
shader.Use();
  glUniformMatrix4fv(shader("PV"),1,GL_FALSE,
  glm::value_ptr(PV));
    glUniform1i(shader("sub_divisions"), sub_divisions);
  glDrawElementsInstanced(GL_TRIANGLES,
  6, GL_UNSIGNED_SHORT, 0, 4);
  shader.UnUse();
  glutSwapBuffers();
}
```

How it works...

First, we need to store the model matrix for each instance separately. Since we have four instances, we store a uniform array of four elements (M[4]). Second, we multiply the per-vertex position (vVertex) with the model matrix for the current instance (M[gl_InstanceID]).

 Note that the gl_InstanceID built-in attribute will be filled with the index of each instance automatically at the time of the glDrawElementsInstanced call. Also note that this built-in attribute is only accessible in the vertex shader.

The MVP matrix is omitted from the geometry shader since now the input vertex positions are in world space. So we only need to multiply them with the combined view projection (PV) matrix. On the application side, the MV matrix is removed. Instead, we store the model matrix array for all four instances (glm::mat4 M[4]). The values of these matrices are initialized in the OnInit() function as follows:

```
M[0] = glm::translate(glm::mat4(1), glm::vec3(-5,0,-5));
M[1] = glm::translate(M[0], glm::vec3(10,0,0));
M[2] = glm::translate(M[1], glm::vec3(0,0,10));
M[3] = glm::translate(M[2], glm::vec3(-10,0,0));
```

The rendering function, OnRender(), creates the combined view projection matrix (PV) and then calls glDrawElementsInsntanced. The first four parameters are similar to the glDrawElements function. The final parameter is the total number of instances desired. Instanced rendering is an efficient mechanism for rendering identical geometry whereby the GL_ARRAY_BUFFER and GL_ELEMENT_ARRAY_BUFFER bindings are shared between instances allowing the GPU to do efficient resource access and sharing.

```
void OnRender() {
  glClear(GL_COLOR_BUFFER_BIT|GL_DEPTH_BUFFER_BIT);
  glm::mat4 T = glm::translate(glm::mat4(1.0f),glm::vec3(0.0f,
  0.0f, dist));
  glm::mat4 Rx = glm::rotate(T,  rX, glm::vec3(1.0f, 0.0f,
  0.0f));
```

```
glm::mat4 V = glm::rotate(Rx, rY, glm::vec3(0.0f, 1.0f, 0.0f));
glm::mat4 PV = P*V;
shader.Use();
    glUniformMatrix4fv(shader("PV"),1,GL_FALSE,
    glm::value_ptr(PV));
    glUniform1i(shader("sub_divisions"), sub_divisions);
    glDrawElementsInstanced(GL_TRIANGLES,6,GL_UNSIGNED_SHORT,0,
    4);
shader.UnUse();
glutSwapBuffers();
}
```

There is always a limit on the maximum number of matrices one can output from the vertex shader and this has some performance implications as well. Some performance improvements can be obtained by replacing the matrix storage with translation and scaling vectors, and an orientation quaternion which can then be converted on the fly into a matrix in the shader.

See also

The official OpenGL wiki can be found at `http://www.opengl.org/wiki/Built-in_Variable_%28GLSL%29`.

An instance rendering tutorial from OGLDev can be found at `http://ogldev.atspace.co.uk/www/tutorial33/tutorial33.html`.

Drawing a 2D image in a window using the fragment shader and the SOIL image loading library

We will wrap up this chapter with a recipe for creating a simple image viewer in the OpenGL v3.3 core profile using the `SOIL` image loading library.

Getting ready

After setting up the Visual Studio environment, we can now work with the SOIL library. The code for this recipe is in the `Chapter1/ImageLoader` directory.

How to do it...

Let us now implement the image loader by following these steps:

1. Load the image using the SOIL library. Since the loaded image from SOIL is inverted vertically, we flip the image on the Y axis.

```
int texture_width = 0, texture_height = 0, channels=0;
GLubyte* pData = SOIL_load_image(filename.c_str(),
&texture_width, &texture_height, &channels,
SOIL_LOAD_AUTO);
if(pData == NULL) {
  cerr<<"Cannot load image: "<<filename.c_str()<<endl;
  exit(EXIT_FAILURE);
}
int i,j;
for( j = 0; j*2 < texture_height; ++j )
{
  int index1 = j * texture_width * channels;
  int index2 = (texture_height - 1 - j) * texture_width *
  channels;
  for( i = texture_width * channels; i > 0; --i )
  {
    GLubyte temp = pData[index1];
    pData[index1] = pData[index2];
    pData[index2] = temp;
    ++index1;
    ++index2;
  }
}
```

2. Set up the OpenGL texture object and free the data allocated by the SOIL library.

```
glGenTextures(1, &textureID);
glActiveTexture(GL_TEXTURE0);
glBindTexture(GL_TEXTURE_2D, textureID);
glTexParameteri(GL_TEXTURE_2D, GL_TEXTURE_MIN_FILTER,
GL_LINEAR);
glTexParameteri(GL_TEXTURE_2D, GL_TEXTURE_MAG_FILTER,
GL_LINEAR);
glTexParameteri(GL_TEXTURE_2D, GL_TEXTURE_WRAP_S,
GL_CLAMP);
glTexParameteri(GL_TEXTURE_2D, GL_TEXTURE_WRAP_T,
GL_CLAMP);
glTexImage2D(GL_TEXTURE_2D, 0, GL_RGB, texture_width,
texture_height, 0, GL_RGB, GL_UNSIGNED_BYTE, pData);
SOIL_free_image_data(pData);
```

3. Set up the vertex shader to output the clip space position (`shaders/shader.vert`).

```
#version 330 core
layout(location=0) in vec2 vVertex;
smooth out vec2 vUV;
void main()
{
  gl_Position = vec4(vVertex*2.0-1,0,1);
  vUV = vVertex;
}
```

4. Set up the fragment shader that samples our image texture (`shaders/shader.frag`).

```
#version 330 core
layout (location=0) out vec4 vFragColor;
smooth in vec2 vUV;
uniform sampler2D textureMap;
void main()
{
  vFragColor = texture(textureMap, vUV);
}
```

5. Set up the application code using the `GLSLShader` shader class.

```
shader.LoadFromFile(GL_VERTEX_SHADER,
"shaders/shader.vert");
shader.LoadFromFile(GL_FRAGMENT_SHADER,"shaders/shader.
frag");
shader.CreateAndLinkProgram();
shader.Use();
  shader.AddAttribute("vVertex");
  shader.AddUniform("textureMap");
  glUniform1i(shader("textureMap"), 0);
shader.UnUse();
```

6. Set up the geometry and topology and pass data to the GPU using buffer objects.

```
vertices[0] = glm::vec2(0.0,0.0);
vertices[1] = glm::vec2(1.0,0.0);
vertices[2] = glm::vec2(1.0,1.0);
vertices[3] = glm::vec2(0.0,1.0);
GLushort* id=&indices[0];
*id++ =0;
*id++ =1;
*id++ =2;
*id++ =0;
*id++ =2;
```

```
   *id++ =3;

   glGenVertexArrays(1, &vaoID);
   glGenBuffers(1, &vboVerticesID);
   glGenBuffers(1, &vboIndicesID);
   glBindVertexArray(vaoID);
   glBindBuffer (GL_ARRAY_BUFFER, vboVerticesID);
   glBufferData (GL_ARRAY_BUFFER, sizeof(vertices),
   &vertices[0], GL_STATIC_DRAW);
   glEnableVertexAttribArray(shader["vVertex"]);
   glVertexAttribPointer(shader["vVertex"], 2, GL_FLOAT,
   GL_FALSE,0,0);
   glBindBuffer(GL_ELEMENT_ARRAY_BUFFER, vboIndicesID);
   glBufferData(GL_ELEMENT_ARRAY_BUFFER, sizeof(indices),
   &indices[0], GL_STATIC_DRAW);
```

7. Set the shader and render the geometry.

```
void OnRender() {
  glClear(GL_COLOR_BUFFER_BIT|GL_DEPTH_BUFFER_BIT);
  shader.Use();
    glDrawElements(GL_TRIANGLES, 6, GL_UNSIGNED_SHORT, 0);
  shader.UnUse();
  glutSwapBuffers();
}
```

8. Release the allocated resources.

```
void OnShutdown() {
  shader.DeleteShaderProgram();
  glDeleteBuffers(1, &vboVerticesID);
  glDeleteBuffers(1, &vboIndicesID);
  glDeleteVertexArrays(1, &vaoID);
  glDeleteTextures(1, &textureID);
}
```

How it works...

The SOIL library provides a lot of functions but for now we are only interested in the SOIL_load_image function.

```
int texture_width = 0, texture_height = 0, channels=0;
GLubyte* pData = SOIL_load_image(filename.c_str(), &texture_width,
&texture_height, &channels, SOIL_LOAD_AUTO);
if(pData == NULL) {
  cerr<<"Cannot load image: "<<filename.c_str()<<endl;
  exit(EXIT_FAILURE);
}
```

The first parameter is the image file name. The next three parameters return the texture width, texture height, and total color channels in the image. These are used when generating the OpenGL texture object. The final parameter is the flag which is used to control further processing on the image. For this simple example, we will use the SOIL_LOAD_AUTO flag which keeps all of the loading settings set to default. If the function succeeds, it returns unsigned char* to the image data. If it fails, the return value is NULL (0). Since the image data loaded by SOIL is vertically flipped, we then use two nested loops to flip the image data on the Y axis.

```
int i,j;
for( j = 0; j*2 < texture_height; ++j )
{
  int index1 = j * texture_width * channels;
  int index2 = (texture_height - 1 - j) * texture_width *
  channels;
  for( i = texture_width * channels; i > 0; --i )
  {
    GLubyte temp = pData[index1];
    pData[index1] = pData[index2];
    pData[index2] = temp;
    ++index1;
    ++index2;
  }
}
```

After the image data is loaded, we generate an OpenGL texture object and pass this data to the texture memory.

```
glGenTextures(1, &textureID);
glActiveTexture(GL_TEXTURE0);
glBindTexture(GL_TEXTURE_2D, textureID);
glTexParameteri(GL_TEXTURE_2D, GL_TEXTURE_MIN_FILTER,
GL_LINEAR);
glTexParameteri(GL_TEXTURE_2D, GL_TEXTURE_MAG_FILTER,
GL_LINEAR);
glTexParameteri(GL_TEXTURE_2D, GL_TEXTURE_WRAP_S, GL_CLAMP);
glTexParameteri(GL_TEXTURE_2D, GL_TEXTURE_WRAP_T, GL_CLAMP);
glTexImage2D(GL_TEXTURE_2D, 0, GL_RGB, texture_width,
texture_height, 0, GL_RGB, GL_UNSIGNED_BYTE, pData);
SOIL_free_image_data(pData);
```

As with every other OpenGL object, we have to first call `glGenTextures`. The first parameter is the total number of texture objects we need and the second parameter holds the ID of the texture object generated. After generation of the texture object, we set the active texture unit by calling `glActiveTexture(GL_TEXTURE0)` and then bind the texture to the active texture unit by calling `glBindTextures(GL_TEXTURE_2D, &textureID)`. Next, we adjust the texture parameters like the texture filtering for minification and magnification, as well as the texture wrapping modes for `S` and `T` texture coordinates. After these calls, we pass the loaded image data to the `glTexImage2D` function.

The `glTexImage2D` function is where the actual allocation of the texture object takes place. The first parameter is the texture target (in our case this is `GL_TEXTURE_2D`). The second parameter is the mipmap level which we keep to `0`. The third parameter is the internal format. We can determine this by looking at the image properties. The fourth and fifth parameters store the texture width and height respectively. The sixth parameter is `0` for no border and `1` for border. The seventh parameter is the image format. The eighth parameter is the type of the image data pointer, and the final parameter is the pointer to the raw image data. After this function, we can safely release the image data allocated by `SOIL` by calling `SOIL_free_image_data(pData)`.

There's more...

In this recipe, we use two shaders, the vertex shader and the fragment shader. The vertex shader outputs the clip space position from the input vertex position (`vVertex`) by simple arithmetic. Using the vertex positions, it also generates the texture coordinates (`vUV`) for sampling of the texture in the fragment shader.

```
gl_Position = vec4(vVertex*2.0-1,0,1);
vUV = vVertex;
```

The fragment shader has the texture coordinates smoothly interpolated from the vertex shader stage through the rasterizer. The image that we loaded using `SOIL` is passed to a texture sampler (`uniform sampler2D textureMap`) which is then sampled using the input texture coordinates (`vFragColor = texture(textureMap, vUV)`). So in the end, we get the image displayed on the screen.

The application side code is similar to the previous recipe. The changes include an addition of the `textureMap` sampler uniform.

```
shader.Use();
  shader.AddAttribute("vVertex");
  shader.AddUniform("textureMap");
  glUniform1i(shader("textureMap"), 0);
shader.UnUse();
```

Since this uniform will not change throughout the lifetime of the application, we initialize it once only. The first parameter of `glUniform1i` is the location of the uniform. We set the value of the sampler uniform to the active texture unit where the texture is bound. In our case, the texture is bound to texture unit 0, that is, `GL_TEXTURE0`. Therefore we pass 0 to the uniform. If it was bound to `GL_TEXTURE1`, we would pass 1 to the uniform.

The `OnShutdown()` function is similar to the earlier recipes. In addition, this code adds deletion of the OpenGL texture object. The rendering code first clears the color and depth buffers. Next, it binds the shader program and then invokes the `glDrawElement` call to render the triangles. Finally the shader is unbound and then the `glutSwapBuffers` function is called to display the current back buffer as the next front buffer. Compiling and running this code displays the image in a window as shown in the following screenshot:

Using image loading libraries like `SOIL` and a fragment shader, we can make a simple image viewer with basic GLSL functionality. More elaborate effects may be achieved by using techniques detailed in the later recipes of this book.

2

3D Viewing and Object Picking

The recipes covered in this chapter include:

- ► Implementing a vector-based camera model with FPS style input support
- ► Implementing the free camera
- ► Implementing target camera
- ► Implementing the view frustum culling
- ► Implementing object picking using the depth buffer
- ► Implementing object picking using color based picking
- ► Implementing object picking using scene intersection queries

Introduction

In this chapter, we will look at the recipes for handling 3D viewing tasks and object picking in OpenGL v3.3 and above. All of the real-time simulations, games, and other graphics applications require a virtual camera or a virtual viewer from the point of view of which the 3D scene is rendered. The virtual camera is itself placed in the 3D world and has a specific direction called the camera look direction. Internally, the virtual camera is itself a collection of translations and rotations, which is stored inside the viewing matrix.

Moreover, projection settings for the virtual camera control how big or small the objects appear on screen. This is the kind of functionality which is controlled through the real world camera lens. These are controlled through the projection matrix. In addition to specifying the viewing and projection matrices, the virtual camera may also help with reducing the amount of geometry pushed to the GPU. This is through a process called view frustum culling. Rather than rendering all of the objects in the scene, only those that are visible to the virtual camera are rendered, thus improving the runtime performance of the application.

Implementing a vector-based camera with FPS style input support

We will begin this chapter by designing a simple class to handle the camera. In a typical OpenGL application, the viewing operations are carried out to place a virtual object on screen. We leave the details of the transformations required in between to a typical graduate text on computer graphics like the one given in the *See also* section of this recipe. This recipe will focus on designing a simple and efficient camera class. We create a simple inheritance from a base class called CAbstractCamera. We will inherit two classes from this parent class, CFreeCamera and CTargetCamera, as shown in the following figure:

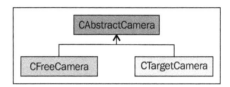

Getting ready

The code for this recipe is in the Chapter2/src directory. The CAbstractCamera class is defined in the AbstractCamera. [h/cpp] files.

```
class CAbstractCamera
{
public:
  CAbstractCamera(void);
  ~CAbstractCamera(void);
  void SetupProjection(const float fovy, const float aspectRatio,
  const float near=0.1f, const float far=1000.0f);
  virtual void Update() = 0;
  virtual void Rotate(const float yaw, const float pitch, const
  float roll);
  const glm::mat4 GetViewMatrix() const;
  const glm::mat4 GetProjectionMatrix() const;
  void SetPosition(const glm::vec3& v);
  const glm::vec3 GetPosition() const;
  void SetFOV(const float fov);
  const float GetFOV() const;
  const float GetAspectRatio() const;
  void CalcFrustumPlanes();
  bool IsPointInFrustum(const glm::vec3& point);
  bool IsSphereInFrustum(const glm::vec3& center, const float
  radius);
  bool IsBoxInFrustum(const glm::vec3& min, const glm::vec3& max);
```

```
   void GetFrustumPlanes(glm::vec4 planes[6]);
   glm::vec3 farPts[4];
   glm::vec3 nearPts[4];
protected:
   float yaw, pitch, roll, fov, aspect_ratio, Znear, Zfar;
   static glm::vec3 UP;
   glm::vec3 look;
   glm::vec3 up;
   glm::vec3 right;
   glm::vec3 position;
   glm::mat4 V;        //view matrix
   glm::mat4 P;        //projection matrix
   CPlane planes[6];   //Frustum planes
};
```

We first declare the constructor/destructor pair. Next, the function for setting the projection for the camera is specified. Then some functions for updating the camera matrices based on rotation values are declared. Following these, the accessors and mutators are defined.

The class declaration is concluded with the view frustum culling-specific functions. Finally, the member fields are declared. The inheriting class needs to provide the implementation of one pure virtual function—Update (to recalculate the matrices and orientation vectors). The movement of the camera is based on three orientation vectors, namely, look, up, and right.

How to do it...

In a typical application, we will not use the CAbstractCamera class. Instead, we will use either the CFreeCamera class or the CTargetCamera class, as detailed in the following recipes. In this recipe, we will see how to handle input using the mouse and keyboard.

In order to handle the keyboard events, we perform the following processing in the idle callback function:

1. Check for the keyboard key press event.

2. If the *W* or *S* key is pressed, move the camera in the look vector direction:

    ```
    if( GetAsyncKeyState(VK_W) & 0x8000)
      cam.Walk(dt);
    if( GetAsyncKeyState(VK_S) & 0x8000)
      cam.Walk(-dt);
    ```

3. If the *A* or *D* key is pressed, move the camera in the right vector direction:

    ```
    if( GetAsyncKeyState(VK_A) & 0x8000)
      cam.Strafe(-dt);
    if( GetAsyncKeyState(VK_D) & 0x8000)
      cam.Strafe(dt);
    ```

4. If the *Q* or *Z* key is pressed, move the camera in the up vector direction:

```
if ( GetAsyncKeyState(VK_Q) & 0x8000)
  cam.Lift(dt);
if ( GetAsyncKeyState(VK_Z) & 0x8000)
  cam.Lift(-dt);
```

For handling mouse events, we attach two callbacks. One for mouse movement and the other for the mouse click event handling:

1. Define the mouse down and mouse move event handlers.

2. Determine the mouse input choice (the zoom or rotate state) in the mouse down event handler based on the mouse button clicked:

```
if(button == GLUT_MIDDLE_BUTTON)
  state = 0;
else
  state = 1;
```

3. If zoom state is chosen, calculate the `fov` value based on the drag amount and then set up the camera projection matrix:

```
if (state == 0) {
  fov += (y - oldY)/5.0f;
  cam.SetupProjection(fov, cam.GetAspectRatio());
}
```

4. If the rotate state is chosen, calculate the rotation amount (pitch and yaw). If mouse filtering is enabled, use the filtered mouse input, otherwise use the raw rotation amount:

```
else {
  rY += (y - oldY)/5.0f;
  rX += (oldX-x)/5.0f;
  if(useFiltering)
    filterMouseMoves(rX, rY);
  else {
    mouseX = rX;
    mouseY = rY;
  }
  cam.Rotate(mouseX,mouseY, 0);
}
```

There's more...

It is always better to use filtered mouse input, which gives smoother movement. In the recipes, we use a simple average filter of the last 10 inputs weighted based on their temporal distance. So the previous input is given more weight and the 5th latest input is given less weight. The filtered result is used as shown in the following code snippet:

```
void filterMouseMoves(float dx, float dy) {
  for (int i = MOUSE_HISTORY_BUFFER_SIZE - 1; i > 0; --i) {
    mouseHistory[i] = mouseHistory[i - 1];
  }
  mouseHistory[0] = glm::vec2(dx, dy);
  float averageX = 0.0f,  averageY = 0.0f, averageTotal = 0.0f,
  currentWeight = 1.0f;

  for (int i = 0; i < MOUSE_HISTORY_BUFFER_SIZE; ++i) {
    glm::vec2 tmp=mouseHistory[i];
    averageX += tmp.x * currentWeight;
    averageY += tmp.y * currentWeight;
    averageTotal += 1.0f * currentWeight;
    currentWeight *= MOUSE_FILTER_WEIGHT;
  }
  mouseX = averageX / averageTotal;
  mouseY = averageY / averageTotal;
}
```

 When using filtered mouse input, make sure that the history buffer is filled with the appropriate initial value; otherwise you will see a sudden jerk in the first few frames.

See also

- Smooth mouse filtering FAQ by Paul Nettle (http://www.flipcode.com/archives/Smooth_Mouse_Filtering.shtml)
- Real-time Rendering 3rd Edition by Tomas Akenine-Moller, Eric Haines, and Naty Hoffman, AK Peters/CRC Press, 2008

Implementing the free camera

Free camera is the first camera type which we will implement in this recipe. A free camera does not have a fixed target. However it does have a fixed position from which it can look in any direction.

The following figure shows a free viewing camera. When we rotate the camera, it rotates at its position. When we move the camera, it keeps looking in the same direction.

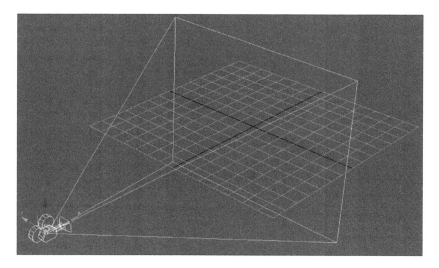

The source code for this recipe is in the `Chapter2/FreeCamera` directory. The `CFreeCamera` class is defined in the `Chapter2/src/FreeCamera.[h/cpp]` files. The class interface is as follows:

```cpp
class CFreeCamera : public CAbstractCamera
{
public:
  CFreeCamera(void);
  ~CFreeCamera(void);
  void Update();
  void Walk(const float dt);
  void Strafe(const float dt);
  void Lift(const float dt);
  void SetTranslation(const glm::vec3& t);
  glm::vec3 GetTranslation() const;
  void SetSpeed(const float speed);
  const float GetSpeed() const;
protected:
  float speed; //move speed of camera in m/s
  glm::vec3 translation;
};
```

How to do it...

The steps needed to implement the free camera are as follows:

1. Define the CFreeCamera class and add a vector to store the current translation.

2. In the Update method, calculate the new orientation (rotation) matrix, using the current camera orientations (that is, yaw, pitch, and roll amount):

   ```
   glm::mat4 R = glm::yawPitchRoll(yaw,pitch,roll);
   ```

    Make sure that the yaw, pitch, and roll angles are in radians.

3. Translate the camera position by the translation amount:

   ```
   position+=translation;
   ```

   If we need to implement a free camera which gradually comes to a halt, we should gradually decay the translation vector by adding the following code after the key events are handled:

   ```
   glm::vec3 t = cam.GetTranslation();
   if(glm::dot(t,t)>EPSILON2) {
       cam.SetTranslation(t*0.95f);
   }
   ```

   If no decay is needed, then we should clear the translation vector to 0 in the CFreeCamera::Update function after translating the position:

   ```
   translation = glm::vec3(0);
   ```

4. Transform the look vector by the current rotation matrix, and determine the right and up vectors to calculate the orthonormal basis:

   ```
   look = glm::vec3(R*glm::vec4(0,0,1,0));
   up = glm::vec3(R*glm::vec4(0,1,0,0));
   right = glm::cross(look, up);
   ```

5. Determine the camera target point:

   ```
   glm::vec3 tgt = position+look;
   ```

6. Use the glm::lookat function to calculate the new view matrix using the camera position, target, and the up vector:

   ```
   V = glm::lookAt(position, tgt, up);
   ```

There's more...

The `Walk` function simply translates the camera in the look direction:

```
void CFreeCamera::Walk(const float dt) {
  translation += (look*dt);
}
```

The `Strafe` function translates the camera in the right direction:

```
void CFreeCamera::Strafe(const float dt) {
  translation += (right*dt);
}
```

The `Lift` function translates the camera in the up direction:

```
void CFreeCamera::Lift(const float dt) {
  translation += (up*dt);
}
```

Running the demo application renders an infinite checkered plane as shown in the following figure. The free camera can be moved around by pressing the keys W, S, A, D, Q, and Z. Left-clicking the mouse rotates the camera at the current position to change the look direction. Middle-click zooms the camera in the look direction.

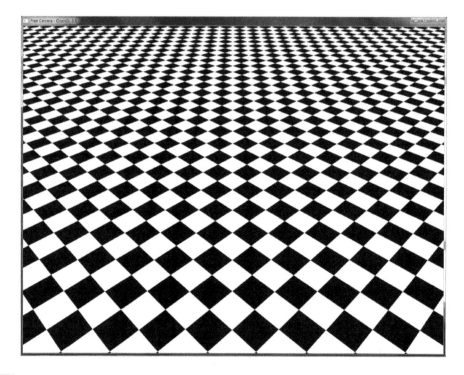

See also

- ▸ DHPOWare OpenGL camera demo – Part 1 (`http://www.dhpoware.com/demos/glCamera1.html`)

- ▸ DHPOWare OpenGL camera demo – Part 2 (`http://www.dhpoware.com/demos/glCamera2.html`)

- ▸ DHPOWare OpenGL camera demo – Part 3 (`http://www.dhpoware.com/demos/glCamera3.html`)

Implementing the target camera

The target camera works the opposite way. Rather than the position, the target remains fixed, while the camera moves or rotates around the target. Some operations like panning, move both the target and the camera position together.

Getting ready

The following figure shows an illustration of a target camera. Note that the small box is the target position for the camera.

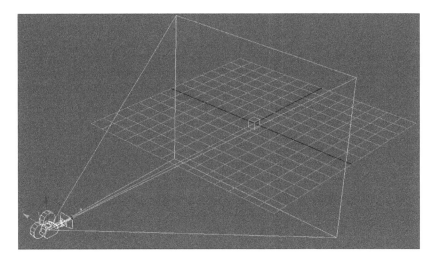

The code for this recipe resides in the `Chapter2/TargetCamera` directory. The `CTargetCamera` class is defined in the `Chapter2/src/TargetCamera.[h/cpp]` files. The class declaration is as follows:

```
class CTargetCamera : public CAbstractCamera
{
public:
```

```
    CTargetCamera(void);
    ~CTargetCamera(void);
    void Update();
    void Rotate(const float yaw, const float pitch, const float
      roll);
    void SetTarget(const glm::vec3 tgt);
    const glm::vec3 GetTarget() const;
    void Pan(const float dx, const float dy);
    void Zoom(const float amount );
    void Move(const float dx, const float dz);
  protected:
    glm::vec3 target;
    float minRy, maxRy;
    float distance;
    float minDistance, maxDistance;
};
```

How to do it...

We implement the target camera as follows:

1. Define the `CTargetCamera` class with a target position (`target`), the rotation limits (`minRy` and `maxRy`), the distance between the target and the camera position (`distance`), and the distance limits (`minDistance` and `maxDistance`).

2. In the `Update` method, calculate the new orientation (rotation) matrix using the current camera orientations (that is, yaw, pitch, and roll amount):

    ```
    glm::mat4 R = glm::yawPitchRoll(yaw,pitch,roll);
    ```

3. Use the distance to get a vector and then translate this vector by the current rotation matrix:

    ```
    glm::vec3 T = glm::vec3(0,0,distance);
    T = glm::vec3(R*glm::vec4(T,0.0f));
    ```

4. Get the new camera position by adding the translation vector to the target position:

    ```
    position = target + T;
    ```

5. Recalculate the orthonormal basis and then the view matrix:

    ```
    look = glm::normalize(target-position);
    up = glm::vec3(R*glm::vec4(UP,0.0f));
    right = glm::cross(look, up);
    V = glm::lookAt(position, target, up);
    ```

There's more...

The Move function moves both the position and target by the same amount in both look and right vector directions.

```
void CTargetCamera::Move(const float dx, const float dy) {
  glm::vec3 X = right*dx;
  glm::vec3 Y = look*dy;
  position += X + Y;
  target += X + Y;
  Update();
}
```

The Pan function moves in the xy plane only, hence the up vector is used instead of the look vector:

```
void CTargetCamera::Pan(const float dx, const float dy) {
  glm::vec3 X = right*dx;
  glm::vec3 Y = up*dy;
  position += X + Y;
  target += X + Y;
  Update();
}
```

The Zoom function moves the position in the look direction:

```
void CTargetCamera::Zoom(const float amount) {
  position += look * amount;
  distance = glm::distance(position, target);
  Distance = std::max(minDistance,
    std::min(distance, maxDistance));
  Update();
}
```

The demonstration for this recipe renders an infinite checkered plane, as in the previous recipe, and is shown in the following figure:

See also

▶ DHPOWare OpenGL camera demo – Part 1 (`http://www.dhpoware.com/demos/glCamera1.html`)

▶ DHPOWare OpenGL camera demo – Part 2 (`http://www.dhpoware.com/demos/glCamera2.html`)

▶ DHPOWare OpenGL camera demo – Part 3 (`http://www.dhpoware.com/demos/glCamera3.html`)

Implementing view frustum culling

When working with a lot of polygonal data, there is a need to reduce the amount of geometry pushed to the GPU for processing. There are several techniques for scene management, such as quadtrees, octrees, and bsp trees. These techniques help in sorting the geometry in visibility order, so that the objects are sorted (and some of these even culled from the display). This helps in reducing the work load on the GPU.

Even before such techniques can be used, there is an additional step which most graphics applications do and that is view frustum culling. This process removes the geometry if it is not in the current camera's view frustum. The idea is that if the object is not viewable, it should not be processed. A frustum is a chopped pyramid with its tip at the camera position and the base is at the far clip plane. The near clip plane is where the pyramid is chopped, as shown in the following figure. Any geometry inside the viewing frustum is displayed.

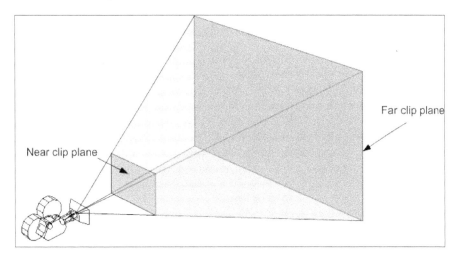

Getting ready

For this recipe, we will create a grid of points that are moved in a sine wave using a simple vertex shader. The geometry shader does the view frustum culling by only emitting vertices that are inside the viewing frustum. The calculation of the viewing frustum is carried out on the CPU, based on the camera projection parameters. We will follow the geometric approach in this tutorial. The code implementing this recipe is in the `Chapter2/ViewFrustumCulling` directory.

How to do it...

We will implement view frustum culling by taking the following steps:

1. Define a vertex shader that displaces the object-space vertex position using a sine wave in the y axis:

```
#version 330 core
layout(location = 0) in vec3 vVertex;
uniform float t;
const float PI = 3.141562;
void main()
```

```
{
  gl_Position=vec4(vVertex,1)+vec4(0,sin(vVertex.x*2*PI+t),0,0);
}
```

2. Define a geometry shader that performs the view frustum culling calculation on each vertex passed in from the vertex shader:

```
#version 330 core
layout (points) in;
layout (points, max_vertices=3) out;
uniform mat4 MVP;
uniform vec4 FrustumPlanes[6];
bool PointInFrustum(in vec3 p) {
  for(int i=0; i < 6; i++)
  {
    vec4 plane=FrustumPlanes[i];
    if ((dot(plane.xyz, p)+plane.w) < 0)
      return false;
  }
  return true;
}
void main()
{
  //get the basic vertices
  for(int i=0;i<gl_in.length(); i++) {
    vec4 vInPos = gl_in[i].gl_Position;
    vec2 tmp = (vInPos.xz*2-1.0)*5;
    vec3 V = vec3(tmp.x, vInPos.y, tmp.y);
    gl_Position = MVP*vec4(V,1);
    if(PointInFrustum(V)) {
      EmitVertex();
    }
  }
  EndPrimitive();
}
```

3. To render particles as rounded points, we do a simple trigonometric calculation by discarding all fragments that fall outside the radius of the circle:

```
#version 330 core
layout(location = 0) out vec4 vFragColor;
void main() {
  vec2 pos = (gl_PointCoord.xy-0.5);
  if(0.25<dot(pos,pos))      discard;
  vFragColor = vec4(0,0,1,1);
}
```

4. On the CPU side, call the `CAbstractCamera::CalcFrustumPlanes()` function to calculate the viewing frustum planes. Get the calculated frustum planes as a `glm::vec4` array by calling `CAbstractCamera::GetFrustumPlanes()`, and then pass these to the shader. The `xyz` components store the plane's normal, and the `w` coordinate stores the distance of the plane. After these calls we draw the points:

```
pCurrentCam->CalcFrustumPlanes();
glm::vec4 p[6];
pCurrentCam->GetFrustumPlanes(p);
pointShader.Use();
  glUniform1f(pointShader("t"), current_time);
  glUniformMatrix4fv(pointShader("MVP"), 1, GL_FALSE,
  glm::value_ptr(MVP));
  glUniform4fv(pointShader("FrustumPlanes"), 6,
  glm::value_ptr(p[0]));
  glBindVertexArray(pointVAOID);
  glDrawArrays(GL_POINTS,0,MAX_POINTS);
pointShader.UnUse();
```

How it works...

There are two main parts of this recipe: calculation of the viewing frustum planes and checking if a given point is in the viewing frustum. The first calculation is carried out in the `CAbstractCamera::CalcFrustumPlanes()` function. Refer to the `Chapter2/src/AbstractCamera.cpp` files for details.

In this function, we follow the geometric approach, whereby we first calculate the eight points of the frustum at the near and far clip planes. Theoretical details about this method are well explained in the reference given in the *See also* section. Once we have the eight frustum points, we use three of these points successively to get the bounding planes of the frustum. Here, we call the `CPlane::FromPoints` function, which generates a `CPlane` object from the given three points. This is repeated to get all six planes.

Testing whether a point is in the viewing frustum is carried out in the geometry shader's `PointInFrustum` function, which is defined as follows:

```
bool PointInFrustum(in vec3 p) {
  for(int i=0; i < 6; i++) {
    vec4 plane=FrustumPlanes[i];
    if ((dot(plane.xyz, p)+plane.w) < 0)
       return false;
  }
  return true;
}
```

This function iterates through all of the six frustum planes. In each iteration, it checks the signed distance of the given point p with respect to the ith frustum plane. This is a simple dot product of the plane normal with the given point and adding the plane distance. If the signed distance is negative for any of the planes, the point is outside the viewing frustum so we can safely reject the point. If the point has a positive signed distance for all of the six frustum planes, it is inside the viewing frustum. Note that the frustum planes are oriented in such a way that their normals point inside the viewing frustum.

There's more...

The demonstration implementing this recipe shows two cameras, the local camera (camera 1) which shows the sine wave and a world camera (camera 2) which shows the whole world, including the first camera frustum. We can toggle the current camera by pressing *1* for camera 1 and *2* for camera 2. When in camera 1 view, dragging the left mouse button rotates the scene, and the information about the total number of points in the viewing frustum are displayed in the title bar. In the camera 2 view, left-clicking rotates camera 1, and the displayed viewing frustum is updated so we can see what the camera view should contain.

In order to see the total number of visible vertices emitted from the geometry shader, we use a hardware query. The whole shader and the rendering code are bracketed in the begin/end query call as shown in the following code:

```
glBeginQuery(GL_PRIMITIVES_GENERATED, query);
pointShader.Use();
  glUniform1f(pointShader("t"), current_time);
  glUniformMatrix4fv(pointShader("MVP"), 1, GL_FALSE,
    glm::value_ptr(MVP));
  glUniform4fv(pointShader("FrustumPlanes"), 6,
  glm::value_ptr(p[0]));
  glBindVertexArray(pointVAOID);
  glDrawArrays(GL_POINTS,0,MAX_POINTS);
pointShader.UnUse();
glEndQuery(GL_PRIMITIVES_GENERATED);
```

After these calls, the query result is retrieved by calling:

```
GLuint res;
glGetQueryObjectuiv(query, GL_QUERY_RESULT, &res);
```

If successful, this call returns the total number of vertices emitted from the geometry shader, and that is the total number of vertices in the viewing frustum.

> Note that for the camera 2 view, all points are emitted. Hence, the total number of points is displayed in the title bar.

When in the camera 1 view (see the following figure), we see the close-up of the wave as it displaces the points in the Y direction. In this view, the points are rendered in blue color. Moreover, the total number of visible points is written in the title bar. The frame rate is also written to show the performance benefit from view frustum culling.

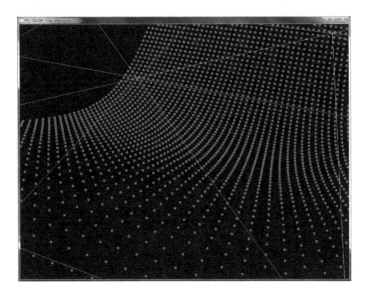

When in the camera 2 view (see the following figure), we can click-and-drag the left mouse button to rotate camera 1. This allows us to see the updated viewing frustum and the visible points. In the camera 2 view, visible points in the camera 1 view frustum are rendered in magenta color, the viewing frustum planes are in red color, and the invisible points (in camera 1 viewing frustum) are in blue color.

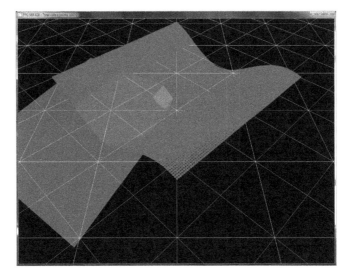

See also

Lighthouse 3D view frustum culling tutorial (`http://www.lighthouse3d.com/tutorials/ view-frustum-culling/geometric-approach-extracting-the-planes/`).

Implementing object picking using the depth buffer

Often when working on projects, we need the ability to pick graphical objects on screen. While in OpenGL versions before OpenGL 3.0, the selection buffer was used for this purpose, this buffer is removed in the modern OpenGL 3.3 core profile. However, this leaves us with some alternate methods. We will implement a simple picking technique using the depth buffer in this recipe.

Getting ready

The code for this recipe is in the `Chapter2/Picking_DepthBuffer` folder. Relevant source files are in the `Chapter2/src` folder.

How to do it...

Picking using depth buffer can be implemented as follows:

1. Enable depth testing:

    ```
    glEnable(GL_DEPTH_TEST);
    ```

2. In the mouse down event handler, read the depth value from the depth buffer using the `glReadPixels` function at the clicked point:

    ```
    glReadPixels( x, HEIGHT-y, 1, 1, GL_DEPTH_COMPONENT,
    GL_FLOAT, &winZ);
    ```

3. Unproject the 3D point, `vec3(x,HEIGHT-y,winZ)`, to obtain the object-space point from the clicked screen-space point `x,y` and the depth value `winZ`. Make sure to invert the `y` value by subtracting `HEIGHT` from the screen-space `y` value:

    ```
    glm::vec3 objPt = glm::unProject(glm::vec3
    (x,HEIGHT-y,winZ), MV, P, glm::vec4(0,0,WIDTH, HEIGHT));
    ```

4. Check the distances of all of the scene objects from the object-space point `objPt`. If the distance is within the bounds of the object and the distance of the object is the nearest to the camera, store the index of the object:

    ```
    size_t i=0;
    float minDist = 1000;
    selected_box=-1;
    ```

```
for(i=0;i<3;i++) {
  float dist = glm::distance(box_positions[i], objPt);
  if( dist<1 && dist<minDist) {
    selected_box = i;
    minDist = dist;
  }
}
```

5. Based on the selected index, color the object as selected:

```
glm::mat4 T = glm::translate(glm::mat4(1),
  box_positions[0]);
cube->color =
  (selected_box==0)?glm::vec3(0,1,1):glm::vec3(1,0,0);
cube->Render(glm::value_ptr(MVP*T));

T = glm::translate(glm::mat4(1), box_positions[1]);
cube->color =
  (selected_box==1)?glm::vec3(0,1,1):glm::vec3(0,1,0);
cube->Render(glm::value_ptr(MVP*T));

T = glm::translate(glm::mat4(1), box_positions[2]);
cube->color =
  (selected_box==2)?glm::vec3(0,1,1):glm::vec3(0,0,1);
cube->Render(glm::value_ptr(MVP*T));
```

How it works...

This recipe renders three cubes in red, green, and blue on the screen. When the user clicks on any of these cubes, the depth buffer is read to find the depth value at the clicked point. The object-space point is then obtained by unprojecting (glm::unProject) the clicked point (x,HEIGHT-y, winZ). A loop is then iterated over all objects in the scene to find the nearest object to the object-space point. The index of the nearest intersected object is then stored.

There's more...

In the demonstration application for this recipe, when the user clicks on any cube, the currently selected box changes color to cyan to signify selection, as shown in the following figure:

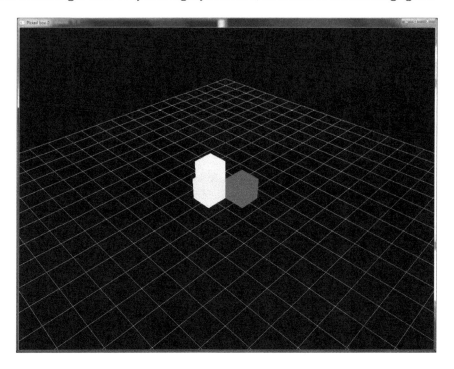

See also

Picking tutorial at OGLDEV (`http://ogldev.atspace.co.uk/www/tutorial29/tutorial29.html`).

Implementing object picking using color

Another method which is used for picking objects in a 3D world is color-based picking. In this recipe, we will use the same scene as in the last recipe.

Getting ready

The code for this recipe is in the `Chapter2/Picking_ColorBuffer` folder. Relevant source files are in the `Chapter2/src` folder.

How to do it...

To enable picking with the color buffer, the following steps are needed:

1. Disable dithering. This is done to prevent any color mismatch during the query:

   ```
   glDisable(GL_DITHER);
   ```

2. In the mouse down event handler, read the color value at the clicked position from the color buffer using the `glReadPixels` function:

   ```
   GLubyte pixel[4];
   glReadPixels(x, HEIGHT-y, 1, 1, GL_RGBA, GL_UNSIGNED_BYTE,
   pixel);
   ```

3. Compare the color value at the clicked point to the color values of all objects to find the intersection:

   ```
   selected_box=-1;
   if(pixel[0]==255 && pixel[1]==0 && pixel[2]==0) {
     cout<<"picked box 1"<<endl;
     selected_box = 0;
   }
   if(pixel[0]==0 && pixel[1]==255 && pixel[2]==0) {
     cout<<"picked box 2"<<endl;
     selected_box = 1;
   }
   if(pixel[0]==0 && pixel[1]==0 && pixel[2]==255) {
     cout<<"picked box 3"<<endl;
     selected_box = 2;
   }
   ```

How it works...

This method is simple to implement. We simply check the color of the pixel where the mouse is clicked. Since dithering might generate a different color value, we disable dithering. The pixel's r, g, and b values are then checked against all of the scene objects and the appropriate object is selected. We could also have used the float data type, GL_FLOAT, when reading and comparing the pixel value. However, due to floating point imprecision, we might not have an accurate test. Therefore, we use the integral data type GL_UNSIGNED_BYTE.

The demonstration application for this recipe uses the scene from the previous recipe. In this demonstration also, the user left-clicks on a box and the selection is highlighted in cyan, as shown in the following figure:

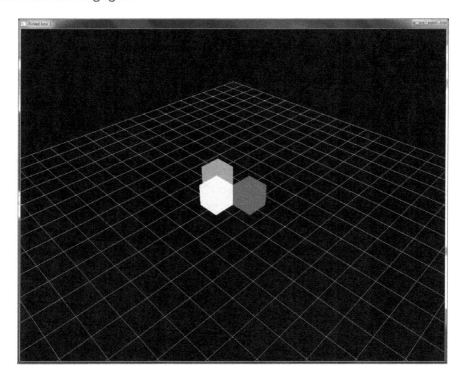

See also

Lighthouse3d color coded picking tutorial (`http://www.lighthouse3d.com/opengl/picking/index.php3?color1`).

Implementing object picking using scene intersection queries

The final method we will cover for picking involves casting rays in the scene to determine the nearest object to the viewer. We will use the same scene as in the last two recipes, three cubes (red, green, and blue colored) placed near the origin.

Getting ready

The code for this recipe is in the `Chapter2/Picking_SceneIntersection` folder. Relevant source files are in the `Chapter2/src` folder.

How to do it...

For picking with scene intersection queries, take the following steps:

1. Get two object-space points by unprojecting the screen-space point (`x`, `HEIGHT-y`), with different depth value, one at z=0 and the other at z=1:

```
glm::vec3 start = glm::unProject(glm::vec3(x,HEIGHT-y,0),
   MV, P, glm::vec4(0,0,WIDTH,HEIGHT));
glm::vec3   end = glm::unProject(glm::vec3(x,HEIGHT-y,1),
   MV, P, glm::vec4(0,0,WIDTH,HEIGHT));
```

2. Get the current camera position as `eyeRay.origin` and get `eyeRay.direction` by subtracting and normalizing the difference of the two object-space points, `end` and `start`, as follows:

```
eyeRay.origin      =  cam.GetPosition();
eyeRay.direction   =  glm::normalize(end-start);
```

3. For all of the objects in the scene, find the intersection of the eye ray with the **Axially Aligned Bounding Box** (**AABB**) of the object. Store the nearest intersected object index:

```
float tMin = numeric_limits<float>::max();
selected_box = -1;
for(int i=0;i<3;i++) {
  glm::vec2 tMinMax = intersectBox(eyeRay, boxes[i]);
  if(tMinMax.x<tMinMax.y && tMinMax.x<tMin) {
    selected_box=i;
    tMin = tMinMax.x;
  }
}
if(selected_box==-1)
  cout<<"No box picked"<<endl;
else
  cout<<"Selected box: "<<selected_box<<endl;
```

How it works...

The method discussed in this recipe first casts a ray from the camera origin in the clicked direction, and then checks all of the scene objects' bounding boxes for intersection. There are two sub parts: estimation of the ray direction from the clicked point and the ray AABB intersection. We first focus on the estimation of the ray direction from the clicked point.

We know that after projection, the x and y values are in the -1 to 1 range. The z or depth values are in the 0 to 1 range, with 0 at the near clip plane and 1 at the far clip plane. We first take the screen-space point and unproject it taking the near clip plane z value of 0. This gives us the object-space point at the near clip plane. Next, we pass the screen-space point and unproject it with the z value of 1. This gives us the object-space point at the far clip plane. Subtracting the two unprojected object-space points gives us the ray direction. We store the camera position as `eyeRay.origin` and normalize the ray direction as `eyeRay.direction`.

After calculating the eye ray, we check it for intersection with all of the scene geometries. If the object-bounding box intersects the eye ray and it is the nearest intersection, we store the index of the object. The `intersectBox` function is defined as follows:

```
glm::vec2 intersectBox(const Ray& ray, const Box& cube) {
  glm::vec3 inv_dir = 1.0f/ray.direction;
  glm::vec3   tMin = (cube.min - ray.origin) * inv_dir;
  glm::vec3   tMax = (cube.max - ray.origin) * inv_dir;
  glm::vec3    t1 = glm::min(tMin, tMax);
  glm::vec3    t2 = glm::max(tMin, tMax);
  float tNear = max(max(t1.x, t1.y), t1.z);
  float  tFar = min(min(t2.x, t2.y), t2.z);
  return glm::vec2(tNear, tFar);
}
```

There's more...

The `intersectBox` function works by finding the intersection of the ray with a pair of slabs for each of the three axes individually. Next it finds the `tNear` and `tFar` values. The box can only intersect with the ray if `tNear` is less than `tFar` for all of the three axes. So the code finds the smallest `tFar` value and the largest `tMin` value. If the smallest `tFar` value is less than the largest `tNear` value, the ray misses the box. For further details, refer to the *See also* section. The output result from the demonstration application for this recipe uses the same scene as in the last two recipes. In this case also, left-clicking the mouse selects the box, which is highlighted in cyan, as shown in the following figure:

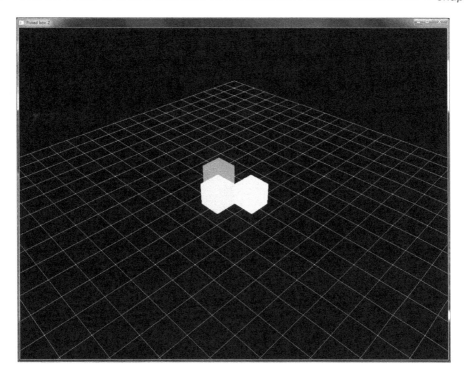

See also

http://www.siggraph.org/education/materials/HyperGraph/raytrace/
rtinter3.htm.

3
Offscreen Rendering and Environment Mapping

In this chapter, we will cover:

- ▶ Implementing the twirl filter using fragment shader
- ▶ Rendering a skybox using static cube mapping
- ▶ Implementing a mirror with render-to-texture using FBO
- ▶ Rendering a reflective object using dynamic cube mapping
- ▶ Implementing area filtering (sharpening/blurring/embossing) on an image using convolution
- ▶ Implementing the glow effect

Introduction

Offscreen rendering functionality is a powerful feature of modern graphics API. In modern OpenGL, this is implemented by using the **Framebuffer objects** (**FBOs**). Some of the applications of the offscreen rendering include post processing effects such as glows, dynamic cubemaps, mirror effect, deferred rendering techniques, image processing techniques, and so on. Nowadays almost all games use this feature to carry out stunning visual effects with high rendering quality and detail. With the FBOs, the offscreen rendering is greatly simplified, as the programmer uses FBO the way he would use any other OpenGL object. This chapter will focus on using FBO to carry out image processing effects for implementing digital convolution and glow. In addition, we will also elaborate on how to use the FBO for mirror effect and dynamic cube mapping.

Implementing the twirl filter using the fragment shader

We will use a simple image manipulation operator in the fragment shader by implementing the twirl filter on the GPU.

Getting ready

This recipe builds up on the image loading recipe from *Chapter 1, Introduction to Modern OpenGL*. The code for this recipe is contained in the `Chapter3/TwirlFilter` directory.

How to do it...

Let us get started with the recipe as follows:

1. Load the image as in the `ImageLoader` recipe from *Chapter 1, Introduction to Modern OpenGL*. Set the texture wrap mode to GL_CLAMP_TO_BORDER.

```
int texture_width = 0, texture_height = 0, channels=0;
GLubyte* pData = SOIL_load_image(filename.c_str(),
&texture_width, &texture_height, &channels,
SOIL_LOAD_AUTO);
int i,j;
for( j = 0; j*2 < texture_height; ++j )
{
  int index1 = j * texture_width * channels;
  int index2 = (texture_height - 1 - j) * texture_width *
  channels;
  for( i = texture_width * channels; i > 0; --i )
  {
    GLubyte temp = pData[index1];
    pData[index1] = pData[index2];
    pData[index2] = temp;
    ++index1;
    ++index2;
  }
}
glGenTextures(1, &textureID);
  glActiveTexture(GL_TEXTURE0);
  glBindTexture(GL_TEXTURE_2D, textureID);
  glTexParameteri(GL_TEXTURE_2D, GL_TEXTURE_MIN_FILTER,
  GL_LINEAR);
```

```
glTexParameteri(GL_TEXTURE_2D, GL_TEXTURE_MAG_FILTER,
GL_LINEAR);
glTexParameteri(GL_TEXTURE_2D, GL_TEXTURE_WRAP_S,
GL_CLAMP_TO_BORDER);
glTexParameteri(GL_TEXTURE_2D, GL_TEXTURE_WRAP_T,
GL_CLAMP_TO_BORDER);
glTexImage2D(GL_TEXTURE_2D, 0, GL_RGB, texture_width,
texture_height, 0, GL_RGB, GL_UNSIGNED_BYTE, pData);
SOIL_free_image_data(pData);
```

2. Set up a simple pass through vertex shader that outputs the texture coordinates for texture lookup in the fragment shader, as given in the `ImageLoader` recipe of *Chapter 1*.

```
void main()
{
  gl_Position = vec4(vVertex*2.0-1,0,1);
  vUV = vVertex;
}
```

3. Set up the fragment shader that first shifts the texture coordinates, performs the twirl transformation, and then converts the shifted texture coordinates back for texture lookup.

```
void main()
{
  vec2 uv = vUV-0.5;
  float angle = atan(uv.y, uv.x);
  float radius = length(uv);
  angle+= radius*twirl_amount;
  vec2 shifted = radius* vec2(cos(angle), sin(angle));
  vFragColor = texture(textureMap, (shifted+0.5));
}
```

4. Render a 2D screen space quad and apply the two shaders as was done in the `ImageLoader` recipe in *Chapter 1*.

```
void OnRender() {
  glClear(GL_COLOR_BUFFER_BIT|GL_DEPTH_BUFFER_BIT);
  shader.Use();
    glUniform1f(shader("twirl_amount"), twirl_amount);
    glDrawElements(GL_TRIANGLES, 6, GL_UNSIGNED_SHORT, 0);
  shader.UnUse();
  glutSwapBuffers();
}
```

How it works...

Twirl is a simple 2D transformation which deforms the image. In polar coordinates, this transformation is given simply as follows:

$$g(r,\theta) = f(r,\theta + r*t)$$

In this equation, *t* is the amount of twirl applied on the input image *f*. In practice, our images are a 2D function *f(x,y)* of Cartesian coordinates. We first convert the Cartesian coordinates to polar coordinates *(r,θ)* by using the following transformation:

$$\theta = \arctan(y,x)$$
$$r = \sqrt{x*x + y*y}$$

Here, *x* and *y* are the two Cartesian coordinates. In the fragment shader, we first offset the texture coordinates so that the origin is at the center of the image. Next, we get the angle *θ* and radius *r*.

```
void main() {
    vec2 uv = vUV-0.5;
    float angle = atan(uv.y, uv.x);
    float radius = length(uv);
```

We then increment the angle by the given amount, multiplied by the radius. Next, we convert the polar coordinates back to Cartesian coordinates.

```
angle+= radius*twirl_amount;
vec2 shifted = radius* vec2(cos(angle), sin(angle));
```

Finally, we offset the texture coordinates back to the original position. The transformed texture coordinates are then used for texture lookup.

```
vFragColor = texture(textureMap, (shifted+0.5));
}
```

There's more...

The demo application implementing this recipe shows a rendered image. Using the - and + keys, we can adjust the twirl amount as shown in the following figure:

Since the texture clamping mode was set to GL_CLAMP_TO_BORDER, the out of image pixels get the black color. In this recipe, we applied the twirl effect to the whole image. As an exercise, we invite the reader to limit the twirl to a specific zone within the image; for example, within a radius of, say, 150 pixels from the center of image. Hint: You can constrain the radius using the given pixel distance.

Rendering a skybox using static cube mapping

This recipe will show how to render a skybox object using static cube mapping. Cube mapping is a simple technique for generating a surrounding environment. There are several methods, such as sky dome, which uses a spherical geometry; skybox, which uses a cubical geometry; and skyplane, which uses a planar geometry. For this recipe, we will focus on skyboxes using the static cube mapping approach. The cube mapping process needs six images that are placed on each face of a cube. The skybox is a very large cube that moves with the camera but does not rotate with it.

Getting ready

The code for this recipe is contained in the Chapter3/Skybox directory.

How to do it...

Let us get started with the recipe as follows:

1. Set up the vertex array and vertex buffer objects to store a unit cube geometry.

2. Load the skybox images using an image loading library, such as SOIL.

```
int texture_widths[6];
int texture_heights[6];
int channels[6];
GLubyte* pData[6];
cout<<"Loading skybox images: ..."<<endl;
for(int i=0;i<6;i++) {
  cout<<"\tLoading: "<<texture_names[i]<<" ... ";
  pData[i] = SOIL_load_image(texture_names[i],
  &texture_widths[i], &texture_heights[i], &channels[i],
  SOIL_LOAD_AUTO);
  cout<<"done."<<endl;
}
```

3. Generate a cubemap OpenGL texture object and bind the six loaded images to the GL_TEXTURE_CUBE_MAP texture targets. Also make sure that the image data loaded by the SOIL library is deleted after the texture data has been stored into the OpenGL texture.

```
glGenTextures(1, &skyboxTextureID);
glActiveTexture(GL_TEXTURE0);
glBindTexture(GL_TEXTURE_CUBE_MAP, skyboxTextureID);
glTexParameteri(GL_TEXTURE_CUBE_MAP, GL_TEXTURE_MIN_FILTER,
GL_LINEAR);
glTexParameteri(GL_TEXTURE_CUBE_MAP, GL_TEXTURE_MAG_FILTER,
GL_LINEAR);
glTexParameteri(GL_TEXTURE_CUBE_MAP, GL_TEXTURE_WRAP_S,
GL_CLAMP_TO_EDGE);
glTexParameteri(GL_TEXTURE_CUBE_MAP, GL_TEXTURE_WRAP_T,
GL_CLAMP_TO_EDGE);
glTexParameteri(GL_TEXTURE_CUBE_MAP, GL_TEXTURE_WRAP_R,
GL_CLAMP_TO_EDGE);
GLint format = (channels[0]==4)?GL_RGBA:GL_RGB;

for(int i=0;i<6;i++) {
  glTexImage2D(GL_TEXTURE_CUBE_MAP_POSITIVE_X + i, 0,
  format,texture_widths[i], texture_heights[i], 0, format,
  GL_UNSIGNED_BYTE, pData[i]);
  SOIL_free_image_data(pData[i]);
}
```

4. Set up a vertex shader (see `Chapter3/Skybox/shaders/skybox.vert`) that outputs the vertex's object space position as the texture coordinate.

```
smooth out vec3 uv;
void main()
{
  gl_Position = MVP*vec4(vVertex,1);
  uv = vVertex;
}
```

5. Add a cubemap sampler to the fragment shader. Use the texture coordinates output from the vertex shader to sample the cubemap sampler object in the fragment shader (see `Chapter3/Skybox/shaders/skybox.frag`).

```
layout(location=0) out vec4 vFragColor;
uniform samplerCube cubeMap;
smooth in vec3 uv;
void main()
{
    vFragColor = texture(cubeMap, uv);
}
```

How it works...

There are two parts of this recipe. The first part, which loads an OpenGL cubemap texture, is self explanatory. We load the six images and bind these to an OpenGL cubemap texture target. There are six cubemap texture targets corresponding to the six sides of a cube. These targets are `GL_TEXTURE_CUBE_MAP_POSITIVE_X`, `GL_TEXTURE_CUBE_MAP_POSITIVE_Y`, `GL_TEXTURE_CUBE_MAP_POSITIVE_Z`, `GL_TEXTURE_CUBE_MAP_NEGATIVE_X`, `GL_TEXTURE_CUBE_MAP_NEGATIVE_Y`, and `GL_TEXTURE_CUBE_MAP_NEGATIVE_Z`. Since their identifiers are linearly generated, we offset the target by the loop variable to move to the next cubemap texture target in the following code:

```
for(int i=0;i<6;i++) {
   glTexImage2D(GL_TEXTURE_CUBE_MAP_POSITIVE_X + i, 0,
   format,texture_widths[i], texture_heights[i], 0, format,
   GL_UNSIGNED_BYTE, pData[i]);
   SOIL_free_image_data(pData[i]);
}
```

The second part is the shader responsible for sampling the cubemap texture. This work is carried out in the fragment shader (`Chapter3/Skybox/shaders/skybox.frag`). In the rendering code, we set the skybox shader and then render the skybox, passing it the MVP matrix, which is obtained as follows:

```
glm::mat4 T = glm::translate(glm::mat4(1.0f),glm::vec3(0.0f,0.0f,
dist));
glm::mat4 Rx  = glm::rotate(glm::mat4(1),   rX, glm::vec3(1.0f,
0.0f, 0.0f));
```

```
glm::mat4 MV  = glm::rotate(Rx, rY, glm::vec3(0.0f, 1.0f, 0.0f));
glm::mat4 S   = glm::scale(glm::mat4(1),glm::vec3(1000.0));
glm::mat4 MVP = P*MV*S;
skybox->Render( glm::value_ptr(MVP));
```

To sample the correct location in the cubemap texture we need a vector. This vector can be obtained from the object space vertex positions that are passed to the vertex shader. These are passed through the `uv` output attribute to the fragment shader.

In this recipe, we scaled a unit cube. While it is not necessary to have a unit cube, one thing that we have to be careful with is that the size of the cube after scaling should not be greater than the far clip plane distance. Otherwise, our skybox will be clipped.

There's more...

The demo application implementing this recipe shows a statically cube mapped skybox which can be looked around by dragging the left mouse button. This gives a surrounded environment feeling to the user as shown in the following figure:

Implementing a mirror with render-to-texture using FBO

We will now use the FBO to render a mirror object on the screen. In a typical offscreen rendering OpenGL application, we set up the FBO first, by calling the `glGenFramebuffers` function and passing it the number of FBOs desired. The second parameter stores the returned identifier. After the FBO object is generated, it has to be bound to the `GL_FRAMEBUFFER`, `GL_DRAW_FRAMEBUFFER,` or `GL_READ_FRAMEBUFFER` target. Following this call, the texture to be bound to the FBOs color attachment is attached by calling the `glFramebufferTexture2D` function.

There can be more than one color attachment on an FBO. The maximum number of color attachments supported on any GPU can be queried using the `GL_MAX_COLOR_ATTACHMENTS` field. The type and dimension of the texture has to be specified and it is not necessary to have the same size as the screen. However, all color attachments on the FBO must have the same dimensions. At any time, only a single FBO can be bound for a drawing operation and similarly, only one can be bound for a reading operation. In addition to the color attachment, there are also depth and stencil attachments on an FBO. The following image shows the different attachment points on an FBO:

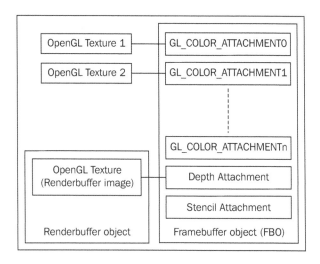

If depth testing is required, a render buffer is also generated and bound by calling `glGenRenderbuffers` followed by the `glBindRenderbuffer` function. For render buffers, the depth buffer's data type and its dimensions have to be specified. After all these steps, the render buffer is attached to the frame buffer by calling the `glFramebufferRenderbuffer` function.

After the setup of the frame buffer and render buffer objects, the frame buffer completeness status has to be checked by calling glCheckFramebufferStatus by passing it the framebuffer target. This ensures that the FBO setup is correct. The function returns the status as an identifier. If this returned value is anything other than GL_FRAMEBUFFER_ COMPLETE, the FBO setup is unsuccessful.

Make sure to check the Framebuffer status after the Framebuffer is bound.

Similar to other OpenGL objects, we must delete the framebuffer and the renderbuffer objects and any texture objects used for offscreen rendering after they are no more needed, by calling the glDeleteFramebuffers and glDeleteRenderbuffers functions. These are the typical steps needed to enable offscreen rendering using FBO objects in modern OpenGL.

Getting ready

The code for this recipe is contained in the Chapter3/MirrorUsingFBO directory.

How to do it...

Let us get started with the recipe as follows:

1. Initialize the framebuffer and renderbuffer objects' color and depth attachments respectively. The render buffer is required if we need depth testing for the offscreen rendering, and the depth precision is specified using the glRenderbufferStorage function.

    ```
    glGenFramebuffers(1, &fboID);
    glBindFramebuffer(GL_DRAW_FRAMEBUFFER, fboID);
    glGenRenderbuffers(1, &rbID);
    glBindRenderbuffer(GL_RENDERBUFFER, rbID);
    glRenderbufferStorage(GL_RENDERBUFFER,
    GL_DEPTH_COMPONENT32,WIDTH, HEIGHT);
    ```

2. Generate the offscreen texture on which FBO will render to. The last parameter of glTexImage2D is NULL, which tells OpenGL that we do not have any content yet, please provide a new block of GPU memory which gets filled when the FBO is used as a render target.

    ```
    glGenTextures(1, &renderTextureID);
    glBindTexture(GL_TEXTURE_2D, renderTextureID);
    glTexParameteri(GL_TEXTURE_2D, GL_TEXTURE_WRAP_S,
    GL_REPEAT);
    glTexParameteri(GL_TEXTURE_2D, GL_TEXTURE_WRAP_T,
    L_REPEAT);
    ```

```
glTexParameteri(GL_TEXTURE_2D, GL_TEXTURE_MIN_FILTER,
GL_NEAREST);
glTexParameteri(GL_TEXTURE_2D, GL_TEXTURE_MAG_FILTER,
GL_NEAREST);
glTexImage2D(GL_TEXTURE_2D, 0, GL_RGBA8, WIDTH, HEIGHT, 0,
GL_BGRA, GL_UNSIGNED_BYTE, NULL);
```

3. Attach `Renderbuffer` to the bound `Framebuffer` object and check for `Framebuffer` completeness.

```
glFramebufferTexture2D(GL_DRAW_FRAMEBUFFER,
GL_COLOR_ATTACHMENT0,GL_TEXTURE_2D, renderTextureID, 0);
glFramebufferRenderbuffer(GL_DRAW_FRAMEBUFFER,
GL_DEPTH_ATTACHMENT,GL_RENDERBUFFER, rbID);
GLuint status = glCheckFramebufferStatus(GL_DRAW_FRAMEBUFFER);
if(status==GL_FRAMEBUFFER_COMPLETE) {
printf("FBO setup succeeded.");
} else {
printf("Error in FBO setup.");
}
```

4. Unbind the `Framebuffer` object as follows:

```
glBindTexture(GL_TEXTURE_2D, 0);
glBindFramebuffer(GL_DRAW_FRAMEBUFFER, 0);
```

5. Create a quad geometry to act as a mirror:

```
mirror = new CQuad(-2);
```

6. Render the scene normally from the point of view of camera. Since the unit color cube is rendered at origin, we translate it on the Y axis to shift it up in Y axis which effectively moves the unit color cube in Y direction so that the unit color cube's image can be viewed completely in the mirror.

```
glClear(GL_COLOR_BUFFER_BIT|GL_DEPTH_BUFFER_BIT);
grid->Render(glm::value_ptr(MVP));
localR[3][1] = 0.5;
cube->Render(glm::value_ptr(P*MV*localR));
```

7. Store the current modelview matrix and then change the modelview matrix such that the camera is placed at the mirror object position. Also make sure to laterally invert this modelview matrix by scaling by -1 on the X axis.

```
glm::mat4 oldMV = MV;
glm::vec3 target;
glm::vec3 V = glm::vec3(-MV[2][0], -MV[2][1], -MV[2][2]);
glm::vec3 R = glm::reflect(V, mirror->normal);
MV = glm::lookAt(mirror->position, mirror->position + R,
glm::vec3(0,1,0));
MV = glm::scale(MV, glm::vec3(-1,1,1));
```

8. Bind the FBO, set up the FBO color attachment for Drawbuffer (GL_COLOR_
    ATTACHMENT0) or any other attachment to which texture is attached, and clear
    the FBO. The glDrawBuffer function enables the code to draw to a specific color
    attachment on the FBO. In our case, there is a single color attachment so we set
    it as the draw buffer.

    ```
    glBindFramebuffer(GL_DRAW_FRAMEBUFFER, fboID);
    glDrawBuffer(GL_COLOR_ATTACHMENT0);
    glClear(GL_COLOR_BUFFER_BIT|GL_DEPTH_BUFFER_BIT);
    ```

9. Set the modified modelview matrix and render the scene again. Also make sure to
    only render from the shiny side of the mirror.

    ```
    if(glm::dot(V,mirror->normal)<0) {
      grid->Render(glm::value_ptr(P*MV));
      cube->Render(glm::value_ptr(P*MV*localR));
    }
    ```

10. Unbind the FBO and restore the default Drawbuffer (GL_BACK_LEFT).

    ```
    glBindFramebuffer(GL_DRAW_FRAMEBUFFER, 0);
    glDrawBuffer(GL_BACK_LEFT);
    ```

> Note that there are several aliases for the back buffer. The real back
> buffer is GL_BACK_LEFT, which is also referred by the GL_BACK
> alias. The default Framebuffer has up to four color buffers, namely
> GL_FRONT_LEFT, GL_FRONT_RIGHT, GL_BACK_LEFT, and
> GL_BACK_RIGHT. If stereo rendering is not active, then only the left
> buffers are active, that is, GL_FRONT_LEFT (the active front color
> buffer) and GL_BACK_LEFT (the active back color buffer).

11. Finally render the mirror quad at the saved modelview matrix.

    ```
    MV = oldMV;
    glBindTexture(GL_TEXTURE_2D, renderTextureID);
    mirror->Render(glm::value_ptr(P*MV));
    ```

How it works...

The mirror algorithm used in the recipe is very simple. We first get the view direction vector
(V) from the viewing matrix. We reflect this vector on the normal of the mirror (N). Next, the
camera position is moved to the place behind the mirror. Finally, the mirror is scaled by -1
on the X axis. This ensures that the image is laterally inverted as in a mirror. Details of the
method are covered in the reference in the *See also* section.

There's more...

Details of the `Framebuffer` object can be obtained from the `Framebuffer` object specifications (see the *See also* section). The output from the demo application implementing this recipe is as follows:

See also

▶ The Official OpenGL registry-Framebuffer object specifications can be found at `http://www.opengl.org/registry/specs/EXT/framebuffer_object.txt`.

▶ *OpenGL Superbible, Fifth Edition, Chapter 8*, pages 354-358, *Richard S. Wright, Addison-Wesley Professional*

▶ FBO tutorial by *Song Ho Ahn*: `http://www.songho.ca/opengl/gl_fbo.html`

Rendering a reflective object using dynamic cube mapping

Now we will see how to use dynamic cube mapping to render a real-time scene to a cubemap render target. This allows us to create reflective surfaces. In modern OpenGL, offscreen rendering (also called render-to-texture) functionality is exposed through FBOs.

Getting ready

In this recipe, we will render a box with encircling particles. The code is contained in the `Chapter3/DynamicCubemap` directory.

How to do it...

Let us get started with the recipe as follows:

1. Create a cubemap texture object.

```
glGenTextures(1, &dynamicCubeMapID);
glActiveTexture(GL_TEXTURE1);
glBindTexture(GL_TEXTURE_CUBE_MAP, dynamicCubeMapID);
glTexParameterf(GL_TEXTURE_CUBE_MAP,GL_TEXTURE_MIN_FILTER,
GL_LINEAR);
glTexParameterf(GL_TEXTURE_CUBE_MAP, GL_TEXTURE_MAG_FILTER,
GL_LINEAR);
glTexParameterf(GL_TEXTURE_CUBE_MAP, GL_TEXTURE_WRAP_S,
GL_CLAMP_TO_EDGE);
glTexParameterf(GL_TEXTURE_CUBE_MAP, GL_TEXTURE_WRAP_T,
GL_CLAMP_TO_EDGE);
glTexParameterf(GL_TEXTURE_CUBE_MAP, GL_TEXTURE_WRAP_R,
GL_CLAMP_TO_EDGE);
for (int face = 0; face < 6; face++) {
  glTexImage2D(GL_TEXTURE_CUBE_MAP_POSITIVE_X + face, 0,
  GL_RGBA,CUBEMAP_SIZE, CUBEMAP_SIZE, 0, GL_RGBA, GL_FLOAT,
  NULL);
}
```

2. Set up an FBO with the cubemap texture as an attachment.

```
glGenFramebuffers(1, &fboID);
glBindFramebuffer(GL_DRAW_FRAMEBUFFER, fboID);
glGenRenderbuffers(1, &rboID);
glBindRenderbuffer(GL_RENDERBUFFER, rboID);
glRenderbufferStorage(GL_RENDERBUFFER, GL_DEPTH_COMPONENT,
CUBEMAP_SIZE, CUBEMAP_SIZE);
glFramebufferRenderbuffer(GL_DRAW_FRAMEBUFFER,
GL_DEPTH_ATTACHMENT, GL_RENDERBUFFER, fboID);
glFramebufferTexture2D(GL_DRAW_FRAMEBUFFER,
GL_COLOR_ATTACHMENT0, GL_TEXTURE_CUBE_MAP_POSITIVE_X,
dynamicCubeMapID, 0);
GLenum status =
glCheckFramebufferStatus(GL_DRAW_FRAMEBUFFER);
if(status != GL_FRAMEBUFFER_COMPLETE) {
  cerr<<"Frame buffer object setup error."<<endl;
  exit(EXIT_FAILURE);
} else {
  cerr<<"FBO setup successfully."<<endl;
}
```

3. Set the viewport to the size of the offscreen texture and render the scene six times without the reflective object to the six sides of the cubemap using FBO.

```
glViewport(0,0,CUBEMAP_SIZE,CUBEMAP_SIZE);
glBindFramebuffer(GL_DRAW_FRAMEBUFFER, fboID);
glFramebufferTexture2D(GL_DRAW_FRAMEBUFFER,
GL_COLOR_ATTACHMENT0,GL_TEXTURE_CUBE_MAP_POSITIVE_X,
dynamicCubeMapID, 0);
glClear(GL_COLOR_BUFFER_BIT|GL_DEPTH_BUFFER_BIT);
glm::mat4   MV1 = glm::lookAt(glm::vec3(0),glm::vec3(1,0,0),glm::v
ec3(0,-
1,0));
DrawScene( MV1*T, Pcubemap);

glFramebufferTexture2D(GL_DRAW_FRAMEBUFFER,
GL_COLOR_ATTACHMENT0, GL_TEXTURE_CUBE_MAP_NEGATIVE_X,
dynamicCubeMapID, 0);
glClear(GL_COLOR_BUFFER_BIT|GL_DEPTH_BUFFER_BIT);
glm::mat4 MV2 = glm::lookAt(glm::vec3(0),glm::vec3(-1,0,0),
glm::vec3(0,-1,0));
DrawScene( MV2*T, Pcubemap);

...//similar for rest of the faces
   glBindFramebuffer(GL_DRAW_FRAMEBUFFER, 0);
```

4. Restore the viewport and the modelview matrix, and render the scene normally.

```
    glViewport(0,0,WIDTH,HEIGHT);
    DrawScene(MV, P);
```

5. Set the cubemap shader and then render the reflective object.

```
glBindVertexArray(sphereVAOID);
cubemapShader.Use();
T = glm::translate(glm::mat4(1), p);
glUniformMatrix4fv(cubemapShader("MVP"), 1, GL_FALSE,
glm::value_ptr(P*(MV*T)));
glUniform3fv(cubemapShader("eyePosition"), 1,
glm::value_ptr(eyePos));
glDrawElements(GL_TRIANGLES,indices.size(),
GL_UNSIGNED_SHORT,0);
cubemapShader.UnUse();
```

How it works...

Dynamic cube mapping renders the scene six times from the reflective object using six cameras at the reflective object's position. For rendering to the cubemap texture, an FBO is used with a cubemap texture attachment. The cubemap texture's GL_TEXTURE_CUBE_MAP_POSITIVE_X target is bound to the GL_COLOR_ATTACHMENT0 color attachment of the FBO. The last parameter of glTexImage2D is NULL since this call just allocates the memory for offscreen rendering and the real data will be populated when the FBO is set as the render target.

The scene is then rendered to the cubemap texture without the reflective object by placing six cameras at the reflective object's position in the six directions. The cubemap projection matrix (Pcubemap) is given a 90 degree fov.

```
Pcubemap = glm::perspective(90.0f,1.0f,0.1f,1000.0f);
```

This renders the scene into the cubemap texture. For each side, a new MVP matrix is obtained by multiplying the new MV matrix (obtained by using glm::lookAt function). This is repeated for all six sides of the cube. Next, the scene is rendered normally and the reflective object is finally rendered using the generated cubemap to render the reflective environment. Rendering each frame six times into an offscreen target hinders performance, especially if there are complex objects in the world. Therefore this technique should be used with caution.

The cubemap vertex shader outputs the object space vertex positions and normals.

```
#version 330 core
layout(location=0) in vec3 vVertex;
layout(location=1) in vec3 vNormal;
uniform mat4 MVP;
smooth out vec3 position;
smooth out vec3 normal;
void main() {
position = vVertex;
normal = vNormal;
    gl_Position = MVP*vec4(vVertex,1);
}
```

The cubemap fragment shader uses the object space vertex positions to determine the view vector. The reflection vector is then obtained by reflecting the view vector at the object space normal.

```
#version 330 core
layout(location=0) out vec4 vFragColor;
uniform samplerCube cubeMap;
smooth in vec3 position;
smooth in vec3 normal;
uniform vec3 eyePosition;
```

```
void main() {
  vec3 N = normalize(normal);
  vec3 V = normalize(position-eyePosition);
  vFragColor = texture(cubeMap, reflect(V,N));
}
```

There's more...

The demo application implementing this recipe renders a reflective sphere with eight cubes pulsating around it, as shown in the following figure:

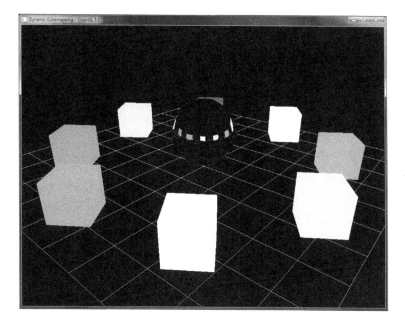

In this recipe, we could also use layered rendering by using the geometry shader to output to a different `Framebuffer` object layer. This can be achieved by outputting to the appropriate `gl_Layer` attribute from the geometry shader and setting the appropriate viewing transformation. This is left as an exercise for the reader.

See also

- Check the OpenGL wiki page at `http://www.opengl.org/wiki/Geometry_Shader#Layered_rendering`
- FBO tutorial by Song Ho Ahn: `http://www.songho.ca/opengl/gl_fbo.html`

Implementing area filtering (sharpening/blurring/embossing) on an image using convolution

We will now see how to do area filtering, that is, 2D image convolution to implement effects like sharpening, blurring, and embossing. There are several ways to achieve image convolution in the spatial domain. The simplest approach is to use a loop that iterates through a given image window and computes the sum of products of the image intensities with the convolution kernel. The more efficient method, as far as the implementation is concerned, is separable convolution which breaks up the 2D convolution into two 1D convolutions. However, this approach requires an additional pass.

Getting ready

This recipe is built on top of the image loading recipe discussed in the first chapter. If you feel a bit lost, we suggest skimming through it to be on page with us. The code for this recipe is contained in the `Chapter3/Convolution` directory. For this recipe, most of the work takes place in the fragment shader.

How to do it...

Let us get started with the recipe as follows:

1. Create a simple pass-through vertex shader that outputs the clip space position and the texture coordinates which are to be passed into the fragment shader for texture lookup.

```
#version 330 core
in vec2 vVertex;
out vec2 vUV;
void main()
{
  gl_Position = vec4(vVertex*2.0-1,0,1);
  vUV = vVertex;
}
```

2. In the fragment shader, we declare a constant array called `kernel` which stores our convolution `kernel`. Changing the convolution `kernel` values dictates the output of convolution. The default `kernel` sets up a sharpening convolution filter. Refer to `Chapter3/Convolution/shaders/shader_convolution.frag` for details.

```
const float kernel[]=float[9] (-1,-1,-1,
                               -1, 8,-1,
                               -1,-1,-1);
```

3. In the fragment shader, we run a nested loop that loops through the current pixel's neighborhood and multiplies the `kernel` value with the current pixel's value. This is continued in an *n x n* neighborhood, where *n* is the width/height of the `kernel`.

```
for(int j=-1;j<=1;j++) {
  for(int i=-1;i<=1;i++) {
    color += kernel[index--] *
    texture(textureMap, vUV+(vec2(i,j)*delta));
  }
}
```

4. After the nested loops, we divide the color value with the total number of values in the `kernel`. For a *3 x 3* `kernel`, we have nine values. Finally, we add the convolved color value to the current pixel's value.

```
color/=9.0;
vFragColor = color + texture(textureMap, vUV);
```

How it works...

For a 2D digital image *f(x,y)*, the processed image *g(x,y)*, after the convolution operation with a kernel *h(x,y)*, is defined mathematically as follows:

$$g(x,y) = \sum_{j=y-w}^{y+w} \sum_{i=x-w}^{x+w} f(i,j) * h(x-i, y-j)$$

For each pixel, we simply sum the product of the current image pixel value with the corresponding coefficient in the kernel in the given neighborhood. For details about the kernel coefficients, we refer the reader to any standard text on digital image processing, like the one given in the *See also* section.

The overall algorithm works like this. We set up our FBO for offscreen rendering. We render our image on the offscreen render target of the FBO, instead of the back buffer. Now the FBO attachment stores our image. Next, we set the output from the first step (that is, the rendered image on the FBO attachment) as input to the convolution shader in the second pass. We render a full-screen quad on the back buffer and apply our convolution shader to it. This performs convolution on the input image. Finally, we swap the back buffer to show the result on the screen.

After the image is loaded and an OpenGL texture has been generated, we render a screen-aligned quad. This allows the fragment shader to run for the whole screen. In the fragment shader, for the current fragment, we iterate through its neighborhood and sum the product of the corresponding entry in the kernel with the look-up value. After the loop is terminated, the sum is divided by the total number of kernel coefficients. Finally, the convolution sum is added to the current pixel's value. There are several different kinds of kernels. We list the ones we will use in this recipe in the following table.

> Based on the wrapping mode set for the texture, for example, GL_CLAMP or GL_REPEAT, the convolution result will be different. In case of the GL_CLAMP wrapping mode, the pixels out of the image are not considered, whereas, in case of the GL_REPEAT wrapping mode, the out of the image pixel information is obtained from the pixel at the wrapping position.

Effect	Kernel matrix
Sharpening	$\begin{bmatrix} -1 & -1 & -1 \\ -1 & 8 & -1 \\ -1 & -1 & -1 \end{bmatrix}$
Blurring / Unweighted Smoothing	$\begin{bmatrix} 1 & 1 & 1 \\ 1 & 1 & 1 \\ 1 & 1 & 1 \end{bmatrix}$
3 x 3 Gaussian blur	$\begin{bmatrix} 0 & 1 & 0 \\ 1 & 5 & 1 \\ 0 & 1 & 0 \end{bmatrix}$
Emboss north-west direction	$\begin{bmatrix} -4 & -4 & 0 \\ -4 & 12 & 0 \\ 0 & 0 & 0 \end{bmatrix}$
Emboss north-east direction	$\begin{bmatrix} 0 & -4 & -4 \\ 0 & 12 & -4 \\ 0 & 0 & 0 \end{bmatrix}$

Effect	Kernel matrix
Emboss south-east direction	$\begin{bmatrix} 0 & 0 & 0 \\ 0 & 12 & -4 \\ 0 & -4 & -4 \end{bmatrix}$
Emboss south-west direction	$\begin{bmatrix} 0 & 0 & 0 \\ -4 & 12 & 0 \\ -4 & -4 & 0 \end{bmatrix}$

There's more...

We just touched the topic of digital image convolution. For details, we refer the reader to the *See also* section. In the demo application, the user can set the required kernel and then press the Space bar key to see the filtered image output. Pressing the Space bar key once again shows the normal unfiltered image.

See also

- *Digital Image Processing, Third Edition, Rafael C. Gonzales and Richard E. Woods, Prentice Hall*
- FBO tutorial by Song Ho Ahn: `http://www.songho.ca/opengl/gl_fbo.html`

Implementing the glow effect

Now that we know how to perform offscreen rendering and blurring, we will put this knowledge to use by implementing the glow effect. The code for this recipe is in the `Chapter3/Glow` directory. In this recipe, we will render a set of points encircling a cube. Every 50 frames, four alternate points glow.

How to do it...

Let us get started with the recipe as follows:

1. Render the scene normally by rendering the points and the cube. The particle shader renders the `GL_POINTS` value (which by default, renders as quads) as circles.

```
grid->Render(glm::value_ptr(MVP));
cube->Render(glm::value_ptr(MVP));
glBindVertexArray(particlesVAO);
particleShader.Use();
```

```
glUniformMatrix4fv(particleShader("MVP"), 1, GL_FALSE,
glm::value_ptr(MVP*Rot));
glDrawArrays(GL_POINTS, 0, 8);
```

The particle vertex shader is as follows:

```
#version 330 core
layout(location=0) in vec3 vVertex;
uniform mat4 MVP;
smooth out vec4 color;
const vec4 colors[8]=vec4[8](vec4(1,0,0,1), vec4(0,1,0,1),
vec4(0,0,1,1),vec4(1,1,0,1), vec4(0,1,1,1), vec4(1,0,1,1),
vec4(0.5,0.5,0.5,1),  vec4(1,1,1,1)) ;

void main() {
  gl_Position = MVP*vec4(vVertex,1);
  color = colors[gl_VertexID/4];
}
```

The particle fragment shader is as follows:

```
#version 330 core
layout(location=0) out vec4 vFragColor;

smooth in vec4 color;

void main() {
  vec2 pos = gl_PointCoord-0.5;
  if(dot(pos,pos)>0.25)
    discard;
  else
    vFragColor = color;
}
```

2. Set up a single FBO with two color attachments. The first attachment is for rendering of scene elements requiring glow and the second attachment is for blurring.

```
glGenFramebuffers(1, &fboID);
glBindFramebuffer(GL_DRAW_FRAMEBUFFER, fboID);
glGenTextures(2, texID);
glActiveTexture(GL_TEXTURE0);
for(int i=0;i<2;i++) {
  glBindTexture(GL_TEXTURE_2D, texID[i]);
  glTexParameterf(GL_TEXTURE_2D,
  GL_TEXTURE_MIN_FILTER,GL_LINEAR);
  glTexParameterf(GL_TXTURE_2D,
  GL_TEXTURE_MAG_FILTER,GL_LINEAR)
```

```
    glTexParameterf(GL_TEXTURE_2D, GL_TEXTURE_WRAP_S,
    GL_CLAMP_TO_EDGE);
    glTexParameterf(GL_TEXTURE_2D, GL_TEXTURE_WRAP_T,
    GL_CLAMP_TO_EDGE);
    glTexImage2D(GL_TEXTURE_2D, 0, GL_RGBA,
    RENDER_TARGET_WIDTH, RENDER_TARGET_HEIGHT, 0,
    GL_RGBA,GL_UNSIGNED_BYTE, NULL);
    glFramebufferTexture2D(GL_DRAW_FRAMEBUFFER,
    GL_COLOR_ATTACHMENT0+i,GL_TEXTURE_2D,texID[i],0);
}
GLenum status =
glCheckFramebufferStatus(GL_DRAW_FRAMEBUFFER);
if(status != GL_FRAMEBUFFER_COMPLETE) {
  cerr<<"Frame buffer object setup error."<<endl;
  exit(EXIT_FAILURE);
} else {
  cerr<<"FBO set up successfully."<<endl;
}
glBindFramebuffer(GL_DRAW_FRAMEBUFFER, 0);
```

3. Bind FBO, set the viewport to the size of the attachment texture, set `Drawbuffer` to render to the first color attachment (`GL_COLOR_ATTACHMENT0`), and render the part of the scene which needs glow.

```
glBindFramebuffer(GL_DRAW_FRAMEBUFFER, fboID);
glViewport(0,0,RENDER_TARGET_WIDTH,RENDER_TARGET_HEIGHT);
glDrawBuffer(GL_COLOR_ATTACHMENT0);
glClear(GL_COLOR_BUFFER_BIT);
  glDrawArrays(GL_POINTS, offset, 4);
particleShader.UnUse();
```

4. Set `Drawbuffer` to render to the second color attachment (`GL_COLOR_ATTACHMENT1`) and bind the FBO texture attached to the first color attachment. Set the blur shader by convolving with a simple unweighted smoothing filter.

```
glDrawBuffer(GL_COLOR_ATTACHMENT1);
glBindTexture(GL_TEXTURE_2D, texID[0]);
```

5. Render a screen-aligned quad and apply the blur shader to the rendering result from the first color attachment of the FBO. This output is written to the second color attachment.

```
blurShader.Use();
glBindVertexArray(quadVAOID);
glDrawElements(GL_TRIANGLES,6,GL_UNSIGNED_SHORT,0);
```

6. Disable FBO rendering, reset the default drawbuffer (GL_BACK_LEFT) and viewport, bind the texture attached to the FBO's second color attachment, draw a screen-aligned quad, and blend the blur output to the existing scene using additive blending.

```
glBindFramebuffer(GL_DRAW_FRAMEBUFFER, 0);
glDrawBuffer(GL_BACK_LEFT);
glBindTexture(GL_TEXTURE_2D, texID[1]);
glViewport(0,0,WIDTH, HEIGHT);
glEnable(GL_BLEND);
glBlendFunc(GL_ONE, GL_ONE);
glDrawElements(GL_TRIANGLES,6,GL_UNSIGNED_SHORT,0);
glBindVertexArray(0);
blurShader.UnUse();
glDisable(GL_BLEND);
```

How it works...

The glow effect works by first rendering the candidate elements of the scene for glow into a separate render target. After rendering, a smoothing filter is applied on the rendered image containing the elements requiring glow. The smoothed output is then additively blended with the current rendering on the frame buffer, as shown in the following figure:

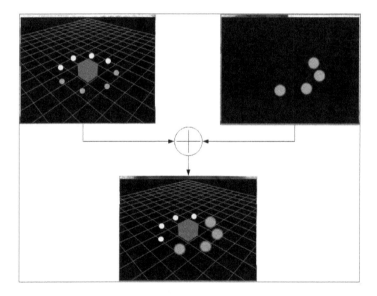

Note that we could also enable blending in the fragment shader. Assuming that the two images to be blended are bound to their texture units and their shader samplers are `texture1` and `texture2`, the additive blending shader code will be like this:

```
#version 330 core
uniform sampler2D texture1;
uniform sampler2D texture2;
layout(location=0) out vec4 vFragColor;
smooth in vec2 vUV;
void main() {
  vec4 color1 = texture(texture1, vUV);
  vec4 color2 = texture(texture2, vUV);
  vFragColor = color1+color2;
}
```

Additionally, we can also apply separable convolution, but that requires two passes. The process requires three color attachments. We first render the scene normally on the first color attachment while the glow effect objects are rendered on the second color attachment. The third color attachment is then set as the render target while the second color attachment acts as input. A full-screen quad is then rendered with the vertical smoothing shader which simply iterates through a row of pixels. This vertically smoothed result is written to the third color attachment.

The second color attachment is then set as output while the output results from the vertical smoothing pass (which was written to the third color attachment) is set as input. The horizontal smoothing shader is then applied on a column of pixels which smoothes the entire image. The image is then rendered to the second color attachment. Finally, the blend shader combines the result from the first color attachment with the result from the second color attachment. Note that the same effect could be carried out by using two separate FBOs: a rendering FBO and a filtering FBO, which gives us more flexibility as we can down sample the filtering result to take advantage of hardware linear filtering. This technique has been used in the *Implementing variance shadow mapping* recipe in *Chapter 4, Lights and Shadows*.

There's more...

The demo application for this recipe shows a simple unit cube encircled by eight points. The first four points are rendered in red and the latter four are rendered in green. The application applies glow to the first four points. After every 50 frames, the glow shifts to the latter four points and so on for the lifetime of the application. The output result from the application is shown in the following figure:

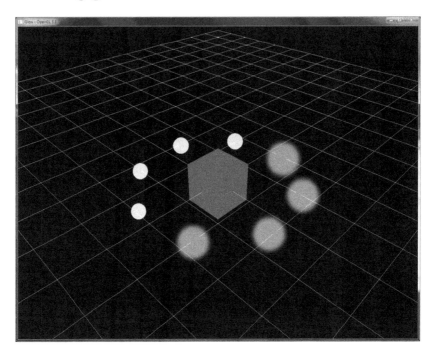

See also

- ▸ Glow sample in NVIDIA OpenGL SDK v10
- ▸ FBO tutorial by Song Ho Ahn: `http://www.songho.ca/opengl/gl_fbo.html`

4
Lights and Shadows

In this chapter, we will cover:

- ▸ Implementing per-vertex and per-fragment point lighting
- ▸ Implementing per-fragment directional light
- ▸ Implementing per-fragment point light with attenuation
- ▸ Implementing per-fragment spot light
- ▸ Implementing shadow mapping with FBO
- ▸ Implementing shadow mapping with percentage closer filtering (PCF)
- ▸ Implementing variance shadow mapping

Introduction

Similar to how the real world would be dark without lights, we require simulated lights to see in our virtual worlds. Visual applications will be incomplete without the presence of lights. There are several kinds of lights; for example, point lights, directional lights, spot lights, and so on. Each of these have some common properties, for example, light position. In addition, they have some specific properties, such as spot direction and spot exponent for spot lights. We will cover all of these light types as well as how to implement them in the vertex shader stage or the fragment shader stage.

Although we can leave the lights to just light the environment, our visual system will start to find problems with such a setting. This is because our eyes are not used to seeing objects lit but casting no shadows. In addition, without shadows, it is very difficult to judge how near or far an object is to the other. Therefore, we detail several shadow generation techniques varying from classic depth shadow mapping to more advanced variance shadow mapping. All of these will be implemented in OpenGL v3.3 and all implementation details will be given to enable the reader to implement the technique on their own.

Implementing per-vertex and per-fragment point lighting

To give more realism to 3D graphic scenes, we add lighting. In OpenGL's fixed function pipeline, per-vertex lighting is provided (which is deprecated in OpenGL v3.3 and above). Using shaders, we can not only replicate the per-vertex lighting of fixed function pipeline but also go a step further by implementing per-fragment lighting. The per-vertex lighting is also known as **Gouraud shading** and the per-fragment shading is known as **Phong shading**. So, without further ado, let's get started.

Getting started

In this recipe, we will render many cubes and a sphere. All of these objects are generated and stored in the buffer objects. For details, refer to the `CreateSphere` and `CreateCube` functions in `Chapter4/PerVertexLighting/main.cpp`. These functions generate both vertex positions as well as per-vertex normals, which are needed for the lighting calculations. All of the lighting calculations take place in the vertex shader of the per-vertex lighting recipe (`Chapter4/PerVertexLighting/`), whereas, for the per-fragment lighting recipe (`Chapter4/PerFragmentLighting/`) they take place in the fragment shader.

How to do it...

Let us start our recipe by following these simple steps:

1. Set up the vertex shader that performs the lighting calculation in the view/eye space. This generates the color after the lighting calculation.

```
#version 330 core
layout(location=0) in vec3 vVertex;
layout(location=1) in vec3 vNormal;
uniform mat4 MVP;
uniform mat4 MV;
uniform mat3 N;
uniform vec3 light_position;  //light position in object
space
uniform vec3 diffuse_color;
uniform vec3 specular_color;
uniform float shininess;
smooth out vec4 color;
const vec3 vEyeSpaceCameraPosition = vec3(0,0,0);
void main()
{
   vec4 vEyeSpaceLightPosition = MV*vec4(light_position,1);
```

```
vec4 vEyeSpacePosition = MV*vec4(vVertex,1);
vec3 vEyeSpaceNormal   = normalize(N*vNormal);
vec3 L = normalize(vEyeSpaceLightPosition.xyz -
vEyeSpacePosition.xyz);
vec3 V = normalize(vEyeSpaceCameraPosition.xyz-
vEyeSpacePosition.xyz);
vec3 H = normalize(L+V);
float diffuse = max(0, dot(vEyeSpaceNormal, L));
float specular = max(0, pow(dot(vEyeSpaceNormal, H),
shininess));
color = diffuse*vec4(diffuse_color,1) +
specular*vec4(specular_color, 1);
gl_Position = MVP*vec4(vVertex,1);
}
```

2. Set up a fragment shader which, inputs the shaded color from the vertex shader interpolated by the rasterizer, and set it as the current output color.

```
#version 330 core
layout(location=0) out vec4 vFragColor;
smooth in vec4 color;
void main() {
  vFragColor = color;
}
```

3. In the rendering code, set the shader and render the objects by passing their modelview/projection matrices to the shader as shader uniforms.

```
shader.Use();
glBindVertexArray(cubeVAOID);
for(int i=0;i<8;i++)
{
  float theta = (float)(i/8.0f*2*M_PI);
  glm::mat4 T = glm::translate(glm::mat4(1),
  glm::vec3(radius*cos(theta), 0.5,radius*sin(theta)));
  glm::mat4 M = T;
  glm::mat4 MV = View*M;
  glm::mat4 MVP = Proj*MV;
  glUniformMatrix4fv(shader("MVP"), 1, GL_FALSE,
  glm::value_ptr(MVP));
  glUniformMatrix4fv(shader("MV"), 1, GL_FALSE,
  glm::value_ptr(MV));
  glUniformMatrix3fv(shader("N"), 1, GL_FALSE,
  glm::value_ptr(glm::inverseTranspose(glm::mat3(MV))));
  glUniform3fv(shader("diffuse_color"),1, &(colors[i].x));
  glUniform3fv(shader("light_position"),1,&(lightPosOS.x));
  glDrawElements(GL_TRIANGLES, 36, GL_UNSIGNED_SHORT, 0);
```

```
        }
        glBindVertexArray(sphereVAOID);
        glm::mat4 T = glm::translate(glm::mat4(1),
        glm::vec3(0,1,0));
        glm::mat4 M = T;
        glm::mat4 MV = View*M;
        glm::mat4 MVP = Proj*MV;
        glUniformMatrix4fv(shader("MVP"), 1, GL_FALSE,
        glm::value_ptr(MVP));
        glUniformMatrix4fv(shader("MV"), 1, GL_FALSE,
        glm::value_ptr(MV));
        glUniformMatrix3fv(shader("N"), 1, GL_FALSE,
        glm::value_ptr(glm::inverseTranspose(glm::mat3(MV))));
        glUniform3f(shader("diffuse_color"), 0.9f, 0.9f, 1.0f);
        glUniform3fv(shader("light_position"),1, &(lightPosOS.x));
        glDrawElements(GL_TRIANGLES, totalSphereTriangles,
        GL_UNSIGNED_SHORT, 0);
        shader.UnUse();
        glBindVertexArray(0);
        grid->Render(glm::value_ptr(Proj*View));
```

How it works...

We can perform the lighting calculations in any coordinate space we wish, that is, object space, world space, or eye/view space. Similar to the lighting in the fixed function OpenGL pipeline, in this recipe we also do our calculations in the eye space. The first step in the vertex shader is to obtain the vertex position and light position in the eye space. This is done by multiplying the current vertex and light position with the modelview (MV) matrix.

```
vec4 vEyeSpaceLightPosition = MV*vec4(light_position,1);
vec4 vEyeSpacePosition = MV*vec4(vVertex,1);
```

Similarly, we transform the per-vertex normals to eye space, but this time we transform them with the inverse transpose of the modelview matrix, which is stored in the normal matrix (N).

```
vec3 vEyeSpaceNormal = normalize(N*vNormal);
```

In the OpenGL versions prior to v3.0, the normal matrix was stored in the gl_NormalMatrix shader uniform, which is the inverse transpose of the modelview matrix. Compared to positions, normals are transformed differently since the scaling transformation may modify the normals in such a way that the normals are not normalized anymore. Multiplying the normals with the inverse transpose of the modelview matrix ensures that the normals are only rotated based on the given matrix, maintaining their unit length.

Next, we obtain the vector from the position of the light in eye space to the position of the vertex in eye space, and do a dot product of this vector with the eye space normal. This gives us the diffuse component.

```
vec3 L = normalize(vEyeSpaceLightPosition.xyz-
vEyeSpacePosition.xyz);
float diffuse = max(0, dot(vEyeSpaceNormal, L));
```

We also calculate two additional vectors, the view vector (V) and the half-way vector (H) between the light and the view vector.

```
vec3 V = normalize(vEyeSpaceCameraPosition.xyz-
vEyeSpacePosition.xyz);
vec3 H = normalize(L+V);
```

These are used for specular component calculation in the **Blinn Phong lighting model**. The specular component is then obtained using $pow(dot(N,H), \sigma)$, where σ is the shininess value; the larger the shininess, the more focused the specular.

```
float specular = max(0, pow(dot(vEyeSpaceNormal, H), shininess));
```

The final color is then obtained by multiplying the diffuse value with the diffuse color and the specular value with the specular color.

```
color =  diffuse*vec4( diffuse_color, 1) +
         specular*vec4(specular_color, 1);
```

The fragment shader in the per-vertex lighting simply outputs the per-vertex color interpolated by the rasterizer as the current fragment color.

```
smooth in vec4 color;
void main() {
  vFragColor = color;
}
```

Alternatively, if we move the lighting calculations to the fragment shader, we get a more pleasing rendering result at the expense of increased processing overhead. Specifically, we transform the per-vertex position, light position, and normals to eye space in the vertex shader, shown as follows:

```
#version 330 core
layout(location=0) in vec3 vVertex;
layout(location=1) in vec3 vNormal;
uniform mat4 MVP;
uniform mat4 MV;
uniform mat3 N;
smooth out vec3 vEyeSpaceNormal;
smooth out vec3 vEyeSpacePosition;
```

```
void main()
{
  vEyeSpacePosition = (MV*vec4(vVertex,1)).xyz;
  vEyeSpaceNormal   = N*vNormal;
  gl_Position = MVP*vec4(vVertex,1);
}
```

In the fragment shader, the rest of the calculation, including the diffuse and specular component contributions, is carried out.

```
#version 330 core
layout(location=0) out vec4 vFragColor;
uniform vec3 light_position;  //light position in object space
uniform vec3 diffuse_color;
uniform vec3 specular_color;
uniform float shininess;
uniform mat4 MV;
smooth in vec3 vEyeSpaceNormal;
smooth in vec3 vEyeSpacePosition;
const vec3 vEyeSpaceCameraPosition = vec3(0,0,0);

void main() {
  vec3 vEyeSpaceLightPosition=(MV*vec4(light_position,1)).xyz;
  vec3 N = normalize(vEyeSpaceNormal);
  vec3 L = normalize(vEyeSpaceLightPosition-vEyeSpacePosition);
  vec3 V = normalize(vEyeSpaceCameraPosition.xyz-
                     vEyeSpacePosition.xyz);
  vec3 H = normalize(L+V);
  float diffuse = max(0, dot(N, L));
  float specular = max(0, pow(dot(N, H), shininess));
  vFragColor = diffuse*vec4(diffuse_color,1) +
               specular*vec4(specular_color, 1);
}
```

We will now dissect the per-fragment lighting fragment shader line-by-line. We first calculate the light position in eye space. Then we calculate the vector from the light to the vertex in eye space. We also calculate the view vector (V) and the half way vector (H).

```
vec3 vEyeSpaceLightPosition = (MV * vec4(light_position,1)).xyz;
vec3 N = normalize(vEyeSpaceNormal);
vec3 L = normalize(vEyeSpaceLightPosition-vEyeSpacePosition);
vec3 V = normalize(vEyeSpaceCameraPosition.xyz-
        vEyeSpacePosition.xyz);
vec3 H = normalize(L+V);
```

Next, the diffuse component is calculated using the dot product with the eye space normal.

```
float diffuse = max(0, dot(vEyeSpaceNormal, L));
```

The specular component is calculated as in the per-vertex case.

```
float specular = max(0, pow(dot(N, H), shininess));
```

Finally, the combined color is obtained by summing the diffuse and specular contributions. The diffuse contribution is obtained by multiplying the diffuse color with the diffuse component and the specular contribution is obtained by multiplying the specular component with the specular color.

```
vFragColor = diffuse*vec4(diffuse_color,1) +
             specular*vec4(specular_color, 1);
```

There's more...

The output from the demo application for this recipe renders a sphere with eight cubes moving in and out, as shown in the following screenshot. The following figure shows the result of the per-vertex lighting. Note the ridge lines clearly visible on the middle sphere, which represents the vertices where the lighting calculations are carried out. Also note the appearance of the specular, which is predominantly visible at vertex positions only.

Now, let us see the result of the same demo application implementing per-fragment lighting:

Note how the per-fragment lighting gives a smoother result compared to the per-vertex lighting. In addition, the specular component is clearly visible.

See also

Learning Modern 3D Graphics Programming, Section III, Jason L. McKesson: http://www.arcsynthesis.org/gltut/Illumination/Illumination.html

Implementing per-fragment directional light

In this recipe, we will now implement directional light. The only difference between a point light and a directional light is that in the case of the directional light source, there is no position, however, there is direction, as shown in the following figure.

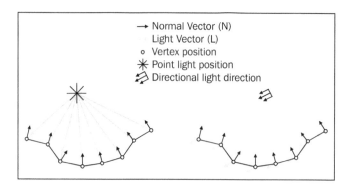

The figure compares directional and point light sources. For a point light source (left-hand side image), the light vector at each vertex is variable, depending on the relative positioning of the vertex with respect to the point light source. For directional light source (right-hand side image), all of the light vectors at vertices are the same and they all point in the direction of the directional light source.

Getting started

We will build on the geometry handling code from the per-fragment lighting recipe, but, instead of the pulsating cubes, we will now render a single cube with a sphere. The code for this recipe is contained in the `Chapter4/DirectionalLight` folder. The same code also works for per-vertex directional light.

How to do it...

Let us start the recipe by following these simple steps:

1. Calculate the light direction in eye space and pass it as shader uniform. Note that the last component is 0 since now we have a light direction vector.

   ```
   lightDirectionES = glm::vec3(MV*
                        glm::vec4(lightDirectionOS,0));
   ```

2. In the vertex shader, output the eye space normal.

   ```
   #version 330 core
   layout(location=0) in vec3 vVertex;
   layout(location=1) in vec3 vNormal;
   uniform mat4 MVP;
   uniform mat3 N;
   smooth out vec3 vEyeSpaceNormal;
   void main()
   {
     vEyeSpaceNormal = N*vNormal;
     gl_Position = MVP*vec4(vVertex,1);
   }
   ```

3. In the fragment shader, compute the diffuse component by calculating the dot product between the light direction vector in eye space with the eye space normal, and multiply with the diffuse color to get the fragment color. Note that here, the light vector is independent of the eye space vertex position.

   ```
   #version 330 core
   layout(location=0) out vec4 vFragColor;
   uniform vec3 light_direction;
   uniform vec3 diffuse_color;
   smooth in vec3 vEyeSpaceNormal;
   ```

```
void main() {
  vec3 L = (light_direction);
  float diffuse = max(0, dot(vEyeSpaceNormal, L));
  vFragColor =  diffuse*vec4(diffuse_color,1);
}
```

How it works...

The only difference between this recipe and the previous one is that we now pass the light direction instead of the position to the fragment shader. The rest of the calculation remains unchanged. If we want to apply attenuation, we can add the relevant shader snippets from the previous recipe.

There's more...

The demo application implementing this recipe shows a sphere and a cube object. In this demo, the direction of the light is shown by using a line segment at origin. The direction of the light can be changed using the right mouse button. The output from this demo application is shown in the following screenshot:

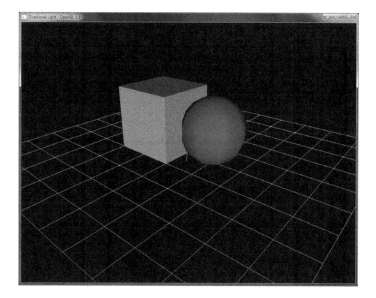

See also

  ▸ The *Implementing per-vertex and per-fragment point lighting* recipe
  ▸ *Learning Modern 3D Graphics Programming, Chapter 9, Lights On, Jason L. McKesson:* http://www.arcsynthesis.org/gltut/Illumination/Tutorial%2009.html

Implementing per-fragment point light with attenuation

The previous recipe handled a directional light source but without attenuation. The relevant changes to enable per-fragment point light with attenuation will be given in this recipe. We start by implementing per-fragment point light, as in the *Implementing per-vertex and per-fragment point lighting* recipe.

Getting started

The code for this recipe is contained in the `Chapter4/PointLight` folder.

How to do it...

Implementing per-fragment point light is demonstrated by following these steps:

1. From the vertex shader, output the eye space vertex position and normal.

    ```
    #version 330 core
    layout(location=0) in vec3 vVertex;
    layout(location=1) in vec3 vNormal;
    uniform mat4 MVP;
    uniform mat4 MV;
    uniform mat3 N;
    smooth out vec3 vEyeSpaceNormal;
    smooth out vec3 vEyeSpacePosition;

    void main() {
        vEyeSpacePosition = (MV*vec4(vVertex,1)).xyz;
        vEyeSpaceNormal   = N*vNormal;
        gl_Position = MVP*vec4(vVertex,1);
    }
    ```

2. In the fragment shader, calculate the light position in eye space, and then calculate the vector from the eye space vertex position to the eye space light position. Store the light distance before normalizing the light vector.

    ```
    #version 330 core
    layout(location=0) out vec4 vFragColor;
    uniform vec3 light_position;  //light position in object space
    uniform vec3 diffuse_color;
    uniform mat4 MV;
    smooth in vec3 vEyeSpaceNormal;
    ```

```
    smooth in vec3 vEyeSpacePosition;
    const float k0 = 1.0;  //constant attenuation
    const float k1 = 0.0;  //linear attenuation
    const float k2 = 0.0;  //quadratic attenuation

    void main() {
      vec3 vEyeSpaceLightPosition =
      (MV*vec4(light_position,1)).xyz;
      vec3 L = (vEyeSpaceLightPosition-vEyeSpacePosition);
      float d = length(L);
      L = normalize(L);
      float diffuse = max(0, dot(vEyeSpaceNormal, L));
      float attenuationAmount = 1.0/(k0 + (k1*d) + (k2*d*d));
      diffuse *= attenuationAmount;
      vFragColor = diffuse*vec4(diffuse_color,1);
    }
```

3. Apply attenuation based on the distance from the light source to the diffuse component.

```
    float attenuationAmount = 1.0/(k0 + (k1*d) + (k2*d*d));
    diffuse *= attenuationAmount;
```

4. Multiply the diffuse component to the diffuse color and set it as the fragment color.

```
    vFragColor = diffuse*vec4(diffuse_color,1);
```

How it works...

The recipe follows the *Implementing per-fragment directional light* recipe. In addition, it performs the attenuation calculation. The attenuation of light is calculated by using the following formula:

$$Attn(d) = \frac{1}{k1 + k2*d + k2*d^2}$$

Here, *d* is the distance from the current position to the light source and *k1*, *k2*, and *k3* are the constant, linear, and quadratic attenuation coefficients respectively. For details about the values and their effect on lighting, we recommend the references in the *See also* section.

There's more...

The output from the demo application implementing this recipe is given in the following screenshot. In this recipe, we render a cube and a sphere. The position of light is shown using a crosshair on the screen. The camera position can be changed using the left mouse button and the light position can be changed by using the right mouse button. The light distance can be changed by using the mouse wheel.

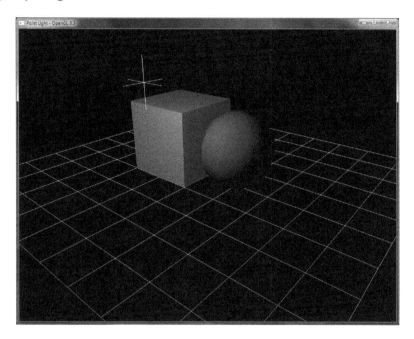

See also

▸ *Real-time Rendering, Third Edition, Tomas Akenine-Moller, Eric Haines, Naty Hoffman, A K Peters/CRC Press*

▸ *Learning Modern 3D Graphics Programming, Chapter 10, Plane Lights, Jason L. McKesson:* http://www.arcsynthesis.org/gltut/Illumination/Tutorial%2010.html

Implementing per-fragment spot light

We will now implement per-fragment spot light. Spot light is a special point light that emits light in a directional cone. The size of this cone is determined by the spot cutoff amount, which is given in angles, as shown in the following figure. In addition, the sharpness of the spot is controlled by the parameter spot exponent. A higher value of the exponent gives a sharper falloff and vice versa.

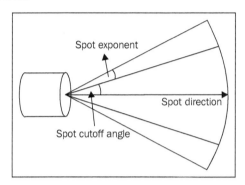

Getting started

The code for this recipe is contained in the `Chapter4/SpotLight` directory. The vertex shader is the same as in the point light recipe. The fragment shader calculates the diffuse component, as in the *Implementing per-vertex and per-fragment point lighting* recipe.

How to do it...

Let us start this recipe by following these simple steps:

1. From the light's object space position and spot light target's position, calculate the spot light direction vector in eye space.

   ```
   spotDirectionES  = glm::normalize(glm::vec3(MV*
                      glm::vec4(spotPositionOS-lightPosOS,0)))
   ```

2. In the fragment shader, calculate the diffuse component as in point light. In addition, calculate the spot effect by finding the angle between the light direction and the spot direction vector.

   ```
   vec3 L = (light_position.xyz-vEyeSpacePosition);
   float d = length(L);
   L = normalize(L);
   vec3 D = normalize(spot_direction);
   vec3 V = -L;
   float diffuse = 1;
   float spotEffect = dot(V,D);
   ```

3. If the angle is greater than the spot cutoff, apply the spot exponent and then use the diffuse shader on the fragment.

```
if(spotEffect > spot_cutoff) {
  spotEffect = pow(spotEffect, spot_exponent);
  diffuse = max(0, dot(vEyeSpaceNormal, L));
  float attenuationAmount = spotEffect/(k0 + (k1*d) +
                            (k2*d*d));
  diffuse *= attenuationAmount;
  vFragColor = diffuse*vec4(diffuse_color,1);
}
```

How it works...

The spot light is a special point light source that illuminates in a certain cone of direction. The amount of cone and the sharpness is controlled using the spot cutoff and spot exponent parameters respectively. Similar to the point light source, we first calculate the diffuse component. Instead of using the vector to light source (L) we use the opposite vector, which points in the direction of light (V=-L). Then we find out if the angle between the spot direction and the light direction vector is within the cutoff angle range. If it is, we apply the diffuse shading calculation. In addition, the sharpness of the spot light is controlled using the spot exponent parameter. This reduces the light in a falloff, giving a more pleasing spot light effect.

There's more...

The demo application implementing this recipe renders the same scene as in the point light demo. We can change the spot light direction using the right mouse button. The output result is shown in the following figure:

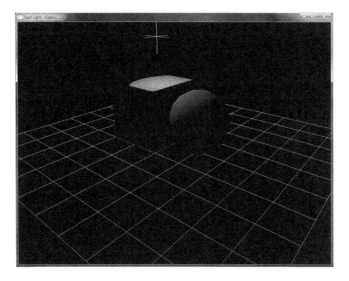

See also

▶ *Real-time Rendering, Third Edition, Tomas Akenine-Moller, Eric Haines, Naty Hoffman, A K Peters/CRC Press*

▶ Spot Light in GLSL tutorial at Ozone3D: `http://www.ozone3d.net/tutorials/glsl_lighting_phong_p3.php`

Implementing shadow mapping with FBO

Shadows give important cues about the relative positioning of graphical objects. There are myriads of shadow generation techniques, including shadow volumes, shadow maps, cascaded shadow maps, and so on. An excellent reference on several shadow generation techniques is given in the *See also* section. We will now see how to carry out basic shadow mapping using FBO.

Getting started

For this recipe, we will use the previous scene but instead of a grid object, we will use a plane object so that the generated shadows can be seen. The code for this recipe is contained in the `Chapter4/ShadowMapping` directory.

How to do it...

Let us start with this recipe by following these simple steps:

1. Create an OpenGL texture object which will be our shadow map texture. Make sure to set the clamp mode to `GL_CLAMP_TO_BORDER`, set the border color to `{1,0,0,0}`, give the texture comparison mode to `GL_COMPARE_REF_TO_TEXTURE`, and set the compare function to `GL_LEQUAL`. Set the texture internal format to `GL_DEPTH_COMPONENT24`.

```
glGenTextures(1, &shadowMapTexID);
glActiveTexture(GL_TEXTURE0);
glBindTexture(GL_TEXTURE_2D, shadowMapTexID);
GLfloat border[4]={1,0,0,0};
glTexParameteri(GL_TEXTURE_2D,GL_TEXTURE_MAG_FILTER,
GL_NEAREST);
glTexParameteri(GL_TEXTURE_2D,GL_TEXTURE_MIN_FILTER,
GL_NEAREST);
glTexParameteri(GL_TEXTURE_2D,GL_TEXTURE_WRAP_S,
GL_CLAMP_TO_BORDER);
glTexParameteri(GL_TEXTURE_2D,GL_TEXTURE_WRAP_T,
GL_CLAMP_TO_BORDER);
```

```
glTexParameteri(GL_TEXTURE_2D,GL_TEXTURE_COMPARE_MODE,
GL_COMPARE_REF_TO_TEXTURE);
glTexParameteri(GL_TEXTURE_2D,GL_TEXTURE_COMPARE_FUNC,
GL_LEQUAL);
glTexParameterfv(GL_TEXTURE_2D,GL_TEXTURE_BORDER_COLOR,
border);
glTexImage2D(GL_TEXTURE_2D,0,GL_DEPTH_COMPONENT24,
SHADOWMAP_WIDTH,SHADOWMAP_HEIGHT,0,GL_DEPTH_COMPONENT,
GL_UNSIGNED_BYTE,NULL);
```

2. Set up an FBO and use the shadow map texture as a single depth attachment. This will store the scene's depth from the point of view of light.

```
glGenFramebuffers(1,&fboID);
glBindFramebuffer(GL_FRAMEBUFFER,fboID);
glFramebufferTexture2D(GL_FRAMEBUFFER,GL_DEPTH_ATTACHMENT,
GL_TEXTURE_2D,shadowMapTexID,0);
GLenum status = glCheckFramebufferStatus(GL_FRAMEBUFFER);
if(status == GL_FRAMEBUFFER_COMPLETE) {
  cout<<"FBO setup successful."<<endl;
} else {
  cout<<"Problem in FBO setup."<<endl;
}
glBindFramebuffer(GL_FRAMEBUFFER,0);
```

3. Using the position and the direction of the light, set up the shadow matrix (S) by combining the light modelview matrix (MV_L), projection matrix (P_L), and bias matrix (B). For reducing runtime calculation, we store the combined projection and bias matrix (BP) at initialization.

```
MV_L = glm::lookAt(lightPosOS,glm::vec3(0,0,0),
       glm::vec3(0,1,0));
P_L  = glm::perspective(50.0f,1.0f,1.0f, 25.0f);
B    = glm::scale(glm::translate(glm::mat4(1),
       glm::vec3(0.5,0.5,0.5)),glm::vec3(0.5,0.5,0.5));
BP   = B*P_L;
S    = BP*MV_L;
```

4. Bind the FBO and render the scene from the point of view of the light. Make sure to enable front-face culling (glEnable(GL_CULL_FACE) and glCullFace(GL_FRONT)) so that the back-face depth values are rendered. Otherwise our objects will suffer from shadow acne.

Normally, a simple shader could be used for rendering of a scene in the depth texture. This may also be achieved by disabling writing to the color buffer (`glDrawBuffer(GL_NONE)`) and then enabling it for normal rendering. In addition, an offset bias can also be added in the shader code to reduce shadow acne.

```
glBindFramebuffer(GL_FRAMEBUFFER,fboID);
glClear(GL_DEPTH_BUFFER_BIT);
glViewport(0,0,SHADOWMAP_WIDTH, SHADOWMAP_HEIGHT);
glCullFace(GL_FRONT);
DrawScene(MV_L, P_L);
glCullFace(GL_BACK);
```

5. Disable FBO, restore default viewport, and render the scene normally from the point of view of the camera.

```
glBindFramebuffer(GL_FRAMEBUFFER,0);
glViewport(0,0,WIDTH, HEIGHT);
DrawScene(MV, P, 0 );
```

6. In the vertex shader, multiply the world space vertex positions (`M*vec4(vVertex,1)`) with the shadow matrix (`S`) to obtain the shadow coordinates. These will be used for lookup of the depth values from the `shadowmap` texture in the fragment shader.

```
#version 330 core
layout(location=0) in vec3 vVertex;
layout(location=1) in vec3 vNormal;

uniform mat4 MVP;    //modelview projection matrix
uniform mat4 MV;     //modelview matrix
uniform mat4 M;      //model matrix
uniform mat3 N;      //normal matrix
uniform mat4 S;      //shadow matrix
smooth out vec3 vEyeSpaceNormal;
smooth out vec3 vEyeSpacePosition;
smooth out vec4 vShadowCoords;
void main()
{
  vEyeSpacePosition = (MV*vec4(vVertex,1)).xyz;
  vEyeSpaceNormal   = N*vNormal;
  vShadowCoords     = S*(M*vec4(vVertex,1));
  gl_Position       = MVP*vec4(vVertex,1);
}
```

7. In the fragment shader, use the shadow coordinates to lookup the depth value in the shadow map sampler which is of the `sampler2Dshadow` type. This sampler can be used with the `textureProj` function to return a comparison outcome. We then use the comparison result to darken the diffuse component, simulating shadows.

```
#version 330 core
layout(location=0) out vec4 vFragColor;
uniform sampler2DShadow shadowMap;
uniform vec3 light_position;  //light position in eye space
uniform vec3 diffuse_color;
smooth in vec3 vEyeSpaceNormal;
smooth in vec3 vEyeSpacePosition;
smooth in vec4 vShadowCoords;
const float k0 = 1.0;  //constant attenuation
const float k1 = 0.0;  //linear attenuation
const float k2 = 0.0;  //quadratic attenuation
uniform bool bIsLightPass; //no shadows in light pass
void main() {
  if(bIsLightPass)
  return;
  vec3 L = (light_position.xyz-vEyeSpacePosition);
  float d = length(L);
  L = normalize(L);
  float attenuationAmount = 1.0/(k0 + (k1*d) + (k2*d*d));
  float diffuse = max(0, dot(vEyeSpaceNormal, L)) *
                  attenuationAmount;
  if(vShadowCoords.w>1) {
    float shadow = textureProj(shadowMap, vShadowCoords);
    diffuse = mix(diffuse, diffuse*shadow, 0.5);
  }
  vFragColor = diffuse*vec4(diffuse_color, 1);
}
```

How it works...

The shadow mapping algorithm works in two passes. In the first pass, the scene is rendered from the point of view of light, and the depth buffer is stored into a texture called `shadowmap`. We use a single FBO with a depth attachment for this purpose. Apart from the conventional minification/magnification texture filtering, we set the texture wrapping mode to `GL_CLAMP_TO_BORDER`, which ensures that the values are clamped to the specified border color. Had we set this as `GL_CLAMP` or `GL_CLAMP_TO_EDGE`, the border pixels forming the shadow map would produce visible artefacts.

The `shadowmap` texture has some additional parameters. The first is the `GL_TEXTURE_COMPARE_MODE` parameter, which is set as the `GL_COMPARE_REF_TO_TEXTURE` value. This enables the texture to be used for depth comparison in the shader. Next, we specify the `GL_TEXTURE_COMPARE_FUNC` parameter, which is set as `GL_LEQUAL`. This compares the currently interpolated texture coordinate value (`r`) with the depth texture's sample value (`D`). It returns 1 if `r<=D`, otherwise it returns 0. This means that if the depth of the current sample is less than or equal to the depth from the `shadowmap` texture, the sample is not in shadow; otherwise, it is in shadow. The `textureProj` GLSL shader function performs this comparison for us and returns 0 or 1 based on whether the point is in shadow or not. These are the texture parameters required for the `shadowmap` texture.

To ensure that we do not have any shadow acne, we enable front-face culling (`glEnable(GL_CULL_FACE)` and `glCullFace(GL_FRONT)`) so that the back-face depth values get written to the `shadowmap` texture. In the second pass, the scene is rendered normally from the point of view of the camera and the shadow map is projected on the scene geometry using shaders.

To render the scene from the point of view of light, the modelview matrix of the light (`MV_L`), the projection matrix (`P_L`), and the bias matrix (`B`) are calculated. After multiplying with the projection matrix, the coordinates are in clip space (that is, they range from [-1,-1,-1]). to [1,1,1]. The bias matrix rescales this range to bring the coordinates from [0,0,0] to [1,1,1] range so that the shadow lookup can be carried out.

If we have the object's vertex position in the object space given as `Vobj`, the shadow coordinates (`UVproj`) for the lookup in the shadow map can be given by multiplying the shadow matrix (`S`) with the world space position of the object (`M*Vobj`). The whole series of transformations is given as follows:

$$UV_{proj} = S * MV * V_{obj}$$
$$S = B * P_L * MV_L$$

Here, *B* is the bias matrix, P_L is the projection matrix of light, and MV_L is the modelview matrix of light. For efficiency, we precompute the bias matrix of the light and the projection matrix, since they are unchanged for the lifetime of the application. Based on the user input, the light's modelview is modified and then the shadow matrix is recalculated. This is then passed to the shader.

In the vertex shader, the `shadowmap` texture coordinates are obtained by multiplying the world space vertex position (`M*Vobj`) with the shadow matrix (`S`). In the fragment shader, the shadow map is looked up using the projected texture coordinate to find if the current fragment is in shadow. Before the texture lookup, we check the value of the w coordinate of the projected texture coordinate. We only do our calculations if the w coordinate is greater than 1. This ensures that we only accept the forward projection and reject the back projection. Try removing this condition to see what we mean.

The shadow map lookup computation is facilitated by the `textureProj` GLSL function. The result from the shadow map lookup returns 1 or 0. This result is multiplied with the shading computation. As it happens in the real world, we never have coal black shadows. Therefore, we combine the shadow outcome with the shading computation by using the `mix` GLSL function.

There's more...

The demo application for this recipe shows a plane, a cube, and a sphere. A point light source, which can be rotated using the right mouse button, is placed. The distance of the light source can be altered using the mouse wheel. The output result from the demo is displayed in the following figure:

This recipe detailed the shadow mapping technique for a single light source. With each additional light source, the processing, as well as storage requirements, increase.

See also

- *Real-time Shadows, Elmar Eisemann, Michael Schwarz, Ulf Assarsson, Michael Wimmer, A K Peters/CRC Press*
- *OpenGL 4.0 Shading Language Cookbook, Chapter 7, Shadows, David Wolff, Packt Publishing*
- *ShadowMapping with GLSL* by Fabien Sanglard: `http://www.fabiensanglard.net/shadowmapping/index.php`

Implemeting shadow mapping with percentage closer filtering (PCF)

The shadow mapping algorithm, though simple to implement, suffers from aliasing artefacts, which are due to the `shadowmap` resolution. In addition, the shadows produced using this approach are hard. These can be minimized either by increasing the `shadowmap` resolution or taking more samples. The latter approach is called **percentage closer filtering** (**PCF**), where more samples are taken for the `shadowmap` lookup and the percentage of the samples is used to estimate if a fragment is in shadow. Thus, in PCF, instead of a single lookup, we sample an n×n neighborhood of `shadowmap` and then average the values.

Getting started

The code for this recipe is contained in the `Chapter4/ShadowMappingPCF` directory. It builds on top of the previous recipe, *Implementing shadow mapping with FBO*. We use the same scene but augment it with PCF.

How to do it...

Let us see how to extend the basic shadow mapping with PCF.

1. Change the `shadowmap` texture minification/magnification filtering modes to `GL_LINEAR`. Here, we exploit the texture filtering capabilities of the GPU to reduce aliasing artefacts during sampling of the shadow map. Even with the linear filtering support, we have to take additional samples to reduce the artefacts.

   ```
   glTexParameteri(GL_TEXTURE_2D,GL_TEXTURE_MAG_FILTER,
   GL_LINEAR);
   glTexParameteri(GL_TEXTURE_2D,GL_TEXTURE_MIN_FILTER,
   GL_LINEAR);
   ```

2. In the fragment shader, instead of a single texture lookup as in the shadow map recipe, we use a number of samples. GLSL provides a convenient function, `textureProjOffset`, to allow calculation of samples using an offset. For this recipe, we look at a 3×3 neighborhood around the current shadow map point. Hence, we use a large offset of 2. This helps to reduce sampling artefacts.

   ```
   if(vShadowCoords.w>1) {
     float sum = 0;
     sum += textureProjOffset(shadowMap,vShadowCoords,
     ivec2(-2,-2));
     sum += textureProjOffset(shadowMap,vShadowCoords,
     ivec2(-2, 0));
     sum += textureProjOffset(shadowMap,vShadowCoords,
     ivec2(-2, 2));
   ```

```
    sum += textureProjOffset(shadowMap,vShadowCoords,
    ivec2( 0,-2));
    sum += textureProjOffset(shadowMap,vShadowCoords,
    ivec2( 0, 0));
    sum += textureProjOffset(shadowMap,vShadowCoords,
    ivec2( 0, 2));
    sum += textureProjOffset(shadowMap,vShadowCoords,
    ivec2( 2,-2));
    sum += textureProjOffset(shadowMap,vShadowCoords,
    ivec2( 2, 0));
    sum += textureProjOffset(shadowMap,vShadowCoords,
    ivec2( 2, 2));
    float shadow = sum/9.0;
    diffuse = mix(diffuse, diffuse*shadow, 0.5);
  }
```

How it works...

In order to implement PCF, the first change we need is to set the texture filtering mode to linear filtering. This change enabled the GPU to bilinearly interpolate the shadow value. This gives smoother edges since the hardware does PCF filtering underneath. However it is not enough for our purpose. Therefore, we have to take additional samples to improve the result.

Fortunately, we can use a convenient function, `textureProjOffset`, which accepts an offset that is added to the given shadow map texture coordinate. Note that the offset given to this function must be a constant literal. Thus, we cannot use a loop variable for dynamic sampling of the shadow map sampler. We, therefore, have to unroll the loop to sample the neighborhood.

We use an offset of 2 units because we wanted to sample at a value of 1.5. However, since the `textureProjOffset` function does not accept a floating point value, we round it to the nearest integer. The offset is then modified to move to the next sample point until the entire 3×3 neighborhood is sampled. We then average the sampling result for the entire neighborhood. The obtained sampling result is then multiplied to the lighting contribution, thus, producing shadows if the current sample happens to be in an occluded region.

Even with adding additional samples, we get sampling artefacts. These can be reduced by shifting the sampling points randomly. To achieve this, we first implement a pseudo-random function in GLSL as follows:

```
  float random(vec4 seed) {
    float dot_product = dot(seed, vec4(12.9898,78.233, 45.164,
                          94.673));
    return fract(sin(dot_product) * 43758.5453);
  }
```

Then, the sampling for PCF uses the noise function to shift the shadow offset, as shown in the following shader code:

```
for(int i=0;i<16;i++) {
  float indexA = (random(vec4(gl_FragCoord.xyx, i))*0.25);
  float indexB = (random(vec4(gl_FragCoord.yxy, i))*0.25);
  sum += textureProj(shadowMap, vShadowCoords +
        vec4(indexA, indexB, 0, 0));
}
shadow = sum/16.0;
```

In the given code, three macros are defined, `STRATIFIED_3x3` (for 3x3 stratified sampling), `STRATIFIED_5x5` (for 5x5 stratified sampling), and `RANDOM_SAMPLING` (for 4x4 random sampling).

There's more...

Making these changes, we get a much better result, as shown in the following figure. If we take a bigger neighborhood, we get a better result. However, the computational requirements also increase.

The following figure compares this result of the PCF-filtered shadow map (right) with a normal shadow map (left). We can see that the PCF-filtered result gives softer shadows with reduced aliasing artefacts.

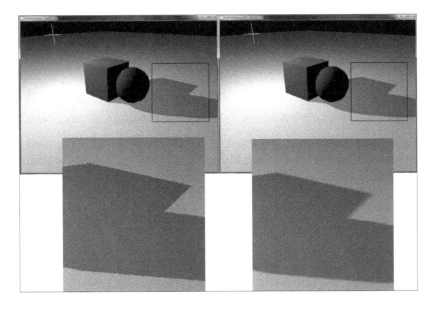

The following figure compares the result of the stratified PCF-filtered image (left) against the random PCF-filtered image (right). As can be seen, the noise-filtered image gives a much better result.

See also

- *GPU Gems, Chapter 11, Shadow Map Antialiasing, Michael Bunnell, Fabio Pellacini,* available online at: `http://http.developer.nvidia.com/GPUGems/gpugems_ch11.html`

- *Shadow mapping,* Tutorial 16: `http://www.opengl-tutorial.org/intermediate-tutorials/tutorial-16-shadow-mapping/`

Implementing variance shadow mapping

In this recipe, we will cover a technique which gives a much better result, has better performance, and at the same time is easier to calculate. The technique is called **variance shadow mapping**. In conventional PCF-filtered shadow mapping, we compare the depth value of the current fragment to the mean depth value in the shadow map, and based on the outcome, we shadow the fragment.

In case of variance shadow mapping, the mean depth value (also called first moment) and the mean squared depth value (also called second moment) are calculated and stored. Then, rather than directly using the mean depth, the variance is used. The variance calculation requires both the mean depth as well as the mean of the squared depth. Using the variance, the probability of whether the given sample is shadowed is estimated. This probability is then compared to the maximum probability to determine if the current sample is shadowed.

Getting started

For this recipe, we will build on top of the shadow mapping recipe, *Implementing shadow mapping with FBO.* The code for this recipe is contained in the `Chapter4/VarianceShadowMapping` folder.

How to do it...

Let us start our recipe by following these simple steps:

1. Set up the `shadowmap` texture as in the shadow map recipe, but this time remove the depth compare mode (`glTexParameteri(GL_TEXTURE_2D,GL_TEXTURE_COMPARE_MODE,GL_COMPARE_REF_TO_TEXTURE)` and `glTexParameteri(GL_TEXTURE_2D,GL_TEXTURE_COMPARE_FUNC,GL_LEQUAL)`). Also set the format of the texture to the `GL_RGBA32F` format. Also enable the mipmap generation for this texture. The mipmaps provide filtered textures across different scales and produces better alias-free shadows. We request five mipmap levels (by specifying the max level as 4).

```
glGenTextures(1, &shadowMapTexID);
glActiveTexture(GL_TEXTURE0);
```

```
glBindTexture(GL_TEXTURE_2D, shadowMapTexID);
glTexParameteri(GL_TEXTURE_2D,GL_TEXTURE_MAG_FILTER,
GL_LINEAR;
glTexParameteri(GL_TEXTURE_2D,GL_TEXTURE_MIN_FILTER,
GL_LINEAR_MIPMAP_LINEAR);
glTexParameteri(GL_TEXTURE_2D,GL_TEXTURE_WRAP_S,
GL_CLAMP_TO_BORDER);
glTexParameteri(GL_TEXTURE_2D,GL_TEXTURE_WRAP_T,
GL_CLAMP_TO_BORDER);
glTexParameterfv(GL_TEXTURE_2D,GL_TEXTURE_BORDER_COLOR,
border;
glTexImage2D(GL_TEXTURE_2D,0,GL_RGBA32F,SHADOWMAP_WIDTH,
SHADOWMAP_HEIGHT,0,GL_RGBA,GL_FLOAT,NULL);
glTexParameteri(GL_TEXTURE_2D, GL_TEXTURE_BASE_LEVEL, 0);
glTexParameteri(GL_TEXTURE_2D, GL_TEXTURE_MAX_LEVEL, 4);
glGenerateMipmap(GL_TEXTURE_2D);
```

2. Set up two FBOs: one for shadowmap generation and another for shadowmap filtering. The shadowmap FBO has a `renderbuffer` attached to it for depth testing. The filtering FBO does not have a `renderbuffer` attached to it but it has two texture attachments.

```
glGenFramebuffers(1,&fboID);
    glGenRenderbuffers(1, &rboID);
    glBindFramebuffer(GL_FRAMEBUFFER,fboID);
    glBindRenderbuffer(GL_RENDERBUFFER, rboID);
    glRenderbufferStorage(GL_RENDERBUFFER,
    GL_DEPTH_COMPONENT32, SHADOWMAP_WIDTH,
    SHADOWMAP_HEIGHT);
glFramebufferTexture2D(GL_FRAMEBUFFER,GL_COLOR_ATTACHMENT0,
GL_TEXTURE_2D,shadowMapTexID,0);
    glFramebufferRenderbuffer(GL_FRAMEBUFFER,
    GL_DEPTH_ATTACHMENT, GL_RENDERBUFFER, rboID);
GLenum status = glCheckFramebufferStatus(GL_FRAMEBUFFER);
if(status == GL_FRAMEBUFFER_COMPLETE) {
  cout<<"FBO setup successful."<<endl;
} else {
  cout<<"Problem in FBO setup."<<endl;
}
glBindFramebuffer(GL_FRAMEBUFFER,0);

glGenFramebuffers(1,&filterFBOID);
glBindFramebuffer(GL_FRAMEBUFFER,filterFBOID);
glGenTextures(2, blurTexID);
for(int i=0;i<2;i++) {
  glActiveTexture(GL_TEXTURE1+i);
```

```
glBindTexture(GL_TEXTURE_2D, blurTexID[i]);
glTexParameteri(GL_TEXTURE_2D,GL_TEXTURE_MAG_FILTER,
GL_LINEAR);
glTexParameteri(GL_TEXTURE_2D,GL_TEXTURE_MIN_FILTER,
GL_LINEAR);
glTexParameteri(GL_TEXTURE_2D,GL_TEXTURE_WRAP_S,
GL_CLAMP_TO_BORDER);
glTexParameteri(GL_TEXTURE_2D,GL_TEXTURE_WRAP_T,
GL_CLAMP_TO_BORDER);
glTexParameterfv(GL_TEXTURE_2D,GL_TEXTURE_BORDER_COLOR,
border);
glTexImage2D(GL_TEXTURE_2D,0,GL_RGBA32F,SHADOWMAP_WIDTH,
SHADOWMAP_HEIGHT,0,GL_RGBA,GL_FLOAT,NULL);
glFramebufferTexture2D(GL_FRAMEBUFFER,
GL_COLOR_ATTACHMENT0+i, GL_TEXTURE_2D,blurTexID[i],0);
}
status = glCheckFramebufferStatus(GL_FRAMEBUFFER);
if(status == GL_FRAMEBUFFER_COMPLETE) {
  cout<<"Filtering FBO setup successful."<<endl;
} else {
  cout<<"Problem in Filtering FBO setup."<<endl;
}
glBindFramebuffer(GL_FRAMEBUFFER,0);
```

3. Bind the `shadowmap` FBO, set the viewport to the size of the `shadowmap` texture, and render the scene from the point of view of the light, as in the *Implementing shadow mapping with FBO* recipe. In this pass, instead of storing the depth as in the shadow mapping recipe, we use a custom fragment shader (`Chapter4/VarianceShadowmapping/shaders/firststep.frag`) to output the *depth* and *depth*depth* values in the **red** and **green** channels of the fragment output color.

```
glBindFramebuffer(GL_FRAMEBUFFER,fboID);
glViewport(0,0,SHADOWMAP_WIDTH, SHADOWMAP_HEIGHT);
glDrawBuffer(GL_COLOR_ATTACHMENT0);
glClear(GL_COLOR_BUFFER_BIT|GL_DEPTH_BUFFER_BIT);
DrawSceneFirstPass(MV_L, P_L);
```

The shader code is as follows:

```
#version 330 core
layout(location=0) out vec4 vFragColor;
smooth in vec4 clipSpacePos;
void main()
{
  vec3 pos = clipSpacePos.xyz/clipSpacePos.w; //-1 to 1
  pos.z += 0.001; //add some offset to remove the shadow
  acne
```

```
float depth = (pos.z +1)*0.5; // 0 to 1
float moment1 = depth;
float moment2 = depth * depth;
vFragColor = vec4(moment1,moment2,0,0);
}
```

4. Bind the filtering **FBO** to filter the `shadowmap` texture generated in the first pass using separable Gaussian smoothing filters, which are more efficient and offer better performance. We first attach the vertical smoothing fragment shader (`Chapter4/VarianceShadowmapping/shaders/GaussV.frag`) to filter the `shadowmap` texture and then the horizontal smoothing fragment shader (`Chapter4/VarianceShadowmapping/shaders/GaussH.frag`) to smooth the output from the vertical Gaussian smoothing filter.

```
glBindFramebuffer(GL_FRAMEBUFFER,filterFBOID);
glDrawBuffer(GL_COLOR_ATTACHMENT0);
glBindVertexArray(quadVAOID);
gaussianV_shader.Use();
glDrawElements(GL_TRIANGLES, 6, GL_UNSIGNED_SHORT, 0);
glDrawBuffer(GL_COLOR_ATTACHMENT1);
gaussianH_shader.Use();
glDrawElements(GL_TRIANGLES, 6, GL_UNSIGNED_SHORT, 0);
glBindFramebuffer(GL_FRAMEBUFFER,0);
```

The horizontal Gaussian blur shader is as follows:

```
#version 330 core
layout(location=0) out vec4 vFragColor;
smooth in vec2 vUV;
uniform sampler2D textureMap;

const float kernel[]=float[21] (0.000272337,  0.00089296,
0.002583865, 0.00659813,  0.014869116, 0.029570767,
0.051898313, 0.080381679, 0.109868729, 0.132526984,
0.14107424,  0.132526984, 0.109868729, 0.080381679,
0.051898313, 0.029570767, 0.014869116, 0.00659813,
0.002583865, 0.00089296, 0.000272337);

void main()
{
  vec2 delta = 1.0/textureSize(textureMap,0);
  vec4 color = vec4(0);
  int  index = 20;

  for(int i=-10;i<=10;i++) {
    color += kernel[index--]*texture(textureMap, vUV +
    (vec2(i*delta.x,0)));
```

```
    }

      vFragColor =   vec4(color.xy,0,0);
  }
```

In the vertical Gaussian shader, the loop statement is modified, whereas the rest of the shader is the same.

```
color += kernel[index--]*texture(textureMap, vUV +
(vec2(0,i*delta.y)));
```

5. Unbind the FBO, reset the default viewport, and then render the scene normally, as in the shadow mapping recipe.

```
glDrawBuffer(GL_BACK_LEFT);
glViewport(0,0,WIDTH, HEIGHT);
DrawScene(MV, P);
```

How it works...

The variance shadowmap technique tries to represent the depth data such that it can be filtered linearly. Instead of storing the depth, it stores the depth and depth*depth value in a floating point texture, which is then filtered to reconstruct the first and second moments of the depth distribution. Using the moments, it estimates the variance in the filtering neighborhood. This helps in finding the probability of a fragment at a specific depth to be occluded using Chebyshev's inequality. For more mathematical details, we refer the reader to the *See also* section of this recipe.

From the implementation point of view, similar to the shadow mapping recipe, the method works in two passes. In the first pass, we render the scene from the point of view of light. Instead of storing the depth, we store the depth and the depth*depth values in a floating point texture using the custom fragment shader (see Chapter4/VarianceShadowmapping/shaders/firststep.frag).

The vertex shader outputs the clip space position to the fragment shader using which the fragment depth value is calculated. To reduce self-shadowing, a small bias is added to the z value.

```
vec3 pos = clipSpacePos.xyz/clipSpacePos.w;
pos.z += 0.001;
float depth = (pos.z +1)*0.5;
float moment1 = depth;
float moment2 = depth * depth;
vFragColor = vec4(moment1,moment2,0,0);
```

After the first pass, the `shadowmap` texture is blurred using a separable Gaussian smoothing filter. First the vertical and then the horizontal filter is applied to the `shadowmap` texture by applying the `shadowmap` texture to a full-screen quad and alternating the filter FBO's color attachment. Note that the `shadowmap` texture is bound to texture unit 0 whereas the textures used for filtering are bound to texture unit 1 (attached to GL_COLOR_ATTTACHMENT0 on the filtering FBO) and texture unit 2 (attached to GL_COLOR_ATTACHMENT1 on the filtering FBO).

```
glBindFramebuffer(GL_FRAMEBUFFER,fboID);
  glViewport(0,0,SHADOWMAP_WIDTH, SHADOWMAP_HEIGHT);
  glDrawBuffer(GL_COLOR_ATTACHMENT0);
  glClear(GL_COLOR_BUFFER_BIT|GL_DEPTH_BUFFER_BIT);
  DrawSceneFirstPass(MV_L, P_L);

glBindFramebuffer(GL_FRAMEBUFFER,filterFBOID);
glDrawBuffer(GL_COLOR_ATTACHMENT0);
glBindVertexArray(quadVAOID);
  gaussianV_shader.Use();
    glDrawElements(GL_TRIANGLES, 6, GL_UNSIGNED_SHORT, 0);

    glDrawBuffer(GL_COLOR_ATTACHMENT1);
  gaussianH_shader.Use();
  glDrawElements(GL_TRIANGLES, 6, GL_UNSIGNED_SHORT, 0);
glBindFramebuffer(GL_FRAMEBUFFER,0);
glDrawBuffer(GL_BACK_LEFT);
glViewport(0,0,WIDTH, HEIGHT);
```

In the second pass, the scene is rendered from the point of view of the camera. The blurred shadowmap is used in the second pass as a texture to lookup the sample value (see `Chapter4/VarianceShadowmapping/shaders/VarianceShadowMap.{vert, frag}`). The variance shadow mapping vertex shader outputs the shadow texture coordinates, as in the shadow mapping recipe.

```
#version 330 core
layout(location=0) in vec3 vVertex;
layout(location=1) in vec3 vNormal;
uniform mat4 MVP;    //modelview projection matrix
uniform mat4 MV;     //modelview matrix
uniform mat4 M;       //model matrix
uniform mat3 N;      //normal matrix
uniform mat4 S;      //shadow matrix
smooth out vec3 vEyeSpaceNormal;
smooth out vec3 vEyeSpacePosition;
smooth out vec4 vShadowCoords;
void main()
```

```
{
  vEyeSpacePosition = (MV*vec4(vVertex,1)).xyz;
  vEyeSpaceNormal   = N*vNormal;
  vShadowCoords     = S*(M*vec4(vVertex,1));
  gl_Position       = MVP*vec4(vVertex,1);
}
```

The variance shadow mapping fragment shader operates differently. We first make sure that the shadow coordinates are in front of the light (to prevent back projection), that is, `shadowCoord.w>1`. Next, the `shadowCoords.xyz` values are divided by the homogeneous coordinate, `shadowCoord.w`, to get the depth value.

```
if(vShadowCoords.w>1) {
  vec3 uv = vShadowCoords.xyz/vShadowCoords.w;
  float depth = uv.z;
```

The texture coordinates after homogeneous division are used to lookup the shadow map storing the two moments. The two moments are used to estimate the variance. The variance is clamped and then the occlusion probability is estimated. The diffuse component is then modulated based on the obtained occlusion probability.

```
  vec4 moments = texture(shadowMap, uv.xy);
  float E_x2 = moments.y;
  float Ex_2 = moments.x*moments.x;
  float var = E_x2-Ex_2;
  var = max(var, 0.00002);
  float mD = depth-moments.x;
  float mD_2 = mD*mD;
  float p_max = var/(var+ mD_2);
  diffuse *= max(p_max, (depth<=moments.x)?1.0:0.2);
}
```

To recap, here is the complete variance shadow mapping fragment shader:

```
#version 330 core
layout(location=0) out vec4 vFragColor;
uniform sampler2D  shadowMap;
uniform vec3 light_position;  //light position in object space
uniform vec3 diffuse_color;
uniform mat4 MV;
smooth in vec3 vEyeSpaceNormal;
smooth in vec3 vEyeSpacePosition;
smooth in vec4 vShadowCoords;
const float k0 = 1.0;  //constant attenuation
const float k1 = 0.0;  //linear attenuation
```

```
const float k2 = 0.0;   //quadratic attenuation
void main() {
  vec4 vEyeSpaceLightPosition = (MV*vec4(light_position,1));
  vec3 L = (vEyeSpaceLightPosition.xyz-vEyeSpacePosition);
  float d = length(L);
   L = normalize(L);
  float attenuationAmount = 1.0/(k0 + (k1*d) + (k2*d*d));
  float diffuse = max(0, dot(vEyeSpaceNormal, L)) *
                  attenuationAmount;
  if(vShadowCoords.w>1) {
    vec3 uv = vShadowCoords.xyz/vShadowCoords.w;
    float depth = uv.z;
    vec4 moments = texture(shadowMap, uv.xy);
    float E_x2 = moments.y;
    float Ex_2 = moments.x*moments.x;
    float var = E_x2-Ex_2;
    var = max(var, 0.00002);
    float mD = depth-moments.x;
    float mD_2 = mD*mD;
    float p_max = var/(var+ mD_2);
    diffuse *= max(p_max, (depth<=moments.x)?1.0:0.2);
  }
  vFragColor = diffuse*vec4(diffuse_color, 1);
}
```

There's more...

Variance shadow mapping is an interesting idea. However, it does suffer from light bleeding artefacts. There have been several improvements to the basic technique, such as summed area variance shadow maps, layered variance shadow maps, and more recently, sample distribution shadow maps, that are referred to in the *See also* section of this recipe. After getting a practical insight into the basic variance shadow mapping idea, we invite the reader to try and implement the different variants of this algorithm, as detailed in the references in the *See also* section.

The demo application for this recipe shows the same scene (a cube and a sphere on a plane) lit by a point light source. Right-clicking the mouse button rotates the point light around the objects. The output result is shown in the following figure:

Comparing this output to the previous shadow mapping recipes, we can see that the output quality is much better if compared to the conventional shadow mapping and the PCF-based technique. When comparing the outputs, variance shadow mapping gives a better output with a significantly less number of samples. Obtaining the same output using PCF or any other technique would require a very large neighborhood lookup with more samples. This makes this technique well-suited for real-time applications such as games.

See also

- *Proceedings of the 2006 symposium on Interactive 3D graphics and games, Variance Shadow Maps, pages 161-165 William Donnelly, Andrew Lauritzen*

- *GPU Gems 3, Chapter 8, Summed-Area Variance Shadow Maps, Andrew Lauritzen:* http://http.developer.nvidia.com/GPUGems3/gpugems3_ch08.html

- *Proceedings of the Graphics Interface 2008, Layered variance shadow maps, pages 139-146, Andrew Lauritzen, Michael McCool*

- *Sample Distribution Shadow Maps, ACM SIGGRAPH Symposium on Interactive 3D Graphics and Games (I3D) 2011, February, Andrew Lauritzen, Marco Salvi, and Aaron Lefohn*

5
Mesh Model Formats and Particle Systems

In this chapter, we will focus on:

- ▸ Implementing terrains using height map
- ▸ Implementing 3ds model loading using separate buffers
- ▸ Implementing OBJ model loading using interleaved buffers
- ▸ Implementing EZMesh model loading
- ▸ Implementing a simple particle system

Introduction

While simple demos and applications can get along with basic primitives like cubes and spheres, most real-world applications and games use 3D mesh models which are modelled in 3D modeling software such as 3ds Max and Maya. For games, the models are then exported into the proprietary game format and then the models are loaded into the game.

While there are many formats available, some formats such as Autodesk® 3ds and Wavefront® OBJ are common formats. In this chapter, we will look at recipes for loading these model formats. We will look at how to load the geometry information, stored in the external files, into the vertex buffer object memory of the GPU. In addition, we will also load material and texture information which is required to improve the fidelity of the model so that it appears more realistic. We will also work on loading terrains which are often used to model outdoor environments. Finally, we will implement a basic particle system for simulating fuzzy phenomena such as fire and smoke. All of the discussed techniques will be implemented in the OpenGL v3.3 and above core profile.

Implementing terrains using the height map

Several demos and applications require rendering of terrains. This recipe will show how to implement terrain generation in modern OpenGL. The height map is loaded using the SOIL image loading library which contains displacement information. A 2D grid is then generated depending on the required terrain resolution. Then, the displacement information contained in the height map is used to displace the 2D grid in the vertex shader. Usually, the obtained displacement value is scaled to increase or decrease the displacement scale as desired.

Getting started

For the terrain, first the 2D grid geometry is generated depending on the terrain resolution. The steps to generate such geometry were previously covered in the *Doing a ripple mesh deformer using vertex shader* recipe in *Chapter 1, Introduction to Modern OpenGL*. The code for this recipe is contained in the Chapter5/TerrainLoading directory.

How to do it...

Let us start our recipe by following these simple steps:

1. Load the height map texture using the SOIL image loading library and generate an OpenGL texture from it. The texture filtering is set to GL_NEAREST as we want to obtain the exact values from the height map. If we had changed this to GL_LINEAR, we would get interpolated values. Since the terrain height map is not tiled, we set the texture wrap mode to GL_CLAMP.

```
int texture_width = 0, texture_height = 0, channels=0;
GLubyte* pData = SOIL_load_image(filename.c_str(),
&texture_width, &texture_height, &channels, SOIL_LOAD_L);
//vertically flip the image data
for( j = 0; j*2 < texture_height; ++j )
{
  int index1 = j * texture_width ;
  int index2 = (texture_height - 1 - j) * texture_width ;
  for( i = texture_width ; i > 0; --i )
  {
    GLubyte temp = pData[index1];
    pData[index1] = pData[index2];
    pData[index2] = temp;
    ++index1;
    ++index2;
  }
}
```

```
glGenTextures(1, &heightMapTextureID);
glActiveTexture(GL_TEXTURE0);
glBindTexture(GL_TEXTURE_2D, heightMapTextureID);
glTexParameteri(GL_TEXTURE_2D, GL_TEXTURE_MIN_FILTER,
GL_NEAREST);
glTexParameteri(GL_TEXTURE_2D, GL_TEXTURE_MAG_FILTER,
GL_NEAREST);
glTexParameteri(GL_TEXTURE_2D, GL_TEXTURE_WRAP_S,
GL_CLAMP);
glTexParameteri(GL_TEXTURE_2D, GL_TEXTURE_WRAP_T,
GL_CLAMP);
glTexImage2D(GL_TEXTURE_2D, 0, GL_RED, texture_width,
texture_height, 0, GL_RED, GL_UNSIGNED_BYTE, pData);
SOIL_free_image_data(pData);
```

2. Set up the terrain geometry by generating a set of points in the XZ plane. The `TERRAIN_WIDTH` parameter controls the total number of vertices in the X axis whereas the `TERRAIN_DEPTH` parameter controls the total number of vertices in the Z axis.

```
for( j=0;j<TERRAIN_DEPTH;j++) {
  for( i=0;i<TERRAIN_WIDTH;i++) {
    vertices[count]=glm::vec3((float(i)/(TERRAIN_WIDTH-
    1)), 0, (float(j)/(TERRAIN_DEPTH-1)));
    count++;
  }
}
```

3. Set up the vertex shader that displaces the 2D terrain mesh. Refer to `Chapter5/TerrainLoading/shaders/shader.vert` for details. The height value is obtained from the height map. This value is then added to the current vertex position and finally multiplied with the combined modelview projection (MVP) matrix to get the clip space position. The `HALF_TERRAIN_SIZE` uniform contains half of the total number of vertices in both the X and Z axes, that is, `HALF_TERRAIN_SIZE = ivec2(TERRAIN_WIDTH/2, TERRAIN_DEPTH/2)`. Similarly the scale uniform is used to scale the height read from the height map. The `half_scale` and `HALF_TERRAIN_SIZE` uniforms are used to position the mesh at origin.

```
#version 330 core
layout (location=0) in vec3 vVertex;
uniform mat4 MVP;
uniform ivec2 HALF_TERRAIN_SIZE;
uniform sampler2D heightMapTexture;
uniform float scale;
uniform float half_scale;
void main()
{
```

```
float height = texture(heightMapTexture,
vVertex.xz).r*scale - half_scale;
vec2 pos  = (vVertex.xz*2.0-1)*HALF_TERRAIN_SIZE;
gl_Position = MVP*vec4(pos.x, height, pos.y, 1);
}
```

4. Load the shaders and the corresponding uniform and attribute locations. Also, set the values of the uniforms that never change during the lifetime of the application, at initialization.

```
shader.LoadFromFile(GL_VERTEX_SHADER,
"shaders/shader.vert");
shader.LoadFromFile(GL_FRAGMENT_SHADER,
"shaders/shader.frag");
shader.CreateAndLinkProgram();
shader.Use();
    shader.AddAttribute("vVertex");
    shader.AddUniform("heightMapTexture");
    shader.AddUniform("scale");
    shader.AddUniform("half_scale");
    shader.AddUniform("HALF_TERRAIN_SIZE");
    shader.AddUniform("MVP");
    glUniform1i(shader("heightMapTexture"), 0);
    glUniform2i(shader("HALF_TERRAIN_SIZE"),
    TERRAIN_WIDTH>>1, TERRAIN_DEPTH>>1);
    glUniform1f(shader("scale"), scale);
    glUniform1f(shader("half_scale"), half_scale);
shader.UnUse();
```

5. In the rendering code, set the shader and render the terrain by passing the modelview/projection matrices to the shader as shader uniforms.

```
shader.Use();
    glUniformMatrix4fv(shader("MVP"), 1, GL_FALSE,
    glm::value_ptr(MVP));
    glDrawElements(GL_TRIANGLES,TOTAL_INDICES,
    GL_UNSIGNED_INT, 0);
shader.UnUse();
```

How it works...

Terrain rendering is relatively straight forward to implement. The geometry is first generated on the CPU and is then stored in the GPU buffer objects. Next, the height map is loaded from an image which is then transferred to the vertex shader as a texture sampler uniform.

In the vertex shader, the height of the vertex is obtained from the height map by texture lookup using the position of the vertex. The final vertex position is obtained by combining the height with the input vertex position. The resulting vector is multiplied with the modelview projection matrix to obtain the clip space position. The vertex displacement technique can also be used to give realistic surface detail to a low resolution 3D model.

The output from the demo application for this recipe renders a wireframe terrain as shown in the following screenshot:

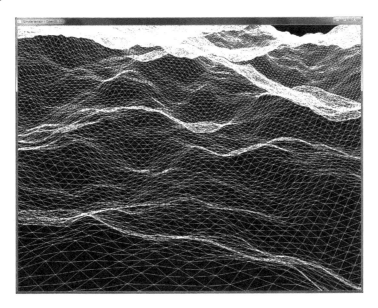

The height map used to generate this terrain is shown in the following screenshot:

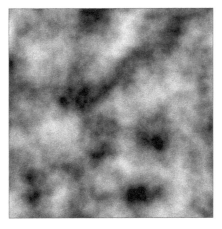

There's more...

The method we have presented in this recipe uses the vertex displacement to generate a terrain from a height map. There are several tools available that can help with the terrain height map generation. One of them is Terragen (`planetside.co.uk`). Another useful tool is World Machine (`http://world-machine.com/`). A general source of information for terrains is available at the virtual terrain project (`http://vterrain.org/`).

We can also use procedural methods to generate terrains such as fractal terrain generation. Noise methods can also be helpful in the generation of the terrains.

See also

To know more about implementing terrains, you can check the following:

▸ *Focus on 3D Terrain Programming*, by *Trent Polack, Premier Press*, 2002

▸ *Chapter 7, Terrain Level of Detail* in *Level of Detail for 3D Graphics* by *David Luebke, Morgan Kaufmann Publishers*, 2003.

Implementing 3ds model loading using separate buffers

We will now create model loader and renderer for Autodesk® 3ds model format which is a simple yet efficient binary model format for storing digital assets.

Getting started

The code for this recipe is contained in the `Chapter5/3DsViewer` folder. This recipe will be using the *Drawing a 2D image in a window using a fragment shader and the SOIL image loading library* recipe from *Chapter 1, Introduction to Modern OpenGL*, for loading the 3ds mesh file's textures using the `SOIL` image loading library.

How to do it...

The steps required to implement a 3ds file viewer are as follows:

1. Create an instance of the `C3dsLoader` class. Then call the `C3dsLoader::Load3DS` function passing it the name of the mesh file and a set of vectors to store the submeshes, vertices, normals, uvs, indices, and materials.

   ```
   if(!loader.Load3DS(mesh_filename.c_str( ), meshes,
   vertices, normals, uvs, faces, indices, materials)) {
   ```

```
        cout<<"Cannot load the 3ds mesh"<<endl;
        exit(EXIT_FAILURE);
    }
```

2. After the mesh is loaded, use the mesh's material list to load the material textures into the OpenGL texture object.

```
for(size_t k=0;k<materials.size();k++) {
    for(size_t m=0;m< materials[k]->textureMaps.size();m++)
    {
        GLuint id = 0;
        glGenTextures(1, &id);
        glBindTexture(GL_TEXTURE_2D, id);
        glTexParameteri(GL_TEXTURE_2D, GL_TEXTURE_MIN_FILTER,
        GL_LINEAR);
        glTexParameteri(GL_TEXTURE_2D, GL_TEXTURE_MAG_FILTER,
        GL_LINEAR);
        glTexParameteri(GL_TEXTURE_2D, GL_TEXTURE_WRAP_S,
        GL_REPEAT);
        glTexParameteri(GL_TEXTURE_2D, GL_TEXTURE_WRAP_T,
        GL_REPEAT);
        int texture_width = 0, texture_height = 0,
        channels=0;
        const string& filename = materials[k]->
        textureMaps[m]->filename;
        std::string full_filename = mesh_path;
        full_filename.append(filename);
        GLubyte* pData = SOIL_load_image
        (full_filename.c_str(), &texture_width,
        &texture_height, &channels, SOIL_LOAD_AUTO);
        if(pData == NULL) {
            cerr<<"Cannot load image: "<<
            full_filename.c_str()<<endl;
                exit(EXIT_FAILURE);
        }
        //Flip the image on Y axis
        int i,j;
        for( j = 0; j*2 < texture_height; ++j ) {
            int index1 = j * texture_width * channels;
            int index2 = (texture_height - 1 - j) *
            texture_width * channels;
            for( i = texture_width * channels; i > 0; --i ){
                GLubyte temp = pData[index1];
                pData[index1] = pData[index2];
                pData[index2] = temp;
                ++index1;
```

```
          ++index2;
        }
      }
      GLenum format = GL_RGBA;
      switch(channels) {
        case 2: format = GL_RG32UI; break;
        case 3: format = GL_RGB; break;
        case 4: format = GL_RGBA; break;
      }
      glTexImage2D(GL_TEXTURE_2D, 0, format, texture_width,
      texture_height, 0, format, GL_UNSIGNED_BYTE, pData);
      SOIL_free_image_data(pData);
      textureMaps[filename]=id;
    }
  }
```

3. Pass the loaded per-vertex attributes; that is, positions (`vertices`), texture coordinates (`uvs`), per-vertex normals (`normals`), and triangle indices (`indices`) to GPU memory by allocating separate buffer objects for each attribute. Note that for easier handling of buffer objects, we bind a single vertex array object (`vaoID`) first.

```
glBindVertexArray(vaoID);
glBindBuffer (GL_ARRAY_BUFFER, vboVerticesID);
glBufferData (GL_ARRAY_BUFFER, sizeof(glm::vec3)*
vertices.size(), &(vertices[0].x), GL_STATIC_DRAW);
glEnableVertexAttribArray(shader["vVertex"]);
glVertexAttribPointer(shader["vVertex"], 3, GL_FLOAT,
GL_FALSE,0,0);
glBindBuffer (GL_ARRAY_BUFFER, vboUVsID);
glBufferData (GL_ARRAY_BUFFER,
sizeof(glm::vec2)*uvs.size(), &(uvs[0].x),
GL_STATIC_DRAW);
glEnableVertexAttribArray(shader["vUV"]);
glVertexAttribPointer(shader["vUV"],2,GL_FLOAT,
GL_FALSE,0, 0);
glBindBuffer (GL_ARRAY_BUFFER, vboNormalsID);
glBufferData (GL_ARRAY_BUFFER, sizeof(glm::vec3)*
normals.size(), &(normals[0].x),  GL_STATIC_DRAW);
glEnableVertexAttribArray(shader["vNormal"]);
glVertexAttribPointer(shader["vNormal"], 3, GL_FLOAT,
GL_FALSE, 0, 0);
```

4. If we have only a single material in the 3ds file, we store the face indices into GL_
ELEMENT_ARRAY_BUFFER so that we can render the whole mesh in a single call.
However, if we have more than one material, we bind the appropriate submeshes
separately. The glBufferData call allocates the GPU memory, however, it is not
initialized. In order to initialize the buffer object memory, we can use the glMapBuffer
function to obtain a direct pointer to the GPU memory. Using this pointer, we can then
write to the GPU memory. An alternative to using glMapBuffer is glBufferSubData
which can modify the GPU memory by copying contents from a CPU buffer.

```
if(materials.size()==1) {
    glBindBuffer(GL_ELEMENT_ARRAY_BUFFER, vboIndicesID);
    glBufferData(GL_ELEMENT_ARRAY_BUFFER,
    sizeof(GLushort)*
    3*faces.size(), 0, GL_STATIC_DRAW);
    GLushort* pIndices = static_cast<GLushort*>(
    glMapBuffer(GL_ELEMENT_ARRAY_BUFFER, GL_WRITE_ONLY));
    for(size_t i=0;i<faces.size();i++) {
        *(pIndices++)=faces[i].a;
        *(pIndices++)=faces[i].b;
        *(pIndices++)=faces[i].c;
    }
    glUnmapBuffer(GL_ELEMENT_ARRAY_BUFFER);
}
```

5. Set up the vertex shader to output the clip space position as well as the per-vertex
texture coordinates. The texture coordinates are then interpolated by the rasterizer
to the fragment shader using an output attribute vUVout.

```
#version 330 core

layout(location = 0) in vec3 vVertex;
layout(location = 1) in vec3 vNormal;
layout(location = 2) in vec2 vUV;

smooth out vec2 vUVout;

uniform mat4 P;
uniform mat4 MV;
uniform mat3 N;

smooth out vec3 vEyeSpaceNormal;
smooth out vec3 vEyeSpacePosition;

void main()
{
```

```
vUVout=vUV;
vEyeSpacePosition = (MV*vec4(vVertex,1)).xyz;
vEyeSpaceNormal = N*vNormal;
gl_Position = P*vec4(vEyeSpacePosition,1);
}
```

6. Set up the fragment shader, which looks up the texture map sampler with the interpolated texture coordinates from the rasterizer. Depending on whether the submesh has a texture, we linearly interpolate between the texture map color and the diffused color of the material, using the GLSL mix function.

```
#version 330 core
uniform sampler2D textureMap;
uniform float hasTexture;
uniform vec3 light_position;//light position in object
space
uniform mat4 MV;
smooth in vec3 vEyeSpaceNormal;
smooth in vec3 vEyeSpacePosition;
smooth in vec2 vUVout;

layout(location=0) out vec4 vFragColor;

const float k0 = 1.0;//constant attenuation
const float k1 = 0.0;//linear attenuation
const float k2 = 0.0;//quadratic attenuation

void main()
{
  vec4 vEyeSpaceLightPosition =
  (MV*vec4(light_position,1));
  vec3 L = (vEyeSpaceLightPosition.xyz-vEyeSpacePosition);
  float d = length(L);
  L = normalize(L);
  float diffuse = max(0, dot(vEyeSpaceNormal, L));
  float attenuationAmount = 1.0/(k0 + (k1*d) + (k2*d*d));
  diffuse *= attenuationAmount;

  vFragColor = diffuse*mix(vec4(1),
  texture(textureMap, vUVout), hasTexture);
}
```

7. The rendering code binds the shader program, sets the shader uniforms, and then renders the mesh, depending on how many materials the 3ds mesh has. If the mesh has only a single material, it is drawn in a single call to glDrawElement by using the indices attached to the GL_ELEMENT_ARRAY_BUFFER binding point.

```
glBindVertexArray(vaoID); {
    shader.Use();
```

```
glUniformMatrix4fv(shader("MV"), 1, GL_FALSE,
glm::value_ptr(MV));
glUniformMatrix3fv(shader("N"), 1, GL_FALSE,
glm::value_ptr(glm::inverseTranspose(glm::mat3(MV))));
glUniformMatrix4fv(shader("P"), 1, GL_FALSE,
glm::value_ptr(P));
glUniform3fv(shader("light_position"),1,
&(lightPosOS.x));
if(materials.size()==1) {
  GLint whichID[1];
  glGetIntegerv(GL_TEXTURE_BINDING_2D, whichID);
  if(textureMaps.size()>0) {
    if(whichID[0] != textureMaps[
    materials[0]->textureMaps[0]->filename]) {
    glBindTexture(GL_TEXTURE_2D,
    textureMaps[materials[0]->textureMaps[0]
    ->filename]);
    glUniform1f(shader("hasTexture"),1.0);
    }
  } else {
    glUniform1f(shader("hasTexture"),0.0);
    glUniform3fv(shader("diffuse_color"),1,
    materials[0]->diffuse);
  }
  glDrawElements(GL_TRIANGLES, meshes[0]->faces.size()*3,
  GL_UNSIGNED_SHORT, 0);
}
```

8. If the mesh contains more than one material, we iterate through the material list, and bind the texture map (if the material has one), otherwise we use the diffuse color stored in the material for the submesh. Finally, we pass the `sub_indices` array stored in the material to the `glDrawElements` function to load those indices only.

```
else {
  for(size_t i=0;i<materials.size();i++) {
    GLint whichID[1];
    glGetIntegerv(GL_TEXTURE_BINDING_2D, whichID);
    if(materials[i]->textureMaps.size()>0) {
      if(whichID[0] != textureMaps[materials[i]
      ->textureMaps[0]->filename]) {
        glBindTexture(GL_TEXTURE_2D, textureMaps
        [materials[i]->textureMaps[0]->filename]);
      }
      glUniform1f(shader("hasTexture"),1.0);
    } else {
      glUniform1f(shader("hasTexture"),0.0);
    }
```

```
        glUniform3fv(shader("diffuse_color"),1,
        materials[i]->diffuse);
        glDrawElements(GL_TRIANGLES,
        materials[i]->sub_indices.size(), GL_UNSIGNED_SHORT,
        &(materials[i]->sub_indices[0]));
    }
}
shader.UnUse();
```

How it works...

The main component of this recipe is the `C3dsLoader::Load3DS` function. The 3ds file is a binary file which is organized into a collection of chunks. Typically, a reader reads the first two bytes from the file which are stored in the chunk ID. The next four bytes store the chunk length in bytes. We continue reading chunks, and their lengths, and then store data appropriately into our vectors/variables until there are no more chunks and we pass reading the end of file. The 3ds specifications detail all of the chunks and their lengths as well as subchunks, as shown in the following figure:

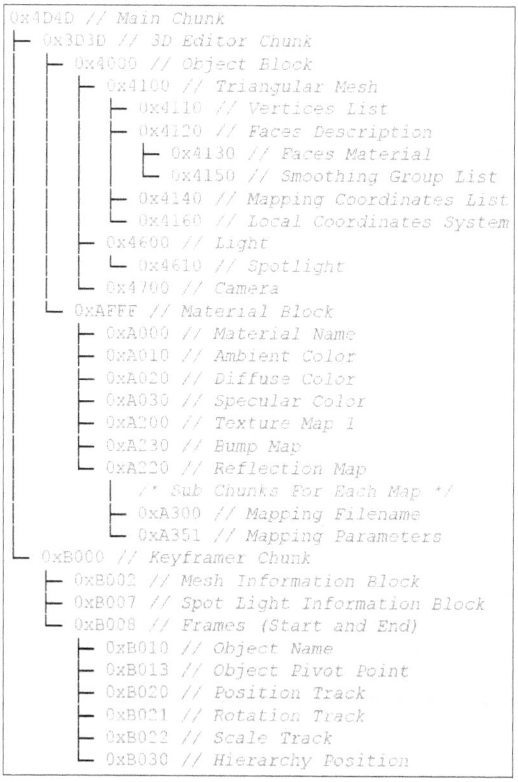

```
0x4D4D // Main Chunk
├─ 0x3D3D // 3D Editor Chunk
│   ├─ 0x4000 // Object Block
│   │   ├─ 0x4100 // Triangular Mesh
│   │   │   ├─ 0x4110 // Vertices List
│   │   │   ├─ 0x4120 // Faces Description
│   │   │   │   ├─ 0x4130 // Faces Material
│   │   │   │   └─ 0x4150 // Smoothing Group List
│   │   │   ├─ 0x4140 // Mapping Coordinates List
│   │   │   └─ 0x4160 // Local Coordinates System
│   │   ├─ 0x4600 // Light
│   │   │   └─ 0x4610 // Spotlight
│   │   └─ 0x4700 // Camera
│   └─ 0xAFFF // Material Block
│       ├─ 0xA000 // Material Name
│       ├─ 0xA010 // Ambient Color
│       ├─ 0xA020 // Diffuse Color
│       ├─ 0xA030 // Specular Color
│       ├─ 0xA200 // Texture Map 1
│       ├─ 0xA230 // Bump Map
│       └─ 0xA220 // Reflection Map
│           │  /* Sub Chunks For Each Map */
│           ├─ 0xA300 // Mapping Filename
│           └─ 0xA351 // Mapping Parameters
└─ 0xB000 // Keyframer Chunk
    ├─ 0xB002 // Mesh Information Block
    ├─ 0xB007 // Spot Light Information Block
    └─ 0xB008 // Frames (Start and End)
        ├─ 0xB010 // Object Name
        ├─ 0xB013 // Object Pivot Point
        ├─ 0xB020 // Position Track
        ├─ 0xB021 // Rotation Track
        ├─ 0xB022 // Scale Track
        └─ 0xB030 // Hierarchy Position
```

Note that if there is a subchunk that we are interested in, we need to read the parent chunk as well, to move the file pointer to the appropriate offset in the file, for our required chunk. The loader first finds the total size of the 3ds mesh file in bytes. Then, it runs a while loop that checks to see if the current file pointer is within the file's size. If it is, it continues to read the first two bytes (the chunk's ID) and the next four bytes (the chunk's length).

```
while(infile.tellg() < fileSize) {
  infile.read(reinterpret_cast<char*>(&chunk_id), 2);
  infile.read(reinterpret_cast<char*>(&chunk_length), 4);
```

Then we start a big switch case with all of the required chunk IDs and then read the bytes from the respective chunks as desired.

```
switch(chunk_id) {
  case 0x4d4d: break;
  case 0x3d3d: break;
  case 0x4000: {
    std::string name = "";
    char c = ' ';
    while(c!='\0') {
      infile.read(&c,1);
      name.push_back(c);
    }
    pMesh = new C3dsMesh(name);
    meshes.push_back(pMesh);
  } break;
  ...//rest of the chunks
}
```

All names (object name, material name, or texture map name) have to be read byte-by-byte until the null terminator character (\0) is found. For reading vertices, we first read two bytes that store the total number of vertices (N). Two bytes means that the maximum number of vertices one mesh can store is 65536. Then, we read the whole chunk of bytes, that is, sizeof(glm::vec3)*N, directly into our mesh's vertices, shown as follows:

```
case 0x4110: {
  unsigned short total_vertices=0;
  infile.read(reinterpret_cast<char*>(&total_vertices), 2);
  pMesh->vertices.resize(total_vertices);
  infile.read(reinterpret_cast<char*>(&pMesh->vertices[0].x),
    sizeof(glm::vec3)   *total_vertices);
}break;
```

Similar to how the vertex information is stored, the face information stores the three unsigned short indices of the triangle and another unsigned short index containing the face flags. Therefore, for a mesh with M triangles, we have to read 4*M unsigned shorts from the file. We store the four unsigned shorts into a Face struct for convenience and then read the contents, as shown in the following code snippet:

```
case 0x4120: {
  unsigned short total_tris=0;
  infile.read(reinterpret_cast<char*>(&total_tris), 2);
  pMesh->faces.resize(total_tris);
  infile.read(reinterpret_cast<char*>(&pMesh->faces[0].a),
  sizeof(Face)*total_tris);
}break;
```

The code for reading the material face IDs and texture coordinates follows in the same way as the total entries are first read and then the appropriate number of bytes are read from the file. Note that, if a chunk has a color chunk (as for chunk IDs: 0xa010 to 0xa030), the color information is contained in a subchunk (IDs: 0x0010 to 0x0013) depending on the data type used to store the color information in the parent chunk.

After the mesh and material information is loaded, we generate global vertices, uvs, and indices vectors. This makes it easy for us to render the submeshes in the render function.

```
size_t total = materials.size();
for(size_t i=0;i<total;i++) {
  if(materials[i]->face_ids.size()==0)
  materials.erase(materials.begin()+i);
}

for(size_t i=0;i<meshes.size();i++) {
  for(size_t j=0;j<meshes[i]->vertices.size();j++)
  vertices.push_back(meshes[i]->vertices[j]);

  for(size_t j=0;j<meshes[i]->uvs.size();j++)
  uvs.push_back(meshes[i]->uvs[j]);

  for(size_t j=0;j<meshes[i]->faces.size();j++) {
    faces.push_back(meshes[i]->faces[j]);
  }
}
```

Note that the 3ds format does not store the per-vertex normal explicitly. It only stores smoothing groups which tell us which faces have shared normals. After we have the vertex positions and face information, we can generate the per-vertex normals by averaging the per-face normals. This is carried out by using the following code snippet in the 3ds.cpp file. We first allocate space for the per-vertex normals. Then we estimate the face's normal by using the cross product of the two edges. Finally, we add the face normal to the appropriate vertex index and then normalize the normal.

```
normals.resize(vertices.size());
for(size_t j=0;j<faces.size();j++) {
  Face f = faces[j];
  glm::vec3 v0 = vertices[f.a];
  glm::vec3 v1 = vertices[f.b];
  glm::vec3 v2 = vertices[f.c];
  glm::vec3 e1 = v1 - v0;
  glm::vec3 e2 = v2 - v0;
  glm::vec3 N = glm::cross(e1,e2);
  normals[f.a] += N;
  normals[f.b] += N;
  normals[f.c] += N;
}
for(size_t i=0;i<normals.size();i++) {
  normals[i]=glm::normalize(normals[i]);
}
```

Once we have all the per-vertex attributes and faces information, we use this to group the triangles by material. We loop through all of the materials and expand their face IDs to include the three vertex IDs and make the face.

```
for(size_t i=0;i<materials.size();i++) {
  Material* pMat = materials[i];
  for(int j=0;j<pMat->face_ids.size();j++) {
    pMat->sub_indices.push_back(faces[pMat->face_ids[j]].a);
    pMat->sub_indices.push_back(faces[pMat->face_ids[j]].b);
    pMat->sub_indices.push_back(faces[pMat->face_ids[j]].c);
  }
}
```

There's more...

The output from the demo application implementing this recipe is given in the following figure. In this recipe, we render three blocks on a quad plane. The camera position can be changed using the left mouse button. The point light source position can be changed using the right mouse button. Each block has six textures attached to it, whereas the plane has no texture, hence it uses the diffuse color value.

Note that the 3ds loader shown in this recipe does not take smoothing groups into consideration. For a more robust loader, we recommend the lib3ds library which provides a more elaborate 3ds file loader with support for smoothing groups, animation tracks, cameras, lights, keyframes, and so on.

See also

For more information on implementing 3ds model loading, you can refer to the following links:

- Lib3ds: http://code.google.com/p/lib3ds/
- 3ds file loader by Damiano Vitulli: http://www.spacesimulator.net/wiki/index.php?title=Tutorials:3ds_Loader
- 3ds file format details on Wikipedia.org: http://en.wikipedia.org/wiki/.3ds

Implementing OBJ model loading using interleaved buffers

In this recipe we will implement the Wavefront ® OBJ model. Instead of using separate buffer objects for storing positions, normals, and texture coordinates as in the previous recipe, we will use a single buffer object with interleaved data. This ensures that we have more chances of a cache hit since related attributes are stored next to each other in the buffer object memory.

Getting started

The code for this recipe is contained in the `Chapter5/ObjViewer` folder.

How to do it...

Let us start the recipe by following these simple steps:

1. Create a global reference of the `ObjLoader` object. Call the `ObjLoader::Load` function, passing it the name of the OBJ file. Pass vectors to store the meshes, vertices, indices, and materials contained in the OBJ file.

```
ObjLoader obj;
if(!obj.Load(mesh_filename.c_str(), meshes, vertices,
indices, materials)) {
  cout<<"Cannot load the 3ds mesh"<<endl;
  exit(EXIT_FAILURE);
}
```

2. Generate OpenGL texture objects for each material using the `SOIL` library if the material has a texture map.

```
for(size_t k=0;k<materials.size();k++) {
  if(materials[k]->map_Kd != "") {
    GLuint id = 0;
    glGenTextures(1, &id);
    glBindTexture(GL_TEXTURE_2D, id);
    glTexParameteri(GL_TEXTURE_2D, GL_TEXTURE_MIN_FILTER,
    GL_LINEAR);
    glTexParameteri(GL_TEXTURE_2D, GL_TEXTURE_MAG_FILTER,
    GL_LINEAR);
    glTexParameteri(GL_TEXTURE_2D, GL_TEXTURE_WRAP_S,
    GL_REPEAT);
    glTexParameteri(GL_TEXTURE_2D, GL_TEXTURE_WRAP_T,
    GL_REPEAT);
```

```
int texture_width = 0, texture_height = 0,
channels=0;
const string& filename =  materials[k]->map_Kd;
std::string full_filename = mesh_path;
full_filename.append(filename);

GLubyte* pData =
SOIL_load_image(full_filename.c_str(),
&texture_width, &texture_height, &channels,
SOIL_LOAD_AUTO);
if(pData == NULL) {
  cerr<<"Cannot load image:
  "<<full_filename.c_str()<<endl;
  exit(EXIT_FAILURE);
}
//… image flipping code
GLenum format = GL_RGBA;
switch(channels) {
  case 2: format = GL_RG32UI; break;
  case 3: format = GL_RGB;  break;
  case 4: format = GL_RGBA;  break;
}
glTexImage2D(GL_TEXTURE_2D, 0, format, texture_width,
texture_height, 0, format, GL_UNSIGNED_BYTE, pData);
SOIL_free_image_data(pData);
textures.push_back(id);
  }
}
```

3. Set up shaders and generate buffer objects to store the mesh file data in the GPU memory. The shader setup is similar to the previous recipes.

```
glGenVertexArrays(1, &vaoID);
glGenBuffers(1, &vboVerticesID);
glGenBuffers(1, &vboIndicesID);
glBindVertexArray(vaoID);
glBindBuffer (GL_ARRAY_BUFFER, vboVerticesID);
glBufferData (GL_ARRAY_BUFFER,
sizeof(Vertex)*vertices.size(),
&(vertices[0].pos.x), GL_STATIC_DRAW);
glEnableVertexAttribArray(shader["vVertex"]);
glVertexAttribPointer(shader["vVertex"], 3, GL_FLOAT,
GL_FALSE,sizeof(Vertex),0);

glEnableVertexAttribArray(shader["vNormal"]);
```

```
glVertexAttribPointer(shader["vNormal"], 3, GL_FLOAT,
GL_FALSE,sizeof(Vertex),(const GLvoid*)(offsetof( Vertex,
normal)) );

glEnableVertexAttribArray(shader["vUV"]);
glVertexAttribPointer(shader["vUV"], 2, GL_FLOAT,
GL_FALSE, sizeof(Vertex), (const
GLvoid*)(offsetof(Vertex, uv)) );
if(materials.size()==1) {
  glBindBuffer(GL_ELEMENT_ARRAY_BUFFER, vboIndicesID);
  glBufferData(GL_ELEMENT_ARRAY_BUFFER,
  sizeof(GLushort)*indices.size(), &(indices[0]),
  GL_STATIC_DRAW);
}
```

4. Bind the vertex array object associated with the mesh, use the shader and pass the shader uniforms, that is, the modelview (MV), projection (P), normal matrices (N) and light position, and so on.

```
glBindVertexArray(vaoID); {
  shader.Use();
  glUniformMatrix4fv(shader("MV"), 1, GL_FALSE,
  glm::value_ptr(MV));
  glUniformMatrix3fv(shader("N"), 1, GL_FALSE,
  glm::value_ptr(glm::inverseTranspose(glm::mat3(MV))));
  glUniformMatrix4fv(shader("P"), 1, GL_FALSE,
  glm::value_ptr(P));
  glUniform3fv(shader("light_position"),1,
  &(lightPosOS.x));
```

5. To draw the mesh/submesh, loop through all of the materials in the mesh and then bind the texture to the GL_TEXTURE_2D target if the material contains a texture map. Otherwise, use a default color for the mesh. Finally, call the glDrawElements function to render the mesh/submesh.

```
for(size_t i=0;i<materials.size();i++) {
  Material* pMat = materials[i];
  if(pMat->map_Kd !="") {
    glUniform1f(shader("useDefault"), 0.0);
    GLint whichID[1];
    glGetIntegerv(GL_TEXTURE_BINDING_2D, whichID);
    if(whichID[0] != textures[i])
      glBindTexture(GL_TEXTURE_2D, textures[i]);
  }
  else
  glUniform1f(shader("useDefault"), 1.0);
```

```
      if(materials.size()==1)
      glDrawElements(GL_TRIANGLES, indices.size(),
      GL_UNSIGNED_SHORT, 0);
      else
      glDrawElements(GL_TRIANGLES, pMat->count,
      GL_UNSIGNED_SHORT, (const GLvoid*)(& indices
      [pMat->offset]));
   }
   shader.UnUse();
```

How it works...

The main component of this recipe is the `ObjLoader::Load` function defined in the `Obj.cpp` file. The Wavefront® OBJ file is a text file which has different text descriptors for different mesh components. Usually, the mesh starts with the geometry definition, that is, vertices that begin with the letter `v` followed by three floating point values. If there are normals, their definitions begin with `vn` followed by three floating point values. If there are texture coordinates, their definitions begin with `vt`, followed by two floating point values. Comments start with the # character, so whenever a line with this character is encountered, it is ignored.

Following the geometry definition, the topology is defined. In this case, the line is prefixed with `f` followed by the indices for the polygon vertices. In case of a triangle, three indices sections are given such that the vertex position indices are given first, followed by texture coordinates indices (if any), and finally the normal indices (if any). Note that the indices start from 1, not 0.

So, for example, say that we have a quad geometry having four position indices (1,2,3,4) having four texture coordinate indices (5,6,7,8), and four normal indices (1,1,1,1) then the topology would be stored as follows:

```
f 1/5/1 2/6/1 3/7/1 4/8/1
```

If the mesh is a triangular mesh with position vertices (1,2,3), texture coordinates (7,8,9), and normals (4,5,6) then the topology would be stored as follows:

```
f 1/7/4 2/8/5 3/9/6
```

Now, if the texture coordinates are omitted from the first example, then the topology would be stored as follows:

```
f 1//1 2//1 3//1 4//1
```

The OBJ file stores material information in a separate material (.mtl) file. This file contains similar text descriptors that define different materials with their ambient, diffuse, and specular color values, texture maps, and so on. The details of the defined elements are given in the OBJ format specifications. The material file for the current OBJ file is declared using the mtllib keyword followed by the name of the .mtl file. Usually, the .mtl file is stored in the same folder as the OBJ file. A polygon definition is preceded with a usemtl keyword followed by the name of the material to use for the upcoming polygon definition. Several polygonal definitions can be grouped using the g or o prefix followed by the name of the group/object respectively.

The ObjLoader::Load function first finds the current prefix. Then, the code branches to the appropriate section depending on the prefix. The suffix strings are then parsed and the extracted data is stored in the corresponding vectors. For efficiency, rather than storing the indices directly, we store them by material so that we can then sort and render the mesh by material. The associated material library file (.mtl) is loaded using the ReadMaterialLibrary function. Refer to the Obj.cpp file for details.

The file parsing is the first piece of the puzzle. The second piece is the transfer of this data to the GPU memory. In this recipe, we use an interleaved buffer, that is, instead of storing each per-vertex attribute separately in its own vertex buffer object, we store them interleaved one after the other in a single buffer object. First positions are followed by normals and then texture coordinates. We achieve this by first defining our vertex format using a custom Vertex struct. Our vertices are a vector of this struct.

```
struct Vertex {
    glm::vec3 pos, normal;
    glm::vec2 uv;
};
```

We generate the vertex array object and then the vertex buffer object. Next, we bind the buffer object passing it our vertices. In this case, we specify the stride of each attribute in the data stream separately as follows:

```
glBindBuffer (GL_ARRAY_BUFFER, vboVerticesID);
glBufferData (GL_ARRAY_BUFFER, sizeof(Vertex)*vertices.size(),
&(vertices[0].pos.x), GL_STATIC_DRAW);
glEnableVertexAttribArray(shader["vVertex"]);
glVertexAttribPointer(shader["vVertex"], 3, GL_FLOAT,
GL_FALSE,sizeof(Vertex),0);
glEnableVertexAttribArray(shader["vNormal"]);
glVertexAttribPointer(shader["vNormal"], 3, GL_FLOAT, GL_FALSE,
sizeof(Vertex), (const GLvoid*)(offsetof(Vertex, normal)) );
glEnableVertexAttribArray(shader["vUV"]);
glVertexAttribPointer(shader["vUV"], 2, GL_FLOAT, GL_FALSE,
sizeof(Vertex), (const GLvoid*)(offsetof(Vertex, uv)) );
```

If the mesh has a single material, we store the mesh indices into a GL_ELEMENT_ARRAY_ BUFFER target. Otherwise, we render the submeshes by material.

```
if(materials.size()==1) {
    glBindBuffer(GL_ELEMENT_ARRAY_BUFFER, vboIndicesID);
    glBufferData(GL_ELEMENT_ARRAY_BUFFER,  sizeof(GLushort) *
    indices.size(), &(indices[0]), GL_STATIC_DRAW);
}
```

At the time of rendering, if we have a single material, we render the whole mesh, otherwise we render the subset stored with the material.

```
if(materials.size()==1)
    glDrawElements(GL_TRIANGLES,indices.size(),GL_UNSIGNED_SHORT,0);
else
    glDrawElements(GL_TRIANGLES, pMat->count, GL_UNSIGNED_SHORT,
    (const GLvoid*)(&indices[pMat->offset]));
```

There's more...

The demo application implementing this recipe shows a scene with three blocks on a planar quad. The camera view can be rotated with the left mouse button. The light source's position is shown by a 3D crosshair that can be moved by dragging the right mouse button. The output from this demo application is shown in the following figure:

See also

You can see the OBJ file specification on Wikipedia at http://en.wikipedia.org/wiki/ Wavefront_.obj_file.

Implementing EZMesh model loading

In this recipe, we will learn how to load and render an EZMesh model. There are several skeletal animation formats such as Quake's md2 (.md2), Autodesk® FBX (.fbx), and Collada (.dae). The conventional model formats such as Collada are overly complicated for doing simple skeletal animation. Therefore, in this recipe, we will learn how to load and render an EZMesh (.ezm) skeletal model.

Getting started

The code for this recipe is contained in the Chapter5/EZMeshViewer directory. For this recipe, we will be using two external libraries to aid with the EZMesh (.ezm) mesh file parsing. The first library is called MeshImport and it can be downloaded from http://code. google.com/p/meshimport/. Make sure to get the latest svn trunk of the code. After downloading, change directory to the compiler subdirectory which contains the visual studio solution files. Double-click to open the solution and build the project dlls. After the library is built successfully, copy MeshImport_[x86/x64].dll and MeshImportEZM_[x86/x64]. dll (subject to your machine configuration) into your current project directory. In addition, also copy the MeshImport.[h/cpp] files which contain some useful library loading routines.

In addition, since EZMesh is an XML format to support loading of textures, we parse the EZMesh XML manually with the help of the pugixml library. You can download it from http://pugixml.org/downloads/. As pugixml is tiny, we can directly include the source files with the project.

How to do it...

Let us start this recipe by following these simple steps:

1. Create a global reference to an EzmLoader object. Call the EzmLoader::Load function passing it the name of the EZMesh (.ezm) file. Pass the vectors to store the submeshes, vertices, indices, and materials-to-image map. The Load function also accepts the min and max vectors to store the EZMesh bounding box.

   ```
   if(!ezm.Load(mesh_filename.c_str(), submeshes, vertices,
      indices, material2ImageMap, min, max)) {
      cout<<"Cannot load the EZMesh mesh"<<endl;
      exit(EXIT_FAILURE);
   }
   ```

2. Using the material information, generate the OpenGL textures for the EZMesh geometry.

```
for(size_t k=0;k<materialNames.size();k++) {
  GLuint id = 0;
  glGenTextures(1, &id);
  glBindTexture(GL_TEXTURE_2D, id);
  glTexParameteri(GL_TEXTURE_2D, GL_TEXTURE_MIN_FILTER,
    GL_LINEAR);
  glTexParameteri(GL_TEXTURE_2D, GL_TEXTURE_MAG_FILTER,
    GL_LINEAR);
  glTexParameteri(GL_TEXTURE_2D, GL_TEXTURE_WRAP_S,
    GL_REPEAT);
  glTexParameteri(GL_TEXTURE_2D, GL_TEXTURE_WRAP_T,
    GL_REPEAT);
  int texture_width = 0, texture_height = 0, channels=0;
  const string& filename =  materialNames[k];

  std::string full_filename = mesh_path;
  full_filename.append(filename);

  //Image loading using SOIL and vertical image flipping
  //...
  GLenum format = GL_RGBA;
  switch(channels) {
    case 2:  format = GL_RG32UI; break;
    case 3: format = GL_RGB;  break;
    case 4: format = GL_RGBA;  break;
  }
  glTexImage2D(GL_TEXTURE_2D, 0, format, texture_width,
  texture_height, 0, format, GL_UNSIGNED_BYTE, pData);
  SOIL_free_image_data(pData);
  materialMap[filename] = id ;
}
```

3. Set up the interleaved buffer object as in the previous recipe, *Implementing OBJ model loading using interleaved buffers*.

```
glBindVertexArray(vaoID);
glBindBuffer (GL_ARRAY_BUFFER, vboVerticesID);
glBufferData (GL_ARRAY_BUFFER,
sizeof(Vertex)*vertices.size(),
&(vertices[0].pos.x), GL_DYNAMIC_DRAW);

glEnableVertexAttribArray(shader["vVertex"]);
glVertexAttribPointer(shader["vVertex"], 3, GL_FLOAT,
GL_FALSE,sizeof(Vertex),0);
```

```
glEnableVertexAttribArray(shader["vNormal"]);
glVertexAttribPointer(shader["vNormal"], 3, GL_FLOAT,
GL_FALSE, sizeof(Vertex), (const
GLvoid*)(offsetof(Vertex, normal)) );

glEnableVertexAttribArray(shader["vUV"]);
glVertexAttribPointer(shader["vUV"], 2, GL_FLOAT,
GL_FALSE, sizeof(Vertex), (const GLvoid*)
(offsetof(Vertex, uv)) );
```

4. To render the EZMesh, bind the mesh's vertex array object, set up the shader, and pass the shader uniforms.

```
glBindVertexArray(vaoID); {
  shader.Use();
  glUniformMatrix4fv(shader("MV"), 1, GL_FALSE,
  glm::value_ptr(MV));
  glUniformMatrix3fv(shader("N"), 1, GL_FALSE,
  glm::value_ptr(glm::inverseTranspose(glm::mat3(MV))));
  glUniformMatrix4fv(shader("P"), 1, GL_FALSE,
  glm::value_ptr(P));
  glUniform3fv(shader("light_position"),1,
  &(lightPosES.x));
```

5. Loop through all submeshes, bind the submesh texture, and then issue the `glDrawEements` call, passing it the submesh indices. If the submesh has no materials, a default solid color material is assigned to the submesh.

```
for(size_t i=0;i<submeshes.size();i++) {
  if(strlen(submeshes[i].materialName)>0) {
    GLuint id = materialMap[material2ImageMap[
    submeshes[i].materialName]];

    GLint whichID[1];
    glGetIntegerv(GL_TEXTURE_BINDING_2D, whichID);

    if(whichID[0] != id)
      glBindTexture(GL_TEXTURE_2D, id);
      glUniform1f(shader("useDefault"), 0.0);
    } else {
      glUniform1f(shader("useDefault"), 1.0);
    }
    glDrawElements(GL_TRIANGLES,
    submeshes[i].indices.size(),
    GL_UNSIGNED_INT, &submeshes[i].indices[0]);
  }
}
```

How it works...

EZMesh is an XML based skeletal animation format. There are two parts to this recipe: parsing of the EZMesh file using the MeshImport/pugixml libraries and handling of the data using OpenGL buffer objects. The first part is handled by the EzmLoader::Load function. Along with the filename, this function accepts vectors to store the submeshes, vertices, indices, and material names map contained in the mesh file.

If we open an EZMesh file, it contains a collection of XML elements. The first element is MeshSystem. This element contains four child elements: Skeletons, Animations, Materials, and Meshes. Each of these subelements has a count attribute that stores the total number of corresponding items in the EZMesh file. Note that we can remove the element as desired. So the hierarchy is typically as follows:

```
<MeshSystem>
    <Skeletons count="N">
    <Animations count="N">
    <Materials count="N">
    <Meshes count="N">
</MeshSystem>
```

For this recipe, we are interested in the last two subelements: Materials and Meshes. We will be using the first two subelements in the skeletal animation recipe in a later chapter of this book. Each Materials element has a counted number of Material elements. Each Material element stores the material's name in the name attribute and the material's details. For example, the texture map file name in the meta_data attribute. In the EZMLoader::Load function, we use pugi_xml to parse the Materials element and its subelements into a material map. This map stores the material's name and its texture file name. Note that the MeshImport library does provide functions for reading material information, but they are broken.

```
pugi::xml_node mats = doc.child("MeshSystem").child("Materials");
int totalMaterials = atoi(mats.attribute("count").value());
pugi::xml_node material = mats.child("Material");
for(int i=0;i<totalMaterials;i++) {
  std::string name = material.attribute("name").value();
  std::string metadata = material.attribute("meta_data").value();
  //clean up metadata
  int len = metadata.length();
  if(len>0) {
    string fullName="";
    int index = metadata.find_last_of("\\");
    if(index == string::npos) {
      fullName.append(metadata);
    } else {
```

```
            std::string fileNameOnly = metadata.substr(index+1,
            metadata.length());
            fullName.append(fileNameOnly);
        }
        bool exists = true;
        if(materialNames.find(name)==materialNames.end() )
            exists = false;
        if(!exists)
            materialNames[name] = (fullName);
            material = material.next_sibling("Material");
        }
    }
```

After the material information is loaded in, we initialize the `MeshImport` library by calling the `NVSHARE::loadMeshImporters` function and passing it the directory where `MeshImport` dlls (`MeshImport_[x86,x64].dll` and `MeshImportEZM_[x86,x64].dll`) are placed. Upon success, this function returns the `NVSHARE::MeshImport` library object. Using the `MeshImport` library object, we first create the mesh system container by calling the `NVSHARE::MeshImport::createMeshSystemContainer` function. This function accepts the object name and the `EZMesh` file contents. If successful, this function returns the `MeshSystemContainer` object which is then passed to the `NVSHARE::MeshImport::get MeshSystem` function which returns the `NVSHARE::MeshSystem` object. This represents the `MeshSystem` node in the `EZMesh` XML file.

Once we have the `MeshSystem` object, we can query all of the subelements. These reside in the `MeshSystem` object as member variables. So let's say we want to traverse through all of the meshes in the current `EZMesh` file and copy the per-vertex attributes to our own vector (`vertices`), we would simply do the following:

```
    for(size_t i=0;i<ms->mMeshCount;i++) {
        NVSHARE::Mesh* pMesh = ms->mMeshes[i];
        vertices.resize(pMesh->mVertexCount);
        for(size_t j=0;j<pMesh->mVertexCount;j++) {
            vertices[j].pos.x = pMesh->mVertices[j].mPos[0];
            vertices[j].pos.y = pMesh->mVertices[j].mPos[1];
            vertices[j].pos.z = pMesh->mVertices[j].mPos[2];

            vertices[j].normal.x = pMesh->mVertices[j].mNormal[0];
            vertices[j].normal.y = pMesh->mVertices[j].mNormal[1];
            vertices[j].normal.z = pMesh->mVertices[j].mNormal[2];

            vertices[j].uv.x = pMesh->mVertices[j].mTexel1[0];
            vertices[j].uv.y = pMesh->mVertices[j].mTexel1[1];
        }
    }
```

In an `EZMesh` file, the indices are sorted by materials into submeshes. We iterate through all of the submeshes and then store their material name and indices into our container.

```
submeshes.resize(pMesh->mSubMeshCount);
for(size_t j=0;j<pMesh->mSubMeshCount;j++) {
  NVSHARE::SubMesh* pSubMesh = pMesh->mSubMeshes[j];
  submeshes[j].materialName = pSubMesh->mMaterialName;
  submeshes[j].indices.resize(pSubMesh->mTriCount * 3);
  memcpy(&(submeshes[j].indices[0]), pSubMesh->mIndices,
  sizeof(unsigned int) *  pSubMesh->mTriCount * 3);
}
```

After the `EZMesh` file is parsed and we have the per-vertex data stored, we first generate the OpenGL textures from the `EZMesh` materials list. Then we store the texture IDs into a material map so that we can refer to the textures by material name.

```
for(size_t k=0;k<materialNames.size();k++) {
  GLuint id = 0;
  glGenTextures(1, &id);
  glBindTexture(GL_TEXTURE_2D, id);
  glTexParameteri(GL_TEXTURE_2D, GL_TEXTURE_MIN_FILTER,
  GL_LINEAR);
  glTexParameteri(GL_TEXTURE_2D, GL_TEXTURE_MAG_FILTER,
  GL_LINEAR);
  glTexParameteri(GL_TEXTURE_2D, GL_TEXTURE_WRAP_S, GL_REPEAT);
  glTexParameteri(GL_TEXTURE_2D, GL_TEXTURE_WRAP_T, GL_REPEAT);
  int texture_width = 0, texture_height = 0, channels=0;
  const string& filename =  materialNames[k];
  std::string full_filename = mesh_path;
  full_filename.append(filename);
  GLubyte* pData = SOIL_load_image(full_filename.c_str(),
  &texture_width, &texture_height, &channels, SOIL_LOAD_AUTO);
  if(pData == NULL) {
    cerr<<"Cannot load image: "<<full_filename.c_str()<<endl;
    exit(EXIT_FAILURE);
  }
  //... Flip the image on Y axis and determine the image format
  glTexImage2D(GL_TEXTURE_2D, 0, format, texture_width,
  texture_height, 0, format, GL_UNSIGNED_BYTE, pData);
  SOIL_free_image_data(pData);
  materialMap[filename] = id ;
}
```

After the materials, the shaders are loaded as in the previous recipes. The per-vertex data is then transferred to the GPU using vertex array and vertex buffer objects. In this case, we use the interleaved vertex buffer format.

```
glGenVertexArrays(1, &vaoID);
glGenBuffers(1, &vboVerticesID);
glGenBuffers(1, &vboIndicesID);

glBindVertexArray(vaoID);
glBindBuffer (GL_ARRAY_BUFFER, vboVerticesID);
glBufferData (GL_ARRAY_BUFFER, sizeof(Vertex)*vertices.size(),
&(vertices[0].pos.x), GL_DYNAMIC_DRAW);
glEnableVertexAttribArray(shader["vVertex"]);

glVertexAttribPointer(shader["vVertex"], 3, GL_FLOAT,
GL_FALSE,sizeof(Vertex),0);
glEnableVertexAttribArray(shader["vNormal"]);
glVertexAttribPointer(shader["vNormal"], 3, GL_FLOAT, GL_FALSE,
sizeof(Vertex), (const GLvoid*)(offsetof(Vertex, normal)) );
glEnableVertexAttribArray(shader["vUV"]);
glVertexAttribPointer(shader["vUV"], 2, GL_FLOAT, GL_FALSE,
sizeof(Vertex), (const GLvoid*)(offsetof(Vertex, uv)) );
```

For rendering of the mesh, we first bind the vertex array object of the mesh, attach our shader and pass the shader uniforms. Then we loop over all of the submeshes and bind the appropriate texture (if the submesh has texture). Otherwise, a default color is used. Finally, the indices of the submesh are used to draw the mesh using the glDrawElements function.

```
glBindVertexArray(vaoID); {
  shader.Use();
  glUniformMatrix4fv(shader("MV"), 1, GL_FALSE,
  glm::value_ptr(MV));
  glUniformMatrix3fv(shader("N"), 1, GL_FALSE,
  glm::value_ptr(glm::inverseTranspose(glm::mat3(MV))));
  glUniformMatrix4fv(shader("P"), 1, GL_FALSE,
  glm::value_ptr(P));
  glUniform3fv(shader("light_position"),1, &(lightPosES.x));
  for(size_t i=0;i<submeshes.size();i++) {
    if(strlen(submeshes[i].materialName)>0) {
      GLuint id =
      materialMap[material2ImageMap[submeshes[i].materialName]];
      GLint whichID[1];
      glGetIntegerv(GL_TEXTURE_BINDING_2D, whichID);
      if(whichID[0] != id)
        glBindTexture(GL_TEXTURE_2D, id);
```

```
        glUniform1f(shader("useDefault"), 0.0);
    } else {
      glUniform1f(shader("useDefault"), 1.0);
    }
    glDrawElements(GL_TRIANGLES, submeshes[i].indices.size(),
    GL_UNSIGNED_INT, &submeshes[i].indices[0]);
  }
  shader.UnUse();
}
```

There's more...

The demo application implementing this recipe renders a skeletal model with textures. The point light source can be moved by dragging the right mouse button. The output result is shown in the following figure:

See also

You can also see John Ratcliff's code repository: A test application for MeshImport library and showcasing EZMesh at http://codesuppository.blogspot.sg/2009/11/test-application-for-meshimport-library.html.

Implementing simple particle system

In this recipe, we will implement a simple particle system. Particle systems are a special category of objects that enable us to simulate fuzzy effects in computer graphics; for example, fire or smoke. In this recipe, we will implement a simple particle system that emits particles at the specified rate from an oriented emitter. In this recipe, we will assign particles with a basic fire color map without texture, to give the effect of fire.

Getting started

The code for this recipe is contained in the `Chapter5/SimpleParticles` directory. All of the work for particle simulation is carried out in the vertex shader.

How to do it...

Let us start this recipe by following these simple steps:

1. Create a vertex shader without any per-vertex attribute. The vertex shader generates the current particle position and outputs a smooth color to the fragment shader for use as the current fragment color.

```
#version 330 core
smooth out vec4 vSmoothColor;
uniform mat4 MVP;
uniform float time;

const vec3 a = vec3(0,2,0);      //acceleration of particles
//vec3 g = vec3(0,-9.8,0);   // acceleration due to gravity

const float rate = 1/500.0;      //rate of emission
const float life = 2;            //life of particle

//constants
const float PI = 3.14159;
const float TWO_PI = 2*PI;

//colormap colours
const vec3 RED = vec3(1,0,0);
const vec3 GREEN = vec3(0,1,0);
const vec3 YELLOW = vec3(1,1,0);

//pseudorandom number generator
float rand(vec2 co){
```

```
    return fract(sin(dot(co.xy ,vec2(12.9898,78.233))) *
    43758.5453);
}

//pseudorandom direction on a sphere
vec3 uniformRadomDir(vec2 v, out vec2 r) {
    r.x = rand(v.xy);
    r.y = rand(v.yx);
    float theta = mix(0.0, PI / 6.0, r.x);
    float phi = mix(0.0, TWO_PI, r.y);
    return vec3(sin(theta) * cos(phi), cos(theta), sin(theta)
    * sin(phi));
}

void main() {
    vec3 pos=vec3(0);
    float t = gl_VertexID*rate;
    float alpha = 1;
    if(time>t) {
        float dt = mod((time-t), life);
        vec2 xy = vec2(gl_VertexID,t);
        vec2 rdm=vec2(0);
        pos = ((uniformRadomDir(xy, rdm) + 0.5*a*dt)*dt);
        alpha = 1.0 - (dt/life);
    }
    vSmoothColor = vec4(mix(RED,YELLOW,alpha),alpha);
    gl_Position = MVP*vec4(pos,1);
}
```

2. The fragment shader outputs the smooth color as the current fragment output color.

```
#version 330 core
smooth in vec4 vSmoothColor;

layout(location=0) out vec4 vFragColor;

void main() {
    vFragColor = vSmoothColor;
}
```

3. Set up a single vertex array object and bind it.

```
glGenVertexArrays(1, &vaoID);
glBindVertexArray(vaoID);
```

4. In the rendering code, set up the shader and pass the shader uniforms. For example, pass the current time to the `time` shader uniform and the combined modelview projection matrix (`MVP`). Here we add an emitter transform matrix (`emitterXForm`) to the combined `MVP` matrix that controls the orientation of our particle emitter.

```
shader.Use();
glUniform1f(shader("time"), time);
glUniformMatrix4fv(shader("MVP"), 1, GL_FALSE,
glm::value_ptr(P*MV*emitterXForm));
```

5. Finally, we render the total number of particles (`MAX_PARTICLES`) with a call to the `glDrawArrays` function and unbind our shader.

```
glDrawArrays(GL_POINTS, 0, MAX_PARTICLES);
shader.UnUse();
```

 Versions of OpenGL prior to OpenGL 3 provided a special particle type called GL_POINT_SPRITE. In OpenGL 3.3 and above core profiles, the GL_POINT_SPRITE enum has been deprecated. Hence, now GL_POINTS acts as point sprites by default.

How it works...

The entire code from generation of particle positions to assignment of colors and forces is carried out in the vertex shader. In this recipe, we do not store any per-vertex attribute as in the previous recipes. Instead, we simply invoke the `glDrawArrays` call with the number of particles (`MAX_PARTICLES`) we need to render. This calls our vertex shader for each particle in turn.

We have two uniforms in the vertex shader, the combined modelview projection matrix (`MVP`) and the current simulation time (`time`). The other variables required for particle simulation are stored as shader constants.

```
#version 330
smooth out vec4 vSmoothColor;
uniform mat4 MVP;
uniform float time;
const vec3 a = vec3(0,2,0);        //acceleration of particles
//vec3 g = vec3(0,-9.8,0);              //acceleration due to gravity
const float rate = 1/500.0;      //rate of emission of particles
const float life = 2;              //particle life
const float PI = 3.14159;
const float TWO_PI = 2*PI;
const vec3 RED = vec3(1,0,0);
const vec3 GREEN = vec3(0,1,0);
const vec3 YELLOW = vec3(1,1,0);
```

In the main function, we calculate the current particle time (t) by multiplying its vertex ID (gl_VertexID) with the emission rate (rate). The gl_VertexID attribute is a unique integer identifier associated with each vertex. We then check the current time (time) against the particle's time (t). If it is greater, we calculate the time step amount (dt) and then calculate the particle's position using a simple kinematics formula.

```
void main() {
  vec3 pos=vec3(0);
  float t = gl_VertexID*rate;
  float alpha = 1;
  if(time>t) {
```

To generate the particle, we need to have its initial velocity. This is generated on the fly by using a pseudorandom generator with the vertex ID and time as the seeds using the function uniformRandomDir which is defined as follows:

```
//pseudorandom number generator
float rand(vec2 co){
    return fract(sin(dot(co.xy ,vec2(12.9898,78.233))) *
    43758.5453);
}
//pseudorandom direction on a sphere
vec3 uniformRadomDir(vec2 v, out vec2 r) {
    r.x = rand(v.xy);
    r.y = rand(v.yx);
    float theta = mix(0.0, PI / 6.0, r.x);
    float phi = mix(0.0, TWO_PI, r.y);
    return vec3(sin(theta) * cos(phi), cos(theta), sin(theta) *
    sin(phi));
}
```

The particle's position is then calculated using the current time and the random initial velocity. To enable respawning, we use the modulus operator (mod) of the difference between the particle's time and the current time (time-t) with the life of particle (life). After calculation of the position, we calculate the particle's alpha to gently fade it when its life is consumed.

```
float dt = mod((time-t), life);
vec2 xy = vec2(gl_VertexID,t);
vec2 rdm;
pos = ((uniformRadomDir(xy, rdm) + 0.5*a*dt)*dt);
alpha = 1.0 - (dt/life);
}
```

The `alpha` value is used to linearly interpolate between red and yellow colors by calling the GLSL `mix` function to give the fire effect. Finally, the generated position is multiplied with the combined modelview projection (`MVP`) matrix to get the clip space position of the particle.

```
    vSmoothColor = vec4(mix(RED,YELLOW,alpha),alpha);
    gl_Position = MVP*vec4(pos,1);
}
```

The fragment shader simply uses the `vSmoothColor` output variable from the vertex shader as the current fragment color.

```
#version 330 core
smooth in vec4 vSmoothColor;
layout(location=0) out vec4 vFragColor;
void main() {
   vFragColor = vSmoothColor;
}
```

Extending to textured billboarded particles requires us to change only the fragment shader. The point sprites provide a varying `gl_PointCoord` that can be used to sample a texture in the fragment shader as shown in the textured particle fragment shader (`Chapter5/ SimpleParticles/shaders/textured.frag`).

```
#version 330 core
smooth in vec4 vSmoothColor;
layout(location=0) out vec4 vFragColor;
uniform sampler2D textureMap;
void main()
{
   vFragColor = texture(textureMap, gl_PointCoord) *
   vSmoothColor.a;
}
```

The application loads a particle texture and generates an OpenGL texture object from it.

```
GLubyte* pData = SOIL_load_image(texture_filename.c_str(),
&texture_width, &texture_height, &channels, SOIL_LOAD_AUTO);
if(pData == NULL) {
  cerr<<"Cannot load image: "<<texture_filename.c_str()<<endl;
  exit(EXIT_FAILURE);
}
//Flip the image on Y axis
int i,j;
for( j = 0; j*2 < texture_height; ++j )
{
   int index1 = j * texture_width * channels;
```

```
    int index2 = (texture_height - 1 - j)*texture_width* channels;
    for( i = texture_width * channels; i > 0; --i )
    {
      GLubyte temp = pData[index1];
      pData[index1] = pData[index2];
      pData[index2] = temp;
      ++index1;
      ++index2;
    }
  }
}
GLenum format = GL_RGBA;
switch(channels) {
  case 2:  format = GL_RG32UI; break;
  case 3: format = GL_RGB;  break;
  case 4: format = GL_RGBA;  break;
}

glGenTextures(1, &textureID);
glBindTexture(GL_TEXTURE_2D, textureID);
  glTexParameteri(GL_TEXTURE_2D, GL_TEXTURE_MIN_FILTER,
  GL_LINEAR);
  glTexParameteri(GL_TEXTURE_2D, GL_TEXTURE_MAG_FILTER,
  GL_LINEAR);
  glTexParameteri(GL_TEXTURE_2D, GL_TEXTURE_WRAP_S, GL_REPEAT);
  glTexParameteri(GL_TEXTURE_2D, GL_TEXTURE_WRAP_T, GL_REPEAT);
  glTexImage2D(GL_TEXTURE_2D, 0, format, texture_width,
  texture_height, 0, format, GL_UNSIGNED_BYTE, pData);
  SOIL_free_image_data(pData);
```

Next, the texture unit to which the texture is bound is passed to the shader.

```
texturedShader.LoadFromFile(GL_VERTEX_SHADER,
"shaders/shader.vert");
texturedShader.LoadFromFile(GL_FRAGMENT_SHADER,
"shaders/textured.frag");
texturedShader.CreateAndLinkProgram();
texturedShader.Use();
  texturedShader.AddUniform("MVP");
  texturedShader.AddUniform("time");
  texturedShader.AddUniform("textureMap");
  glUniform1i(texturedShader("textureMap"),0);
texturedShader.UnUse();
```

Finally, the particles are rendered using the `glDrawArrays` call as shown earlier.

There's more...

The demo application for this recipe renders a particle system to simulate fire emitting from a point emitter as would typically come out from a rocket's exhaust. We can press the space bar key to toggle display of textured particles. The current view can be rotated and zoomed by dragging the left and middle mouse buttons respectively. The output result from the demo is displayed in the following figure:

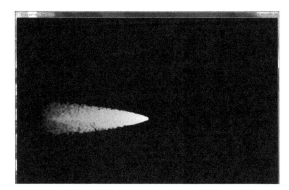

If the textured particles shader is used, we get the following output:

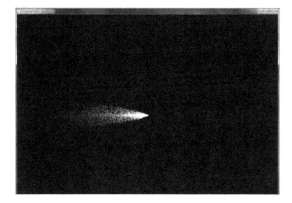

The orientation and position of the emitter is controlled using the emitter transformation matrix (`emitterXForm`). We can change this matrix to reorient/reposition the particle system in the 3D space.

The shader code given in the previous subsection generates a particle system from a point emitter source. If we want to change the source to a rectangular emitter, we can replace the position calculation with the following shader code snippet:

```
pos = ( uniformRadomDir(xy, rdm) + 0.5*a*dt)*dt;
vec2 rect = (rdm*2.0 - 1.0);
pos += vec3(rect.x, 0, rect.y) ;
```

This gives the following output:

Changing the emitter to a disc shape further filters the points spawned in the rectangle emitter by only accepting those which lie inside the circle of a given radius, as given in the following code snippet:

```
pos = ( uniformRadomDir(xy, rdm) + 0.5*a*dt)*dt;
vec2 rect = (rdm*2.0 - 1.0);
float dotP = dot(rect, rect);
if(dotP<1)
  pos += vec3(rect.x, 0, rect.y);
```

Using this position calculation gives a disc emitter as shown in the following output:

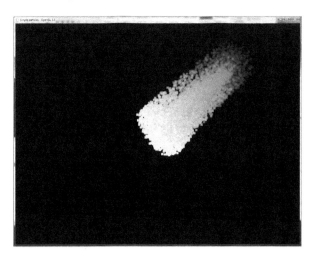

We can also add additional forces such as air drag, wind, vortex, and so on, by simply adding to the acceleration or velocity component of the particle system. Another option could be to direct the emitter to a specific path such as a b-spline. We could also add deflectors to deflect the generated particles or create particles that spawn other particles as is typically used in a fireworks particle system. Particle systems are an extremely interesting area in computer graphics which help us obtain wonderful effects easily.

The recipe detailed here shows how to do a very simple particle system entirely on the GPU. While such a particle system might be useful for basic effects, more detailed effects would need more elaborate treatment as detailed in the references in the *See also* section.

See also

To know more about detailed effects you can refer to the following links:

- Real-time particle systems on the GPU in Dynamic Environment SIGGRAPH 2007 Talk: `http://developer.amd.com/wordpress/media/2012/10/Drone-Real-Time_Particles_Systems_on_the_GPU_in_Dynamic_Environments%28Siggraph07%29.pdf`

- GPU Gems 3 Chapter 23-High speed offscreen particles: `http://http.developer.nvidia.com/GPUGems3/gpugems3_ch23.html`

- Building a million particle system by Lutz Latta: `http://www.gamasutra.com/view/feature/130535/building_a_millionparticle_system.php?print=1`

- CG Tutorial chapter 6: `http://http.developer.nvidia.com/CgTutorial/cg_tutorial_chapter06.html`

6
GPU-based Alpha Blending and Global Illumination

In this chapter, we will focus on:

- ▶ Implementing order-independent transparency using front-to-back peeling
- ▶ Implementing order-independent transparency with dual depth peeling
- ▶ Implementing screen space ambient occlusion (SSAO)
- ▶ Implementing global illumination using spherical harmonics lighting
- ▶ Implementing GPU-based ray tracing
- ▶ Implementing GPU-based path tracing

Introduction

Even with the introduction of lighting, our virtual objects don't look and feel real. This is because our lights are a simple approximation of the reflection behavior of the surface. There is a specific category of algorithms that help bridge the gap between the real-world lighting and the virtual-world lighting. These are called **global illumination methods**. Although these methods had been proven to be expensive to evaluate in real time, new methods have been proposed that fake the global illumination using clever techniques. One such technique is spherical harmonics lighting that uses HDR light probes to light a virtual scene having no light source. The idea is to extract the lighting information from the light probe and give a feeling that the virtual objects are in the same environment.

In addition, rendering of transparent geometry is also problematic since this requires sorting of geometry in the depth order. If the scene complexity increases, it becomes not only difficult to maintain the depth order, but the processing overhead also increases. To circumvent these scenarios and handle the alpha blending for order-independent transparency of the 3D geometry efficiently, we implement depth peeling and the more efficient dual depth peeling, on the modern GPU. All of these techniques will be implemented in OpenGL 3.3 core profile.

Implementing order-independent transparency using front-to-back peeling

When we have to render translucent geometry, for example, a glass window in a graphics application, care has to be taken to make sure that the geometry is properly rendered in the depth order such that the opaque objects in the scene are rendered first and the transparent objects are rendered last. This unfortunately incurs additional overhead where the CPU is busy sorting objects. In addition, the blending result will be correct only from a specific viewing direction, as shown in the following figure. Note that the image on the left is the result if we view from the direction of the Z axis. There is no blending at all in the left image. If the same scene is viewed from the opposite side, we can see the correct alpha blending result.

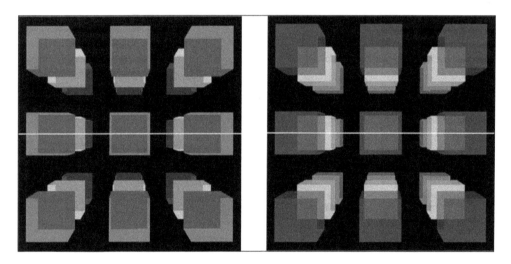

Depth peeling (also called front-to-back peeling) is one technique that helps in this process. In this technique, the scene is rendered in slices in such a way that slices are rendered one after another from front to back until the whole object is processed, as shown in the following figure, which is a 2D side view of the same scene as in the previous figure.

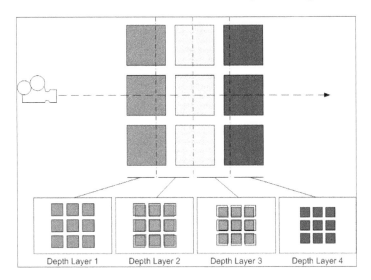

The number of layers to use for peeling is dependent on the depth complexity of the scene. This recipe will show how to implement this technique in modern OpenGL.

Getting ready

The code for this recipe is contained in the `Chapter6/FrontToBackPeeling` directory.

How to do it...

Let us start our recipe by following these simple steps:

1. Set up two frame buffer objects (FBOs) with two color and depth attachments. For this recipe, we will use rectangle textures (`GL_TEXTURE_RECTANGLE`) since they enable easier handling of images (samplers) in the fragment shader. With rectangle textures we can access texture values using pixel positions directly. In case of normal texture (`GL_TEXTUR_2D`), we have to normalize the texture coordinates.

    ```
    glGenFramebuffers(2, fbo);
      glGenTextures (2, texID);
      glGenTextures (2, depthTexID);
      for(int i=0;i<2;i++) {
        glBindTexture(GL_TEXTURE_RECTANGLE, depthTexID[i]);
        //set texture parameters like minification etc.
    ```

```
glTexImage2D(GL_TEXTURE_RECTANGLE , 0,
GL_DEPTH_COMPONENT32F, WIDTH, HEIGHT, 0,
GL_DEPTH_COMPONENT, GL_FLOAT, NULL);
glBindTexture(GL_TEXTURE_RECTANGLE,texID[i]);
//set texture parameters like minification etc.
glTexImage2D(GL_TEXTURE_RECTANGLE , 0,GL_RGBA, WIDTH,
HEIGHT, 0, GL_RGBA, GL_FLOAT, NULL);
glBindFramebuffer(GL_FRAMEBUFFER, fbo[i]);
glFramebufferTexture2D(GL_FRAMEBUFFER,
GL_DEPTH_ATTACHMENT, GL_TEXTURE_RECTANGLE,
depthTexID[i], 0);
glFramebufferTexture2D(GL_FRAMEBUFFER,
GL_COLOR_ATTACHMENT0, GL_TEXTURE_RECTANGLE,
texID[i], 0);
}
glGenTextures(1, &colorBlenderTexID);
glBindTexture(GL_TEXTURE_RECTANGLE, colorBlenderTexID);
//set texture parameters like minification etc.
glTexImage2D(GL_TEXTURE_RECTANGLE, 0, GL_RGBA, WIDTH,
HEIGHT, 0, GL_RGBA, GL_FLOAT, 0);
```

2. Set another FBO for color blending and check the FBO for completeness. The color blending FBO uses the depth texture from the first FBO as a depth attachment, as it uses the depth output from the first step during blending.

```
glGenFramebuffers(1, &colorBlenderFBOID);
glBindFramebuffer(GL_FRAMEBUFFER, colorBlenderFBOID);
glFramebufferTexture2D(GL_FRAMEBUFFER,
GL_DEPTH_ATTACHMENT, GL_TEXTURE_RECTANGLE,
depthTexID[0], 0);
glFramebufferTexture2D(GL_FRAMEBUFFER,
GL_COLOR_ATTACHMENT0, GL_TEXTURE_RECTANGLE,
colorBlenderTexID, 0);
GLenum status = glCheckFramebufferStatus(GL_FRAMEBUFFER);
if(status == GL_FRAMEBUFFER_COMPLETE )
  printf("FBO setup successful !!! \n");
else
  printf("Problem with FBO setup");

glBindFramebuffer(GL_FRAMEBUFFER, 0);
```

3. In the rendering function, set the color blending FBO as the current render target and then render the scene normally with depth testing enabled.

```
glBindFramebuffer(GL_FRAMEBUFFER, colorBlenderFBOID);
glDrawBuffer(GL_COLOR_ATTACHMENT0);
glClear(GL_COLOR_BUFFER_BIT | GL_DEPTH_BUFFER_BIT );
glEnable(GL_DEPTH_TEST);
DrawScene(MVP, cubeShader);
```

4. Next, bind the other FBO pair alternatively, clear the render target, and enable depth testing, but disable alpha blending. This is to render the nearest surface in the offscreen render target. The number of passes dictate the number of layers the given geometry is peeled into. The more the number of passes, the more continuous the depth peeling result. For the demo in this recipe, the number of passes is set as 6. The number of passes is dependent on the depth complexity of the scene. If the user wants to check the number of samples output from the depth peeling step, then based on the value of the flag (bUseOQ) an occlusion query is used to find the number of samples output from the depth peeling step.

```
int numLayers = (NUM_PASSES - 1) * 2;
for (int layer = 1; bUseOQ || layer < numLayers; layer++) {
   int currId = layer % 2;
   int prevId = 1 - currId;
   glBindFramebuffer(GL_FRAMEBUFFER, fbo[currId]);
   glDrawBuffer(GL_COLOR_ATTACHMENT0);
   glClearColor(0, 0, 0, 0);
   glClear(GL_COLOR_BUFFER_BIT | GL_DEPTH_BUFFER_BIT);
   glDisable(GL_BLEND);
   glEnable(GL_DEPTH_TEST);
if (bUseOQ) {
     glBeginQuery(GL_SAMPLES_PASSED_ARB, queryId);
}
```

5. Bind the depth texture from the first step so that the nearest fragment can be used with the attached shaders and then render the scene with the front peeling shaders. Refer to Chapter6/FrontToBackPeeling/shaders/front_peel.{vert,frag} for details. We then end the hardware query if the query was initiated.

```
glBindTexture(GL_TEXTURE_RECTANGLE, depthTexID[prevId]);
DrawScene(MVP, frontPeelShader);
if (bUseOQ) {
   glEndQuery(GL_SAMPLES_PASSED_ARB);
}
```

6. Bind the color blender FBO again, disable depth testing, and enable additive blending; however, specify separate blending so that the color and alpha can be blended separately. Finally, bind the rendered output from step 5 and then using a full-screen quad and the blend shader (Chapter6/FrontToBackPeeling/shaders/blend.{vert,frag}), blend the whole scene.

```
glBindFramebuffer(GL_FRAMEBUFFER, colorBlenderFBOID);
glDrawBuffer(GL_COLOR_ATTACHMENT0);
glDisable(GL_DEPTH_TEST);
glEnable(GL_BLEND);
glBlendEquation(GL_FUNC_ADD);
```

```
glBlendFuncSeparate(GL_DST_ALPHA, GL_ONE,GL_ZERO,
GL_ONE_MINUS_SRC_ALPHA);
glBindTexture(GL_TEXTURE_RECTANGLE, texID[currId]);
blendShader.Use();
  DrawFullScreenQuad();
blendShader.UnUse();
glDisable(GL_BLEND);
```

7. In the final step, restore the default draw buffer (GL_BACK_LEFT) and disable alpha blending and depth testing. Use a full-screen quad and a final shader (Chapter6/ FrontToBackPeeling/shaders/final.frag) to blend the output from the color blending FBO.

```
glBindFramebuffer(GL_FRAMEBUFFER, 0);
glDrawBuffer(GL_BACK_LEFT);
glDisable(GL_DEPTH_TEST);
glDisable(GL_BLEND);

glBindTexture(GL_TEXTURE_RECTANGLE, colorBlenderTexID);
finalShader.Use();
  glUniform4fv(finalShader("vBackgroundColor"), 1,
  &bg.x);
  DrawFullScreenQuad();
finalShader.UnUse();
```

How it works...

The front-to-back depth peeling works in three steps. First, the scene is rendered normally on a depth FBO with depth testing enabled. This ensures that the scene depth values are stored in the depth attachment of the FBO. In the second pass, we bind the depth FBO, bind the depth texture from the first step, and then iteratively clip parts of the geometry by using a fragment shader (see Chapter6/FrontToBackPeeling/shaders/front_peel.frag) as shown in the following code snippet:

```
#version 330 core
layout(location = 0) out vec4 vFragColor;
uniform vec4 vColor;
uniform sampler2DRect  depthTexture;
void main() {
  float frontDepth = texture(depthTexture, gl_FragCoord.xy).r;
  if(gl_FragCoord.z <= frontDepth)
    discard;
  vFragColor = vColor;
}
```

This shader simply compares the incoming fragment's depth against the depth value stored in the depth texture. If the current fragment's depth is less than or equal to the depth in the depth texture, the fragment is discarded. Otherwise, the fragment color is output.

```
float frontDepth = texture(depthTexture, gl_FragCoord.xy).r;
if(gl_FragCoord.z <= frontDepth)
  discard;
```

After this step, we bind the color blend FBO, disable depth test, and then enable alpha blending with separate blending of colors and alpha values. The `glBlendFunctionSeparate` function is used here as it enables us to handle color and alpha channels for source and destination separately. The first parameter is the source RGB, which is assigned the alpha value of the pixel in the frame buffer. This blends the incoming fragment with the existing color in the frame buffer. The second parameter, that is, the destination RGB, is set as `GL_ONE`, which keeps the value in the destination as is. The third parameter is set as `GL_ZERO`, which removes the source alpha component as we already applied the alpha from the destination using the first parameter. The final parameter, that is, the destination alpha is set as the conventional over-compositing alpha value (`GL_ONE_MINUS_SRC_ALPHA`).

We then bind the texture from the previous step output and then use the blend shader (see `Chapter6/FrontToBackPeeling/shaders/blend.frag`) on a full-screen quad to alpha blend the current fragments with the existing fragments on the frame buffer. The blend shader is defined as follows:

```
#version 330 core
uniform sampler2DRect tempTexture;
layout(location = 0) out vec4 vFragColor;
void main() {
  vFragColor = texture(tempTexture, gl_FragCoord.xy);
}
```

The `tempTexture` sampler contains the output from the depth peeling step stored in the `colorBlenderFBO` attachment. After this step, the alpha blending is disabled, as shown in the code snippet in step 6 of the *How to do it...* section.

In the final step, the default draw buffer is restored, depth testing and alpha blending is disabled, and the final output from the color blend FBO is blended with the background color using a simple fragment shader. The code snippet is as shown in step 7 of the *How to do it...* section. The final fragment shader is defined as follows:

```
#version 330 core
uniform sampler2DRect colorTexture;
uniform vec4 vBackgroundColor;
layout(location = 0) out vec4 vFragColor;
void main() {
  vec4 color = texture(colorTexture, gl_FragCoord.xy);
  vFragColor = color + vBackgroundColor*color.a;
}
```

The final shader takes the front peeled result and blends it with the background color using the alpha value from the front peeled result. This way rather than taking the nearest depth fragment all fragments are taken into consideration showing a correctly blended result.

There's more...

The output from the demo application for this recipe renders 27 translucent cubes at the origin. The camera position can be changed using the left mouse button. The front-to-back depth peeling gives the following output. Note the blended color, for example, the yellow color where the green boxes overlay the red ones.

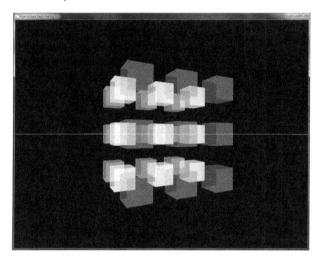

Pressing the Space bar disables front-to-back peeling so that we can see the normal alpha blending without back-to-front sorting which gives the following output. Note that we do not see the yellow blended color where the green and red boxes overlap.

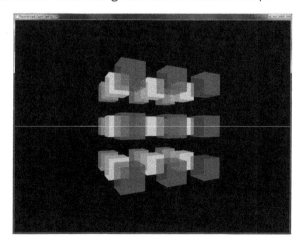

Even though the output produced by front-to-back peeling is correct, it requires multiple passes through the geometry that incur additional processing overhead. The next recipe details the more robust method called **dual depth peeling** which tackles this problem.

See also

▸ *Interactive Order-Independent Transparency, Cass Everitt*: http://gamedevs.org/uploads/interactive-order-independent-transparency.pdf

Implementing order-independent transparency using dual depth peeling

In this recipe, we will implement dual depth peeling. The main idea behind this method is to peel two depth layers at the same time. This results in a much better performance with the same output, as dual depth peeling peels two layers at a time; one from the front and one from the back.

Getting ready

The code for this recipe is contained in the `Chapter6/DualDepthPeeling` folder.

How to do it...

The steps required to implement dual depth peeling are as follows:

1. Create an FBO and attach six textures in all: two for storing the front buffer, two for storing the back buffer, and two for storing the depth buffer values.

```
glGenFramebuffers(1, &dualDepthFBOID);
glGenTextures (2, texID);
glGenTextures (2, backTexID);
glGenTextures (2, depthTexID);
for(int i=0;i<2;i++) {
glBindTexture(GL_TEXTURE_RECTANGLE, depthTexID[i]);
//set texture parameters
glTexImage2D(GL_TEXTURE_RECTANGLE , 0, GL_FLOAT_RG32_NV,
WIDTH, HEIGHT, 0, GL_RGB, GL_FLOAT, NULL);
glBindTexture(GL_TEXTURE_RECTANGLE,texID[i]);
//set texture parameters
glTexImage2D(GL_TEXTURE_RECTANGLE , 0, GL_RGBA, WIDTH,
HEIGHT, 0, GL_RGBA, GL_FLOAT, NULL);
glBindTexture(GL_TEXTURE_RECTANGLE,backTexID[i]);
    //set texture parameters
```

```
glTexImage2D(GL_TEXTURE_RECTANGLE , 0, GL_RGBA, WIDTH,
HEIGHT, 0, GL_RGBA, GL_FLOAT, NULL);
}
```

2. Bind the six textures to the appropriate attachment points on the FBO.

```
glBindFramebuffer(GL_FRAMEBUFFER, dualDepthFBOID);
for(int i=0;i<2;i++) {
  glFramebufferTexture2D(GL_FRAMEBUFFER, attachID[i],
  GL_TEXTURE_RECTANGLE, depthTexID[i], 0);
  glFramebufferTexture2D(GL_FRAMEBUFFER, attachID[i]+1,
  GL_TEXTURE_RECTANGLE, texID[i], 0);
  glFramebufferTexture2D(GL_FRAMEBUFFER, attachID[i]+2,
  GL_TEXTURE_RECTANGLE, backTexID[i], 0);
}
```

3. Create another FBO for color blending and attach a new texture to it. Also attach this texture to the first FBO and check the FBO completeness.

```
glGenTextures(1, &colorBlenderTexID);
glBindTexture(GL_TEXTURE_RECTANGLE, colorBlenderTexID);
//set texture parameters
glTexImage2D(GL_TEXTURE_RECTANGLE, 0, GL_RGBA, WIDTH,
HEIGHT, 0, GL_RGBA, GL_FLOAT, 0);
glGenFramebuffers(1, &colorBlenderFBOID);
glBindFramebuffer(GL_FRAMEBUFFER, colorBlenderFBOID);
glFramebufferTexture2D(GL_FRAMEBUFFER,
GL_COLOR_ATTACHMENT0, GL_TEXTURE_RECTANGLE,
colorBlenderTexID, 0);
glFramebufferTexture2D(GL_FRAMEBUFFER,
GL_COLOR_ATTACHMENT6, GL_TEXTURE_RECTANGLE,
colorBlenderTexID, 0);
GLenum status = glCheckFramebufferStatus(GL_FRAMEBUFFER);
if(status == GL_FRAMEBUFFER_COMPLETE )
  printf("FBO setup successful !!! \n");
else
  printf("Problem with FBO setup");
glBindFramebuffer(GL_FRAMEBUFFER, 0);
```

4. In the render function, first disable depth testing and enable blending and then bind the depth FBO. Initialize and clear DrawBuffer to write on the render target attached to GL_COLOR_ATTACHMENT1 and GL_COLOR_ATTACHMENT2.

```
glDisable(GL_DEPTH_TEST);
glEnable(GL_BLEND);
glBindFramebuffer(GL_FRAMEBUFFER, dualDepthFBOID);
glDrawBuffers(2, &drawBuffers[1]);
glClearColor(0, 0, 0, 0);
glClear(GL_COLOR_BUFFER_BIT);
```

5. Next, set `GL_COLOR_ATTACHMENT0` as the draw buffer, enable min/max blending (`glBlendEquation(GL_MAX)`), and initialize the color attachment using fragment shader (see `Chapter6/DualDepthPeeling/shaders/dual_init.frag`). This completes the first step of dual depth peeling, that is, initialization of the buffers.

```
glDrawBuffer(drawBuffers[0]);
glClearColor(-MAX_DEPTH, -MAX_DEPTH, 0, 0);
glClear(GL_COLOR_BUFFER_BIT);
glBlendEquation(GL_MAX);
DrawScene(MVP, initShader);
```

6. Next, set `GL_COLOR_ATTACHMENT6` as the draw buffer and clear it with background color. Then, run a loop that alternates two draw buffers and then uses min/max blending. Then draw the scene again.

```
glDrawBuffer(drawBuffers[6]);
glClearColor(bg.x, bg.y, bg.z, bg.w);
glClear(GL_COLOR_BUFFER_BIT);
int numLayers = (NUM_PASSES - 1) * 2;
int currId = 0;
for (int layer = 1; bUseOQ || layer < numLayers; layer++) {
  currId = layer % 2;
  int prevId = 1 - currId;
  int bufId = currId * 3;
  glDrawBuffers(2, &drawBuffers[bufId+1]);
  glClearColor(0, 0, 0, 0);
  glClear(GL_COLOR_BUFFER_BIT);
  glDrawBuffer(drawBuffers[bufId+0]);
  glClearColor(-MAX_DEPTH, -MAX_DEPTH, 0, 0);
  glClear(GL_COLOR_BUFFER_BIT);
  glDrawBuffers(3, &drawBuffers[bufId+0]);
  glBlendEquation(GL_MAX);
  glActiveTexture(GL_TEXTURE0);
  glBindTexture(GL_TEXTURE_RECTANGLE, depthTexID[prevId]);
  glActiveTexture(GL_TEXTURE1);
  glBindTexture(GL_TEXTURE_RECTANGLE, texID[prevId]);
  DrawScene(MVP, dualPeelShader, true,true);
```

7. Finally, enable additive blending (`glBlendFunc(GL_FUNC_ADD)`) and then draw a full screen quad with the blend shader. This peels away fragments from the front as well as the back layer of the rendered geometry and blends the result on the current draw buffer.

```
glDrawBuffer(drawBuffers[6]);
glBlendEquation(GL_FUNC_ADD);
glBlendFunc(GL_SRC_ALPHA, GL_ONE_MINUS_SRC_ALPHA);
if (bUseOQ) {
```

```
        glBeginQuery(GL_SAMPLES_PASSED_ARB, queryId);
    }
    glActiveTexture(GL_TEXTURE0);
    glBindTexture(GL_TEXTURE_RECTANGLE, backTexID[currId]);
    blendShader.Use();
        DrawFullScreenQuad();
    blendShader.UnUse();
        }
```

8. In the final step, we unbind the FBO and enable rendering on the default back buffer (GL_BACK_LEFT). Next, we bind the outputs from the depth peeling and blending steps to their appropriate texture location. Finally, we use a final blending shader to combine the two peeled and blended fragments.

```
glBindFramebuffer(GL_FRAMEBUFFER, 0);
glDrawBuffer(GL_BACK_LEFT);
glBindTexture(GL_TEXTURE_RECTANGLE, colorBlenderTexID);
glActiveTexture(GL_TEXTURE0);
glBindTexture(GL_TEXTURE_RECTANGLE, depthTexID[currId]);
glActiveTexture(GL_TEXTURE1);
glBindTexture(GL_TEXTURE_RECTANGLE, texID[currId]);
glActiveTexture(GL_TEXTURE2);
glBindTexture(GL_TEXTURE_RECTANGLE, colorBlenderTexID);
finalShader.Use();
    DrawFullScreenQuad();
finalShader.UnUse();
```

How it works...

Dual depth peeling works in a similar fashion as the front-to-back peeling. However, the difference is in the way it operates. It peels away depths from both the front and the back layer at the same time using min/max blending. First, we initialize the fragment depth values using the fragment shader (Chapter6/DualDepthPeeling/shaders/dual_init.frag) and min/max blending.

```
    vFragColor.xy = vec2(-gl_FragCoord.z, gl_FragCoord.z);
```

This initializes the blending buffers. Next, a loop is run but instead of peeling depth layers front-to-back, we first peel back depths and then the front depths. This is carried out in the fragment shader (Chapter6/DualDepthPeeling/shaders/dual_peel.frag) along with max blending.

```
    float fragDepth = gl_FragCoord.z;
    vec2 depthBlender = texture(depthBlenderTex, gl_FragCoord.xy).xy;
    vec4 forwardTemp = texture(frontBlenderTex, gl_FragCoord.xy);
    //initialize variables …
```

```
  if (fragDepth < nearestDepth || fragDepth > farthestDepth) {
    vFragColor0.xy = vec2(-MAX_DEPTH);
    return;
  }
  if(fragDepth > nearestDepth && fragDepth < farthestDepth) {
    vFragColor0.xy = vec2(-fragDepth, fragDepth);
    return;
  }
  vFragColor0.xy = vec2(-MAX_DEPTH);

  if (fragDepth == nearestDepth) {
    vFragColor1.xyz += vColor.rgb * alpha * alphaMultiplier;
    vFragColor1.w = 1.0 - alphaMultiplier * (1.0 - alpha);
  } else {
    vFragColor2 += vec4(vColor.rgb,alpha);
  }
```

The blend shader (`Chapter6/DualDepthPeeling/shaders/blend.frag`) simply discards fragments whose alpha values are zero. This ensures that the occlusion query is not incremented, which would give a wrong number of samples than the actual fragment used in the depth blending.

```
vFragColor = texture(tempTexture, gl_FragCoord.xy);
if(vFragColor.a == 0)
  discard;
```

Finally, the last blend shader (`Chapter6/DualDepthPeeling/shaders/final.frag`) takes the blended fragments from the front and back blend textures and blends the results to get the final fragment color.

```
vec4 frontColor = texture(frontBlenderTex, gl_FragCoord.xy);
vec3 backColor = texture(backBlenderTex, gl_FragCoord.xy).rgb;
vFragColor.rgb = frontColor.rgb + backColor * frontColor.a;
```

There's more...

The demo application for this demo is similar to the one shown in the previous recipe. If dual depth peeling is enabled, we get the result as shown in the following figure:

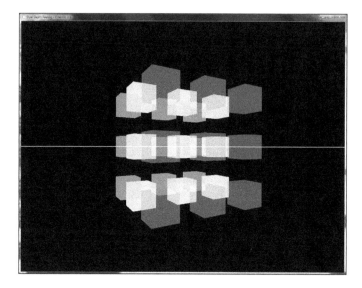

Pressing the Space bar enables/disables dual depth peeling. If dual peeling is disabled, the result is as follows:

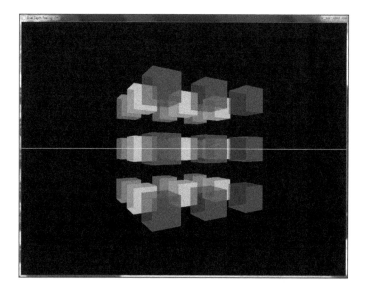

See also

▶ Louis Bavoil and Kevin Myers, *Order Independent Transparency with Dual Depth Peeling* demo in NVIDIA OpenGL 10 sdk: `http://developer.download.nvidia.com/ SDK/10/opengl/src/dual_depth_peeling/doc/DualDepthPeeling.pdf`

Implementing screen space ambient occlusion (SSAO)

We have implemented simple lighting recipes in previous chapters. These unfortunately approximate some aspects of lighting. However, effects such as global illumination are not handled by the basic lights, as discussed earlier. In this respect, several techniques have been developed over the years which fake the global illumination effects. One such technique is **Screen Space Ambient Occlusion** (**SSAO**) which we will implement in this recipe.

As the name suggests, this method works in screen space. For any given pixel onscreen, the amount of occlusion due to its neighboring pixels can be obtained by looking at the difference in their depth value. In order to reduce the sampling artefacts, the neighbor coordinates are randomly offset. For a pixel whose depth values are close to one another, they belong to the geometry which is spatially lying close. Based on the difference of the depth values, an occlusion value is determined. Given in pseudocode, the algorithm may be given as follows:

```
Get the position (p), normal (n) and depth (d) value at current pixel
position
For each pixel in the neighborhood of current pixel
    Get the position (p0) of the neighborhood pixel
    Call proc. CalcAO(p, p0, n)
End for
Return the ambient occlusion amount as color
```

The ambient occlusion procedure is defined as follows:

```
const float DEPTH_TOLERANCE = 0.00001;
proc CalcAO(p,p0,n)
    diff = p0-p-DEPTH_TOLERANCE;
    v = normalize(diff);
    d = length(diff)*scale;
    return max(0.1, dot(n,v)-bias)*(1.0/(1.0+d))*intensity;
end proc
```

Note that we have three artist control parameters: scale, bias, and intensity. The scale parameter controls the size of the occlusion area, bias shifts the occlusion, and intensity controls the strength of the occlusion. The DEPTH_TOLERANCE constant is added to remove depth-fighting artefacts.

The whole recipe proceeds as follows. We load our 3D model and render it into an offscreen texture using FBO. We use two FBOs: one for storing the eye space normals and depth, and another FBO is for filtering of intermediate results. For both the color attachment and the depth attachment of first FBO, floating point texture formats are used. For the color attachment, GL_RGBA32F is used, whereas for depth texture, the GL_DEPTH_COMPONENT32F floating point format is used. Floating point texture formats are used as we require more precision, otherwise truncation errors will show up in the rendering result. The second FBO is used for separable Gaussian smoothing as was carried out in the *Implementing variance shadow mapping* recipe in *Chapter 4, Lights and Shadows*. This FBO has two color attachments with the floating point texture format GL_RGBA32F.

In the rendering function, the scene is first rendered normally. Then, the first shader is used to output the eye space normals. This is stored in the color attachment and the depth values are stored in the depth attachment of the first FBO. After this step, the filtering FBO is bound and the second shader is used, which uses the depth and normal textures from the first FBO to calculate the ambient occlusion result. Since the neighbor points are randomly offset, noise is introduced. The noisy result is then smoothed by applying separable gaussian smoothing. Finally, the filtered result is blended with the existing rendering by using conventional alpha blending.

Getting ready

The code for this recipe is contained in the Chapter6/SSAO folder. We will be using the Obj model viewer from *Chapter 5, Mesh Model Formats and and Particle Systems*. We will add SSAO to the Obj model.

How to do it...

Let us start the recipe by following these simple steps:

1. Create a global reference of the ObjLoader object. Call the ObjLoader::Load function passing it the name of the OBJ file. Pass vectors to store the meshes, vertices, indices, and materials contained in the OBJ file.

2. Create a framebuffer object (FBO) with two attachments: first to store the scene normals and second to store the depth. We will use a floating point texture format (GL_RGBA32F) for both of these. In addition, we create a second FBO for Gaussian smoothing of the SSAO output. We are using multiple texture units here as the second shader expects normal and depth textures to be bound to texture units 1 and 3 respectively.

```
glGenFramebuffers(1, &fboID);
glBindFramebuffer(GL_FRAMEBUFFER, fboID);
glGenTextures(1, &normalTextureID);
glGenTextures(1, &depthTextureID);
glActiveTexture(GL_TEXTURE1);
```

```
glBindTexture(GL_TEXTURE_2D, normalTextureID);
//set texture parameters
glTexImage2D(GL_TEXTURE_2D, 0, GL_RGBA32F, WIDTH, HEIGHT,
0, GL_BGRA, GL_FLOAT, NULL);
glActiveTexture(GL_TEXTURE3);
glBindTexture(GL_TEXTURE_2D, depthTextureID);
//set texture parameters
glTexImage2D(GL_TEXTURE_2D, 0, GL_DEPTH_COMPONENT32F,
WIDTH, HEIGHT, 0, GL_DEPTH_COMPONENT, GL_FLOAT, NULL);
glFramebufferTexture2D(GL_FRAMEBUFFER,
GL_COLOR_ATTACHMENT0, GL_TEXTURE_2D, normalTextureID, 0);
glFramebufferTexture2D(GL_FRAMEBUFFER,
GL_DEPTH_ATTACHMENT,GL_TEXTURE_2D, depthTextureID, 0);
glGenFramebuffers(1,&filterFBOID);
glBindFramebuffer(GL_FRAMEBUFFER,filterFBOID);
glGenTextures(2, blurTexID);
for(int i=0;i<2;i++) {
    glActiveTexture(GL_TEXTURE4+i);
    glBindTexture(GL_TEXTURE_2D, blurTexID[i]);
    //set texture parameters
    glTexImage2D(GL_TEXTURE_2D,0,GL_RGBA32F,RTT_WIDTH,
    RTT_HEIGHT,0,GL_RGBA,GL_FLOAT,NULL);
    glFramebufferTexture2D(GL_FRAMEBUFFER,
    GL_COLOR_ATTACHMENT0+i,GL_TEXTURE_2D,blurTexID[i],0);
}
```

3. In the render function, render the scene meshes normally. After this step, bind the first FBO and then use the first shader program. This program takes the per-vertex positions/normals of the mesh and outputs the view space normals from the fragment shader.

```
glBindFramebuffer(GL_FRAMEBUFFER, fboID);
glViewport(0,0,RTT_WIDTH, RTT_HEIGHT);
glDrawBuffer(GL_COLOR_ATTACHMENT0);
glClear(GL_COLOR_BUFFER_BIT|GL_DEPTH_BUFFER_BIT);
glBindVertexArray(vaoID); {
ssaoFirstShader.Use();
glUniformMatrix4fv(ssaoFirstShader("MVP"), 1, GL_FALSE,
glm::value_ptr(P*MV));
glUniformMatrix3fv(ssaoFirstShader("N"), 1, GL_FALSE,
glm::value_ptr(glm::inverseTranspose(glm::mat3(MV))));
for(size_t i=0;i<materials.size();i++) {
Material* pMat = materials[i];
if(materials.size()==1)
  glDrawElements(GL_TRIANGLES, indices.size(),
  GL_UNSIGNED_SHORT, 0);
```

```
else
  glDrawElements(GL_TRIANGLES, pMat->count,
  GL_UNSIGNED_SHORT, (const GLvoid*)(&indices
  [pMat->offset]));
}
ssaoFirstShader.UnUse();
}
```

The first vertex shader (`Chapter6/SSAO/shaders/SSAO_FirstStep.vert`) outputs the eye space normal as shown in the following code snippet:

```
#version 330 core
layout(location = 0) in vec3 vVertex;
layout(location = 1) in vec3 vNormal;
uniform mat4 MVP;
uniform mat3 N;
smooth out vec3 vEyeSpaceNormal;
void main() {
    vEyeSpaceNormal = N*vNormal;
    gl_Position = MVP*vec4(vVertex,1);

}
```

The fragment shader (`Chapter6/SSAO/shaders/SSAO_FirstStep.frag`) returns the interpolated normal, as the fragment color, shown as follows:

```
#version 330 core
smooth in vec3 vEyeSpaceNormal;
layout(location=0) out vec4 vFragColor;
void main() {
    vFragColor = vec4(normalize(vEyeSpaceNormal)*0.5 + 0.5,
    1);
}
```

4. Bind the filtering FBO and use the second shader (`Chapter6/SSAO/shaders/SSAO_SecondStep.frag`). This shader does the actual SSAO calculation. The input to the shader is the normals texture from step 3. This shader is invoked on a full screen quad.

```
glBindFramebuffer(GL_FRAMEBUFFER,filterFBOID);
glDrawBuffer(GL_COLOR_ATTACHMENT0);
glBindVertexArray(quadVAOID);
ssaoSecondShader.Use();
glUniform1f(ssaoSecondShader("radius"), sampling_radius);
glDrawElements(GL_TRIANGLES, 6, GL_UNSIGNED_SHORT, 0);
ssaoSecondShader.UnUse();
```

5. Filter the output from step 4 by using separable Gaussian convolution using two fragment shaders (`Chapter6/SSAO/shaders/GaussH.frag` and `Chapter6/SSAO/shaders/GaussV.frag`). The separable Gaussian smoothing is added in to smooth out the ambient occlusion result.

```
glDrawBuffer(GL_COLOR_ATTACHMENT1);
glBindVertexArray(quadVAOID);
gaussianV_shader.Use();
glDrawElements(GL_TRIANGLES, 6, GL_UNSIGNED_SHORT, 0);
glDrawBuffer(GL_COLOR_ATTACHMENT0);
gaussianH_shader.Use();
glDrawElements(GL_TRIANGLES, 6, GL_UNSIGNED_SHORT, 0);
```

6. Unbind the filtering FBO, reset the default viewport, and then the default draw buffer. Enable alpha blending and then use the final shader (`Chapter6/SSAO/shaders/final.frag`) to blend the output from steps 3 and 5. This shader simply renders the final output from the filtering stage using a full-screen quad.

```
glBindFramebuffer(GL_FRAMEBUFFER,0);
glViewport(0,0,WIDTH, HEIGHT);
glDrawBuffer(GL_BACK_LEFT);
glEnable(GL_BLEND);
glBlendFunc(GL_SRC_ALPHA, GL_ONE_MINUS_SRC_ALPHA);
finalShader.Use();
glDrawElements(GL_TRIANGLES, 6, GL_UNSIGNED_SHORT, 0);
finalShader.UnUse();
glDisable(GL_BLEND);
```

How it works...

There are three steps in the SSAO calculation. The first step is the preparation of inputs, that is, the view space normals and depth. The normals are stored using the first step vertex shader (`Chapter6/SSAO/shaders/SSAO_FirstStep.vert`).

```
vEyeSpaceNormal_Depth = N*vNormal;
vec4 esPos = MV*vec4(vVertex,1);
gl_Position = P*esPos;
```

The fragment shader (`Chapter6/SSAO/shaders/SSAO_FirstStep.frag`) then outputs these values. The depth is extracted from the depth attachment of the FBO.

The second step is the actual SSAO calculation. We use a fragment shader (`Chapter6/SSAO/shaders/SSAO_SecondStep.frag`) to perform this by first rendering a screen-aligned quad. Then, for each fragment, the corresponding normal and depth values are obtained from the render target, from the first step. Next, a loop is run to compare the depth values of the neighboring fragments and then an occlusion value is estimated.

```
float depth = texture(depthTex, vUV).r;
if(depth<1.0)
{

    vec3 n = normalize(texture(normalTex, vUV).xyz*2.0 - 1.0);
    vec4 p = invP*vec4(vUV,depth,1);
    p.xyz /= p.w;

    vec2 random = normalize(texture(noiseTex,
    viewportSize/random_size * vUV).rg * 2.0 - 1.0);
    float ao = 0.0;

    for(int i = 0; i < NUM_SAMPLES; i++)
    {
      float npw = (pw + radius * samples[i].x * random.x);
      float nph = (ph + radius * samples[i].y * random.y);

      vec2 uv = vUV + vec2(npw, nph);
      vec4 p0 = invP * vec4(vUV,texture2D(depthTex, uv ).r, 1.0);
      p0.xyz /= p0.w;
      ao += calcAO(p0, p, n);
      //calculate similar depth points from the neighborhood
      //and calcualte ambient occlusion amount
    }
    ao *= INV_NUM_SAMPLES/8.0;

    vFragColor = vec4(vec3(0), ao);
}
```

After the second shader, we filter the SSAO output using separable Gaussian convolution. The default draw buffer is then restored and then the Gaussian filtered SSAO output is alpha blended with the normal rendering.

There's more...

The demo application implementing this recipe shows the scene with three blocks on a planar quad. When run, the output is as shown in the following screenshot:

Pressing the Space bar disables SSAO to produce the following output. As can be seen, ambient occlusion helps in giving shaded cues that approximate how near or far objects are. We can also change the sampling radius by using the + and - keys.

See also

▸ *A Simple and Practical Approach to SSAO* by Jose Maria Mendez: http://www.gamedev.net/page/resources/_/technical/graphics-programming-and-theory/a-simple-and-practical-approach-to-ssao-r2753

▸ SSAO Article at GameRendering.com: http://www.gamerendering.com/category/lighting/ssao-lighting/

Implementing global illumination using spherical harmonics lighting

In this recipe, we will learn about implementing simple global illumination using spherical harmonics. Spherical harmonics is a class of methods that enable approximation of functions as a product of a set of coefficients with a set of basis functions. Rather than calculating the lighting contribution by evaluating the **bi-directional reflectance distribution function (BRDF)**, this method uses special HDR/RGBE images that store the lighting information. The only attribute required for this method is the per-vertex normal. These are multiplied with the spherical harmonics coefficients that are extracted from the HDR/RGBE images.

The RGBE image format was invented by *Greg Ward*. These images store three bytes for the RGB value (that is, the red, green, and blue channel) and an additional byte which stores a shared exponent. This enables these files to have an extended range and precision of floating point values. For details about the theory behind the spherical harmonics method and the RGBE format, refer to the references in the *See also* section of this recipe.

To give an overview of the recipe, using the probe image, the SH coefficients (C1 to C5) are estimated by projection. Details of the projection method are given in the references in the *See also* section. For most of the common lighting HDR probes, the spherical harmonic coefficients are documented. We use these values as constants in our vertex shader.

Getting ready

The code for this recipe is contained in the `Chapter6/SphericalHarmonics` directory. For this recipe, we will be using the Obj mesh loader discussed in the previous chapter.

How to do it...

Let us start this recipe by following these simple steps:

1. Load an `obj` mesh using the `ObjLoader` class and fill the OpenGL buffer objects and the OpenGL textures, using the material information loaded from the file, as in the previous recipes.

2. In the vertex shader that is used for the mesh, perform the lighting calculation using spherical harmonics. The vertex shader is detailed as follows:

```
#version 330 core
layout(location = 0) in vec3 vVertex;
layout(location = 1) in vec3 vNormal;
layout(location = 2) in vec2 vUV;

smooth out vec2 vUVout;
smooth out vec4 diffuse;
```

```
uniform mat4 P;
uniform mat4 MV;
uniform mat3 N;

const float C1 = 0.429043;
const float C2 = 0.511664;
const float C3 = 0.743125;
const float C4 = 0.886227;
const float C5 = 0.247708;
const float PI = 3.14159265358979323846426433832795;

//Old town square probe
const vec3 L00 = vec3( 0.871297, 0.875222, 0.864470);
const vec3 L1m1 = vec3( 0.175058, 0.245335, 0.312891);
const vec3 L10 = vec3( 0.034675, 0.036107, 0.037362);
const vec3 L11 = vec3(-0.004629, -0.029448, -0.048028);
const vec3 L2m2 = vec3(-0.120535, -0.121160, -0.117507);
const vec3 L2m1 = vec3( 0.003242, 0.003624, 0.007511);
const vec3 L20 = vec3(-0.028667, -0.024926, -0.020998);
const vec3 L21 = vec3(-0.077539, -0.086325, -0.091591);
const vec3 L22 = vec3(-0.161784, -0.191783, -0.219152);
const vec3 scaleFactor = vec3(0.161784/
(0.871297+0.161784), 0.191783/(0.875222+0.191783),
0.219152/(0.864470+0.219152));

void main()
{
    vUVout=vUV;
    vec3 tmpN = normalize(N*vNormal);
    vec3 diff = C1 * L22 * (tmpN.x*tmpN.x -
    tmpN.y*tmpN.y) +
            C3 * L20 * tmpN.z*tmpN.z +
            C4 * L00 -
            C5 * L20 +
            2.0 * C1 * L2m2*tmpN.x*tmpN.y +
            2.0 * C1 * L21*tmpN.x*tmpN.z +
            2.0 * C1 * L2m1*tmpN.y*tmpN.z +
            2.0 * C2 * L11*tmpN.x +
            2.0 * C2 * L1m1*tmpN.y +
            2.0 * C2 * L10*tmpN.z;
    diff *= scaleFactor;
    diffuse = vec4(diff, 1);
    gl_Position = P*(MV*vec4(vVertex,1));
}
```

3. The per-vertex color calculated by the vertex shader is interpolated by the rasterizer and then the fragment shader sets the color as the current fragment color.

```
#version 330 core
uniform sampler2D textureMap;
uniform float useDefault;
smooth in vec4 diffuse;
smooth in vec2 vUVout;
layout(location=0) out vec4 vFragColor;
void main() {
    vFragColor = mix(texture(textureMap, vUVout)*diffuse,
                    diffuse, useDefault);
}
```

How it works...

Spherical harmonics is a technique that approximates the lighting, using coefficients and spherical harmonics basis. The coefficients are obtained at initialization from an HDR/RGBE image file that contains information about lighting. This allows us to approximate the same light so the graphical scene feels more immersive.

The method reproduces accurate diffuse reflection using information extracted from an HDR/RGBE light probe. The light probe itself is not accessed in the code. The spherical harmonics basis and coefficients are extracted from the original light probe using projection. Since this is a mathematically involved process, we refer the interested readers to the references in the See also section. The code for generating the spherical harmonics coefficients is available online. We used this code to generate the spherical harmonics coefficients for the shader.

The spherical harmonics is a frequency space representation of an image on a sphere. As was shown by Ramamoorthi and Hanrahan, only the first nine spherical harmonic coefficients are enough to give a reasonable approximation of the diffuse reflection component of a surface. These coefficients are obtained by constant, linear, and quadratic polynomial interpolation of the surface normal. The interpolation result gives us the diffuse component which has to be normalized by a scale factor which is obtained by summing all of the coefficients as shown in the following code snippet:

```
vec3 tmpN = normalize(N*vNormal);
vec3 diff = C1 * L22 * (tmpN.x*tmpN.x - tmpN.y*tmpN.y) +
            C3 * L20 * tmpN.z*tmpN.z +
            C4 * L00 -
            C5 * L20 +
            2.0 * C1 * L2m2*tmpN.x*tmpN.y +
            2.0 * C1 * L21*tmpN.x*tmpN.z +
            2.0 * C1 * L2m1*tmpN.y*tmpN.z +
            2.0 * C2 * L11*tmpN.x +
            2.0 * C2 * L1m1*tmpN.y +
            2.0 * C2 * L10*tmpN.z;
diff *= scaleFactor;
```

The obtained per-vertex diffuse component is then forwarded through the rasterizer to the fragment shader where it is directly multiplied by the texture of the surface.

```
vFragColor = mix(texture(textureMap, vUVout)*diffuse,
            diffuse, useDefault);
```

There's more...

The demo application implementing this recipe renders the same scene as in the previous recipes, as shown in the following figure. We can rotate the camera view using the left mouse button, whereas, the point light source can be rotated using the right mouse button. Pressing the Space bar toggles the use of spherical harmonics. When spherical harmonics lighting is on, we get the following result:

Without the spherical harmonics lighting, the result is as follows:

The probe image used for this image is shown in the following figure:

Note that this method approximates global illumination by modifying the diffuse component using the spherical harmonics coefficients. We can also add the conventional Blinn Phong lighting model as we did in the earlier recipes. For that we would only need to evaluate the Blinn Phong lighting model using the normal and light position, as we did in the previous recipe.

See also

- *Ravi Ramamoorthi* and *Pat Hanrahan*, An Efficient Representation for Irradiance Environment Maps: `http://www1.cs.columbia.edu/~ravir/papers/envmap/index.html`

- *Randi J. Rost*, *Mill M. Licea-Kane*, *Dan Ginsburg*, *John M. Kessenich*, *Barthold Lichtenbelt*, *Hugh Malan*, *Mike Weiblen*, OpenGL Shading Language, Third Edition, Section 12.3, Lighting and Spherical Harmonics, Addison-Wesley Professional

- *Kelly Dempski* and *Emmanuel Viale*, *Advanced Lighting and Materials with Shaders*, *Chapter 8*, *Spherical Harmonic Lighting*, Jones & Bartlett Publishers

- The RGBE image format specifications: `http://www.graphics.cornell.edu/online/formats/rgbe/`

- Paul Debevec HDR light probes: `http://www.pauldebevec.com/Probes/`

- Spherical harmonics lighting tutorial: `http://www.paulsprojects.net/opengl/sh/sh.html`

Implementing GPU-based ray tracing

To this point, all of the recipes rendered 3D geometry using rasterization. In this recipe, we will implement another method for rendering geometry, which is called **ray tracing**. Simply put, ray tracing uses a probing ray from the camera position into the graphical scene. The intersections of this ray are obtained for each geometry. The good thing with this method is that only the visible objects are rendered.

The ray tracing algorithm can be given in pseudocode as follows:

```
For each pixel on screen
  Get the eye ray origin and direction using camera position
  For the amount of traces required
    Cast the ray into scene
    For each object in the scene
      Check eye ray for intersection
      If intersection found
        Determine the hit point and surface normal
        For each light source
          Calculate diffuse and specular comp. at hit point
          Cast shadow ray from hit point to light
        End For
```

```
        Darken diffuse component based on shadow result
        Set the hit point as the new ray origin
        Reflect the eye ray direction at surface normal
      End If
    End For
  End For
End For
```

Getting ready

The code for this recipe is contained in the `Chapter6/GPURaytracing` directory.

How to do it...

Let us start with this recipe by following these simple steps:

1. Load the Obj mesh model using the Obj loader and store mesh geometry in vectors. Note that for the GPU ray tracer we use the original vertices and indices lists stored in the OBJ file.

    ```
    vector<unsigned short> indices2;
    vector<glm::vec3> vertices2;
    if(!obj.Load(mesh_filename.c_str(), meshes, vertices,
    indices, materials, aabb, vertices2, indices2)) {
      cout<<"Cannot load the 3ds mesh"<<endl;
      exit(EXIT_FAILURE);
    }
    ```

2. Load the material texture maps into an OpenGL texture array instead of loading each texture separately, as in previous recipes. We opted for texture arrays because this helps in simplifying the shader code and we would have no way in determining the total samplers we would require, as that is dependent on the material textures we have in the model. In previous recipes, there was a single texture sampler which was modified for each sub-mesh.

    ```
    for(size_t k=0;k<materials.size();k++) {
    if(materials[k]->map_Kd != "") {
    if(k==0) {
      glGenTextures(1, &textureID);
      glBindTexture(GL_TEXTURE_2D_ARRAY, textureID);
      glTexParameteri(GL_TEXTURE_2D_ARRAY,
      GL_TEXTURE_MIN_FILTER, GL_LINEAR);
     //set other texture parameters
    }
    //set image name
    ```

```
GLubyte* pData = SOIL_load_image(full_filename.c_str(),
&texture_width, &texture_height, &channels,
SOIL_LOAD_AUTO);
 if(pData == NULL) {
  cerr<<"Cannot load image: "<<full_filename.c_str()<<endl;
  exit(EXIT_FAILURE);
 }
 //flip the image and set the image format
 if(k==0) {
  glTexImage3D(GL_TEXTURE_2D_ARRAY, 0, format,
  texture_width, texture_height, total, 0, format,
  GL_UNSIGNED_BYTE, NULL);
 }
  glTexSubImage3D(GL_TEXTURE_2D_ARRAY, 0,0,0,k,
  texture_width, texture_height, 1, format,
  GL_UNSIGNED_BYTE, pData);
  SOIL_free_image_data(pData);
 }
}
```

3. Store the vertex positions into a texture for the ray tracing shader. We use a floating point texture with the GL_RGBA32F internal format.

```
glGenTextures(1, &texVerticesID);
glActiveTexture(GL_TEXTURE1);
glBindTexture( GL_TEXTURE_2D, texVerticesID);
//set the texture formats
GLfloat* pData = new GLfloat[vertices2.size()*4];
int count = 0;
for(size_t i=0;i<vertices2.size();i++) {
pData[count++] = vertices2[i].x;
pData[count++] = vertices2[i].y;
pData[count++] = vertices2[i].z;
pData[count++] = 0;
}
glTexImage2D(GL_TEXTURE_2D, 0, GL_RGBA32F,
vertices2.size(),1, 0, GL_RGBA, GL_FLOAT, pData);
delete [] pData;
```

4. Store the list of indices into an integral texture for the ray tracing shader. Note that for this texture, the internal format is GL_RGBA16I and the format is GL_RGBA_INTEGER.

```
glGenTextures(1, &texTrianglesID);
glActiveTexture(GL_TEXTURE2);
glBindTexture( GL_TEXTURE_2D, texTrianglesID);
//set the texture formats
```

```
        GLushort* pData2 = new GLushort[indices2.size()];
        count = 0;
        for(size_t i=0;i<indices2.size();i+=4) {
          pData2[count++] = (indices2[i]);
          pData2[count++] = (indices2[i+1]);
          pData2[count++] = (indices2[i+2]);
          pData2[count++] = (indices2[i+3]);
        }
        glTexImage2D(GL_TEXTURE_2D, 0, GL_RGBA16I,
        indices2.size()/4, 1, 0, GL_RGBA_INTEGER,
        GL_UNSIGNED_SHORT, pData2);
        delete [] pData2;
```

5. In the `render` function, bind the ray tracing shader and then draw a full-screen quad to invoke the fragment shader for the entire screen.

How it works...

The main code for ray tracing is the ray tracing fragment shader (`Chapter6/GPURaytracing/shaders/raytracer.frag`). We first set up the camera ray origin and direction using the parameters passed to the shader as shader uniforms.

```
    eyeRay.origin = eyePos;
    cam.U = (invMVP*vec4(1,0,0,0)).xyz;
    cam.V = (invMVP*vec4(0,1,0,0)).xyz;
    cam.W = (invMVP*vec4(0,0,1,0)).xyz;
    cam.d = 1;
    eyeRay.dir = get_direction(uv , cam);
    eyeRay.dir += cam.U*uv.x;
    eyeRay.dir += cam.V*uv.y;
```

After the eye ray is set up, we check the ray against the axially aligned bounding box of the scene. If there is an intersection, we continue further. For this simple example, we use a brute force method of looping through all of the triangles and testing each of them in turn for ray intersection.

In ray tracing, we try to find the neatest intersection of a parametric ray with the given triangle. Any point along the ray is obtained by using a parameter t. We are looking for the nearest intersection (smallest t value). If there is an intersection and it is the closest so far, we store the collision information and the normal at the intersection point. The t parameter gives us the exact position where the intersection occurs.

```
    vec4 val=vec4(t,0,0,0);
    vec3 N;
    for(int i=0;i<int(TRIANGLE_TEXTURE_SIZE);i++)
    {
```

```
    vec3 normal;
    vec4 res = intersectTriangle(eyeRay.origin, eyeRay.dir, i,
    normal);
    if(res.x>0 && res.x <= val.x) {
      val = res;
      N = normal;
    }
  }
}
```

When we plug its value into the parametric equation of a ray, we get the hit point. Then, we calculate a vector to light from the hit point. This vector is then used to estimate the diffuse component and the attenuation amount.

```
  if(val.x != t) {
    vec3 hit = eyeRay.origin + eyeRay.dir*val.x;
    vec3 jitteredLight = light_position +
    uniformlyRandomVector(gl_FragCoord.x);
    vec3 L = (jitteredLight.xyz-hit);
    float d = length(L);
    L = normalize(L);
    float diffuse = max(0, dot(N, L));
    float attenuationAmount = 1.0/(k0 + (k1*d) + (k2*d*d));
    diffuse *= attenuationAmount;
```

With ray tracing, shadows are very easy to calculate. We simply cast another ray, but this time, just look at if the ray intersects any object on its way to the light source. If it does, we darken the final color, otherwise we leave the color as is. Note that to prevent the shadow acne, we add a slight offset to the ray start position.

```
    float inShadow = shadow(hit+ N*0.0001, L);
    vFragColor = inShadow*diffuse*mix(texture(textureMaps,
    val.yzw), vec4(1), (val.w==255) );
    return;
  }
```

There's more...

The demo application for this recipe renders the same scene as in previous recipes. The scene can be toggled between rasterization and GPU ray tracing by pressing the Space bar. We can see that the shadows are clearly visible in the ray tracing scene. Note that the performance of GPU ray tracing is directly related to how close or far the object is from the camera, as well as how many triangles are there in the rendered mesh. For better performance, some acceleration structure, such as uniform grid or kd-tree should be employed. Also note, soft shadows require us to cast more shadow rays, which also add additional strain on the ray tracing fragment shader.

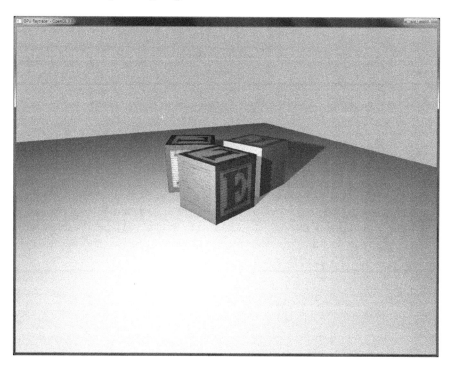

See also

- ▸ *Timothy Purcell, Ian Buck, William R. Mark*, and *Pat Hanrahan*, ACM Transactions on Graphics 21 (3), Ray Tracing on Programmable Graphics Hardware, pages 703-712: http://graphics.stanford.edu/papers/rtongfx/

- ▸ *Real-time GPU Ray-Tracer* at Icare3D: http://www.icare3d.org/codes-and-projects/codes/raytracer_gpu_full_1-0.html

Implementing GPU-based path tracing

In this recipe, we will implement another method, called path tracing, for rendering geometry. Similar to ray tracing, path tracing casts rays but these rays are shot randomly from the light position(s). Since it is usually difficult to approximate real lighting, we can approximate it using Monte Carlo-based integration schemes. These methods use random sampling and if there are enough samples, the integration result converges to the true solution.

We can give the path tracing pseudocode as follows:

```
For each pixel on screen
  Create a light ray from light position in a random direction
  For the amount of traces required
    For each object in the scene
      Check light ray for intersection
      If intersection found
        Determine the hit point and surface normal
        Calculate diffuse and specular comp. at hit point
        Cast shadow ray in random direction from hit point
        Darken diffuse component based on shadow result
        Set the randomly jittered hit point as new ray origin
        Reflect the light ray direction at surface normal
      End If
    End For
  End For
End For
```

Getting ready

The code for this recipe is contained in the `Chapter6/GPUPathtracing` directory.

How to do it...

Let us start with this recipe by following these simple steps:

1. Load the Obj mesh model using the Obj loader and store the mesh geometry in vectors. Note that for the GPU path tracer we use the original vertices and indices lists stored in the OBJ file, as in the previous recipe.

2. Load the material texture maps into an OpenGL texture array instead of loading each texture separately as in the previous recipe.

3. Store the vertex positions into a texture for the path tracing shader, similar to how we stored them for ray tracing in the previous recipe. We use a floating point texture with the GL_RGBA32F internal format.

```
glGenTextures(1, &texVerticesID);
glActiveTexture(GL_TEXTURE1);
glBindTexture( GL_TEXTURE_2D, texVerticesID);
//set the texture formats
GLfloat* pData = new GLfloat[vertices2.size()*4];
int count = 0;
for(size_t i=0;i<vertices2.size();i++) {
  pData[count++] = vertices2[i].x;
  pData[count++] = vertices2[i].y;
  pData[count++] = vertices2[i].z;
  pData[count++] = 0;
}
glTexImage2D(GL_TEXTURE_2D, 0, GL_RGBA32F,
vertices2.size(),1, 0, GL_RGBA, GL_FLOAT, pData);
delete [] pData;
```

4. Store the indices list into an integral texture for the path tracing shader, as was done for the ray tracing recipe. Note that for this texture, the internal format is GL_RGBA16I and format is GL_RGBA_INTEGER.

```
glGenTextures(1, &texTrianglesID);
glActiveTexture(GL_TEXTURE2);
glBindTexture( GL_TEXTURE_2D, texTrianglesID);
//set the texture formats
GLushort* pData2 = new GLushort[indices2.size()];
count = 0;
for(size_t i=0;i<indices2.size();i+=4) {
  pData2[count++] = (indices2[i]);
  pData2[count++] = (indices2[i+1]);
  pData2[count++] = (indices2[i+2]);
  pData2[count++] = (indices2[i+3]);
}
glTexImage2D(GL_TEXTURE_2D, 0, GL_RGBA16I,
indices2.size()/4, 1, 0, GL_RGBA_INTEGER,
GL_UNSIGNED_SHORT, pData2);
delete [] pData2;
```

5. In the render function, bind the path tracing shader and then draw a full-screen quad to invoke the fragment shader for the entire screen.

```
pathtraceShader.Use();
  glUniform3fv(pathtraceShader("eyePos"), 1,
  glm::value_ptr(eyePos));
```

```
glUniform1f(pathtraceShader("time"), current);
glUniform3fv(pathtraceShader("light_position"),1,
&(lightPosOS.x));
glUniformMatrix4fv(pathtraceShader("invMVP"), 1,
GL_FALSE, glm::value_ptr(invMVP));
DrawFullScreenQuad();
pathtraceShader.UnUse();
```

How it works...

The main code for path tracing is carried out in the path tracing fragment shader (Chapter6/ GPUPathtracing/shaders/pathtracer.frag). We first set up the camera ray origin and direction using the parameters passed to the shader as shader uniforms.

```
eyeRay.origin = eyePos;
cam.U = (invMVP*vec4(1,0,0,0)).xyz;
cam.V = (invMVP*vec4(0,1,0,0)).xyz;
cam.W = (invMVP*vec4(0,0,1,0)).xyz;
cam.d = 1;
eyeRay.dir = get_direction(uv , cam);
eyeRay.dir += cam.U*uv.x;
eyeRay.dir += cam.V*uv.y;
```

After the eye ray is set up, we check the ray against the scene's axially aligned bounding box. If there is an intersection, we call our path trace function.

```
vec2 tNearFar = intersectCube(eyeRay.origin, eyeRay.dir,  aabb);
if(tNearFar.x<tNearFar.y  ) {
  t = tNearFar.y+1;
  vec3 light = light_position + uniformlyRandomVector(time) *
  0.1;
  vFragColor = vec4(pathtrace(eyeRay.origin, eyeRay.dir, light,
  t),1);
}
```

In the path trace function, we run a loop that iterates for a number of passes. In each pass, we check the scene geometry for an intersection with the ray. We use a brute force method of looping through all of the triangles and testing each of them in turn for collision. If we have an intersection, we check to see if this is the nearest intersection. If it is, we store the normal and the texture coordinates at the intersection point.

```
for(int bounce = 0; bounce < MAX_BOUNCES; bounce++) {
  vec2 tNearFar = intersectCube(origin, ray,  aabb);
  if(  tNearFar.x > tNearFar.y)
    continue;
  if(tNearFar.y<t)
```

```
    t = tNearFar.y+1;
vec3 N;
vec4 val=vec4(t,0,0,0);
for(int i=0;i<int(TRIANGLE_TEXTURE_SIZE);i++)
{
  vec3 normal;
  vec4 res = intersectTriangle(origin, ray, i, normal);
  if(res.x>0.001 && res.x <  val.x) {
    val = res;
    N = normal;
  }
}
```

We then check the t parameter value to find the nearest intersection and then use the texture array to sample the appropriate texture for the output color value for the current fragment. We then change the current ray origin to the current hit point and then change the current ray direction to a uniform random direction in the hemisphere above the intersection point.

```
if(val.x < t) {
  surfaceColor = mix(texture(textureMaps, val.yzw), vec4(1),
  (val.w==255) ).xyz;
  vec3 hit = origin + ray * val.x;
  origin = hit;
  ray = uniformlyRandomDirection(time + float(bounce));
```

The diffuse component is then estimated and then the color is accumulated. At the end of the loop, the final accumulated color is returned.

```
  vec3  jitteredLight  =  light + ray;
  vec3 L = normalize(jitteredLight - hit);
  diffuse = max(0.0, dot(L, N));
  colorMask *= surfaceColor;
  float inShadow = shadow(hit+ N*0.0001, L);
  accumulatedColor += colorMask * diffuse * inShadow;
  t = val.x;
}
  }
  if(accumulatedColor == vec3(0))
    return surfaceColor*diffuse;
  else
    return accumulatedColor/float(MAX_BOUNCES-1);}
```

Note that the path tracing output is noisy and a large number of samples are needed to get a less noisy result.

There's more...

The demo application for this recipe renders the same scene as in previous recipes. The scene can be toggled between rasterization and GPU path tracing by pressing the Space bar, as shown below:

Note that the performance of GPU path tracing is directly related to how close or far the object is from camera, as well as how many triangles are there in the rendered mesh. In order to reduce the amount of testing, some acceleration structure, such as uniform grid or kd-tree should be employed. In addition, since the results obtained from path tracing are generally noisier as compared to the ray tracing results, noise removal filters, such as Gaussian smoothing could be carried out on the path traced result.

Ray tracing is poor at approximating global illumination and soft shadows. Path tracing, on the other hand, handles global illumination and soft shadows well, but it suffers from noise. To get a good result, it requires a large number of random sampling points. There are other techniques, such as Metropolis light transport, which uses heuristics to only accept good sample points and reject bad sampling points. As a result, it converges to a less noisier result faster as compared to naïve path tracing.

See also

▶ *Tim Purcell, Ian Buck, William Mark*, and *Pat Hanrahan*, Ray Tracing on Programmable Graphics Hardware, ACM Transactions on Graphics 21(3), pp: 703-712, 2002. Available online: `http://graphics.stanford.edu/papers/rtongfx/`

▶ Peter and Karl's GPU Path Tracer: `http://gpupathtracer.blogspot.sg/`

▶ Real-time path traced Brigade demo at Siggraph 2012: `http://raytracey.blogspot.co.nz/2012/08/real-time-path-traced-brigade-demo-at.html`

7

GPU-based Volume Rendering Techniques

In this chapter, we will focus on:

- ▸ Implementing volume rendering using 3D texture slicing
- ▸ Implementing volume rendering using single-pass GPU ray casting
- ▸ Implementing pseudo isosurface rendering in single-pass GPU ray casting
- ▸ Implementing volume rendering using splatting
- ▸ Implementing the transfer function for volume classification
- ▸ Implementing polygonal isosurface extraction using the Marching Tetrahedra algorithm
- ▸ Implementing volumetric lighting using half-angle slicing

Introduction

Volume rendering techniques are used in various domains in biomedical and engineering disciplines. They are often used in biomedical imaging to visualize the CT/MRI datasets. In mechanical engineering, they are used to visualize intermediate results from FEM simulations, flow, and structural analysis. With the advent of GPU, all of the existing models and methods of visualization were ported to GPU to harness their computational power. This chapter will detail several algorithms that are used for volume visualization on the GPU in OpenGL Version 3.3 and above. Specifically, we will look at three widely used methods including 3D texture slicing, single-pass ray casting with alpha compositing as well as isosurface rendering, and splatting.

After looking at the volume rendering methods, we will look at volume classification by implementing transfer functions. Polygonal isosurfaces are also often generated to extract out classified regions, for example, cellular boundaries. We, therefore, implement the Marching Tetrahedra algorithm. Finally, volume lighting is another area that is actively researched in the volume rendering community. As there are very few implementations of volume lighting, and especially half-angle slicing, we detail how to implement volume lighting through the half-angle slicing technique in modern OpenGL.

Implementing volume rendering using 3D texture slicing

Volume rendering is a special class of rendering algorithms that allows us to portray fuzzy phenomena, such as smoke. There are numerous algorithms for volume rendering. To start our quest, we will focus on the simplest method called 3D texture slicing. This method approximates the volume-density function by slicing the dataset in front-to-back or back-to-front order and then blends the proxy slices using hardware-supported blending. Since it relies on the rasterization hardware, this method is very fast on the modern GPU.

The pseudo code for view-aligned 3D texture slicing is as follows:

1. Get the current view direction vector.

2. Calculate the min/max distance of unit cube vertices by doing a dot product of each unit cube vertex with the view direction vector.

3. Calculate all possible intersections parameter (λ) of the plane perpendicular to the view direction with all edges of the unit cube going from the nearest to farthest vertex, using min/max distances from step 1.

4. Use the intersection parameter λ (from step 3) to move in the viewing direction and find the intersection points. Three to six intersection vertices will be generated.

5. Store the intersection points in the specified order to generate triangular primitives, which are the proxy geometries.

6. Update the buffer object memory with the new vertices.

Getting ready

The code for this recipe is in the `Chapter7/3DTextureSlicing` directory.

How to do it...

Let us start our recipe by following these simple steps:

1. Load the volume dataset by reading the external volume datafile and passing the data into an OpenGL texture. Also enable hardware mipmap generation. Typically, the volume datafiles store densities that are obtained from using a cross-sectional imaging modality such as CT or MRI scans. Each CT/MRI scan is a 2D slice. We accumulate these slices in Z direction to obtain a 3D texture, which is simply an array of 2D textures. The densities store different material types, for example, values ranging from 0 to 20 are typically occupied by air. As we have an 8-bit unsigned dataset, we store the dataset into a local array of GLubyte type. If we had an unsigned 16-bit dataset, we would have stored it into a local array of GLushort type. In case of 3D textures, in addition to the S and T parameters, we have an additional parameter R that controls the slice we are at in the 3D texture.

```
std::ifstream infile(volume_file.c_str(), std::ios_base::binary);
if(infile.good()) {
    GLubyte* pData = new GLubyte[XDIM*YDIM*ZDIM];
    infile.read(reinterpret_cast<char*>(pData),
    XDIM*YDIM*ZDIM*sizeof(GLubyte));
    infile.close();
    glGenTextures(1, &textureID);
    glBindTexture(GL_TEXTURE_3D, textureID);
    glTexParameteri(GL_TEXTURE_3D, GL_TEXTURE_WRAP_S,
    GL_CLAMP);
    glTexParameteri(GL_TEXTURE_3D, GL_TEXTURE_WRAP_T,
    GL_CLAMP);
    glTexParameteri(GL_TEXTURE_3D, GL_TEXTURE_WRAP_R,
    GL_CLAMP);
    glTexParameteri(GL_TEXTURE_3D, GL_TEXTURE_MAG_FILTER,
                GL_LINEAR);
    glTexParameteri(GL_TEXTURE_3D, GL_TEXTURE_MIN_FILTER,
                GL_LINEAR_MIPMAP_LINEAR);
    glTexParameteri(GL_TEXTURE_3D, GL_TEXTURE_BASE_LEVEL, 0);
    glTexParameteri(GL_TEXTURE_3D, GL_TEXTURE_MAX_LEVEL, 4);
glTexImage3D(GL_TEXTURE_3D,0,GL_RED,XDIM,YDIM,ZDIM,0,GL_RED,GL_
UNSIGNED_BYTE,pData);
    glGenerateMipmap(GL_TEXTURE_3D);
    return true;
} else {
    return false;
}
```

The filtering parameters for 3D textures are similar to the 2D texture parameters that we have seen before. Mipmaps are collections of down-sampled versions of a texture that are used for **level of detail** (**LOD**) functionality. That is, they help to use a down-sampled version of the texture if the viewer is very far from the object on which the texture is applied. This helps improve the performance of the application. We have to specify the max number of levels (GL_TEXTURE_MAX_LEVEL), which is the maximum number of mipmaps generated from the given texture. In addition, the base level (GL_TEXTURE_BASE_LEVEL) denotes the first level for the mipmap that is used when the object is closest.

The glGenerateMipMap function works by generating derived arrays by repeated filtered reduction operation on the previous level. So let's say that we have three mipmap levels and our 3D texture has a resolution of 256×256×256 at level 0. For level 1 mipmap, the level 0 data will be reduced to half the size by filtered reduction to 128×128×128. For level 2 mipmap, the level 1 data will be filtered and reduced to 64×64×64. Finally, for level 3 mipmap, the level 2 data will be filtered and reduced to 32×32×32.

2. Setup a vertex array object and a vertex buffer object to store the geometry of the proxy slices. Make sure that the buffer object usage is specified as GL_DYNAMIC_DRAW. The initial glBufferData call allocates GPU memory for the maximum number of slices. The vTextureSlices array is defined globally and it stores the vertices produced by texture slicing operation for triangulation. The glBufferData is initialized with 0 as the data will be filled at runtime dynamically.

```
const int MAX_SLICES = 512;
glm::vec3 vTextureSlices[MAX_SLICES*12];

glGenVertexArrays(1, &volumeVAO);
glGenBuffers(1, &volumeVBO);
glBindVertexArray(volumeVAO);
glBindBuffer (GL_ARRAY_BUFFER, volumeVBO);
glBufferData (GL_ARRAY_BUFFER, sizeof(vTextureSlices), 0, GL_
DYNAMIC_DRAW);
glEnableVertexAttribArray(0);
glVertexAttribPointer(0, 3, GL_FLOAT, GL_FALSE,0,0);
glBindVertexArray(0);
```

3. Implement slicing of volume by finding intersections of a unit cube with proxy slices perpendicular to the viewing direction. This is carried out by the SliceVolume function. We use a unit cube since our data has equal size in all three axes that is, 256×256×256. If we have a non-equal sized dataset, we can scale the unit cube appropriately.

```
//determine max and min distances
  glm::vec3 vecStart[12];
  glm::vec3 vecDir[12];
```

```
float lambda[12];
float lambda_inc[12];
float denom = 0;
float plane_dist = min_dist;
float plane_dist_inc = (max_dist-min_dist)/float(num_slices);

//determine vecStart and vecDir values
glm::vec3 intersection[6];
float dL[12];

for(int i=num_slices-1;i>=0;i--) {
    for(int e = 0; e < 12; e++)
    {
        dL[e] = lambda[e] + i*lambda_inc[e];
    }

    if ((dL[0] >= 0.0) && (dL[0] < 1.0))    {
        intersection[0] = vecStart[0] +
        dL[0]*vecDir[0];
    }
    //like wise for all intersection points
    int indices[]={0,1,2, 0,2,3, 0,3,4, 0,4,5};
    for(int i=0;i<12;i++)
    vTextureSlices[count++]=intersection[indices[i]];
}
//update buffer object
glBindBuffer(GL_ARRAY_BUFFER, volumeVBO);
glBufferSubData(GL_ARRAY_BUFFER, 0,
sizeof(vTextureSlices),  &(vTextureSlices[0].x));
```

4. In the render function, set the over blending, bind the volume vertex array object, bind the shader, and then call the `glDrawArrays` function.

```
glEnable(GL_BLEND);
glBlendFunc(GL_SRC_ALPHA, GL_ONE_MINUS_SRC_ALPHA);
glBindVertexArray(volumeVAO);
shader.Use();
glUniformMatrix4fv(shader("MVP"), 1, GL_FALSE, glm::value_
ptr(MVP));
glDrawArrays(GL_TRIANGLES, 0, sizeof(vTextureSlices)/
sizeof(vTextureSlices[0]));
shader.UnUse();
glDisable(GL_BLEND);
```

How it works...

Volume rendering using 3D texture slicing approximates the volume rendering integral by alpha-blending textured slices. The first step is loading and generating a 3D texture from the volume data. After loading the volume dataset, the slicing of the volume is carried out using proxy slices. These are oriented perpendicular to the viewing direction. Moreover, we have to find the intersection of the proxy polygons with the unit cube boundaries. This is carried out by the SliceVolume function. Note that slicing is carried out only when the view is rotated.

We first obtain the view direction vector (viewDir), which is the third column in the model-view matrix. The first column of the model-view matrix stores the right vector and the second column stores the up vector. We will now detail how the SliceVolume function works internally. We find the minimum and maximum vertex in the current viewing direction by calculating the maximum and minimum distance of the 8 unit vertices in the viewing direction. These distances are obtained using the dot product of each unit cube vertex with the view direction vector:

```
float max_dist = glm::dot(viewDir, vertexList[0]);
float min_dist = max_dist;
int max_index = 0;
int count = 0;
for(int i=1;i<8;i++) {
    float dist = glm::dot(viewDir, vertexList[i]);
    if(dist > max_dist) {
        max_dist = dist;
        max_index = i;
    }
    if(dist<min_dist)
        min_dist = dist;
}
int max_dim = FindAbsMax(viewDir);
min_dist -= EPSILON;
max_dist += EPSILON;
```

There are only three unique paths when going from the nearest vertex to the farthest vertex from the camera. We store all possible paths for each vertex into an edge table, which is defined as follows:

```
int edgeList[8][12]={{0,1,5,6,  4,8,11,9,  3,7,2,10 }, //v0 is front
                     {0,4,3,11,  1,2,6,7,   5,9,8,10 }, //v1 is front
                     {1,5,0,8,   2,3,7,4,   6,10,9,11}, //v2 is front
              { 7,11,10,8, 2,6,1,9,   3,0,4,5  }, // v3 is front
              { 8,5,9,1,   11,10,7,6, 4,3,0,2  }, // v4 is front
              { 9,6,10,2,  8,11,4,7,  5,0,1,3  }, // v5 is front
              { 9,8,5,4,   6,1,2,0,   10,7,11,3}, // v6 is front
              { 10,9,6,5,  7,2,3,1,   11,4,8,0 } // v7 is front
```

Next, plane intersection distances are estimated for the 12 edge indices of the unit cube:

```
glm::vec3 vecStart[12];
glm::vec3 vecDir[12];
float lambda[12];
float lambda_inc[12];
float denom = 0;
float plane_dist = min_dist;
float plane_dist_inc = (max_dist-min_dist)/float(num_slices);
for(int i=0;i<12;i++) {
    vecStart[i]=vertexList[edges[edgeList[max_index][i]][0]];
    vecDir[i]=vertexList[edges[edgeList[max_index][i]][1]]-
            vecStart[i];
    denom = glm::dot(vecDir[i], viewDir);
    if (1.0 + denom != 1.0) {
      lambda_inc[i] =  plane_dist_inc/denom;
      lambda[i]=(plane_dist-glm::dot(vecStart[i],viewDir))/denom;
    } else {
        lambda[i]       = -1.0;
        lambda_inc[i] =   0.0;
    }
}
```

Finally, the interpolated intersections with the unit cube edges are carried out by moving back-to-front in the viewing direction. After proxy slices have been generated, the vertex buffer object is updated with the new data.

```
for(int i=num_slices-1;i>=0;i--) {
    for(int e = 0; e < 12; e++) {
        dL[e] = lambda[e] + i*lambda_inc[e];
    }
    if  ((dL[0] >= 0.0) && (dL[0] < 1.0))  {
        intersection[0] = vecStart[0] + dL[0]*vecDir[0];
    } else if ((dL[1] >= 0.0) && (dL[1] < 1.0))  {
        intersection[0] = vecStart[1] + dL[1]*vecDir[1];
    } else if ((dL[3] >= 0.0) && (dL[3] < 1.0))  {
        intersection[0] = vecStart[3] + dL[3]*vecDir[3];
    } else continue;

    if ((dL[2] >= 0.0) && (dL[2] < 1.0)){
        intersection[1] = vecStart[2] + dL[2]*vecDir[2];
    } else if ((dL[0] >= 0.0) && (dL[0] < 1.0)){
        intersection[1] = vecStart[0] + dL[0]*vecDir[0];
    } else if ((dL[1] >= 0.0) && (dL[1] < 1.0)){
        intersection[1] = vecStart[1] + dL[1]*vecDir[1];
    } else {
```

```
        intersection[1] = vecStart[3] + dL[3]*vecDir[3];
    }
    //similarly for others edges unit1 intersection[5]
    int indices[]={0,1,2, 0,2,3, 0,3,4, 0,4,5};
    for(int i=0;i<12;i++)
        vTextureSlices[count++]=intersection[indices[i]];
}

    glBindBuffer(GL_ARRAY_BUFFER, volumeVBO);
    glBufferSubData(GL_ARRAY_BUFFER, 0,  sizeof(vTextureSlices),
    &(vTextureSlices[0].x));
```

In the rendering function, the appropriate shader is bound. The vertex shader calculates the clip space position by multiplying the object space vertex position (vPosition) with the combined model view projection (MVP) matrix. It also calculates the 3D texture coordinates (vUV) for the volume data. Since we render a unit cube, the minimum vertex position will be (-0.5,-0.5,-0.5) and the maximum vertex position will be (0.5,0.5,0.5). Since our 3D texture lookup requires coordinates from (0,0,0) to (1,1,1), we add (0.5,0.5,0.5) to the object space vertex position to obtain the correct 3D texture coordinates.

```
    smooth out vec3 vUV;
    void main() {
        gl_Position = MVP*vec4(vVertex.xyz,1);
        vUV = vVertex + vec3(0.5);
    }
```

The fragment shader then uses the 3D texture coordinates to sample the volume data (which is now accessed through a new sampler type sampler3D for 3D textures) to display the density. At the time of creation of the 3D texture, we specified the internal format as GL_RED (the third parameter of the glTexImage3D function). Therefore, we can now access our densities through the red channel of the texture sampler. To get a shader of grey, we set the same value for green, blue, and alpha channels as well.

```
    smooth in vec3 vUV;
    uniform sampler3D volume;
    void main(void) {

        vFragColor = texture(volume, vUV).rrrr;
    }
```

In previous OpenGL versions, we would store the volume densities in a special internal format GL_INTENSITY. This is deprecated in the OpenGL3.3 core profile. So now we have to use GL_RED, GL_GREEN, GL_BLUE, or GL_ALPHA internal formats.

There's more...

The output from the demo application for this recipe volume renders the engine dataset using 3D texture slicing. In the demo code, we can change the number of slices by pressing the + and - keys.

We now show how we obtain the result by showing an image containing successive 3D texture slicing images in the same viewing direction from **8 slices** all the way to **256 slices**. The results are given in the following screenshot. The wireframe view is shown in the top row, whereas the alpha-blended result is shown in the bottom row.

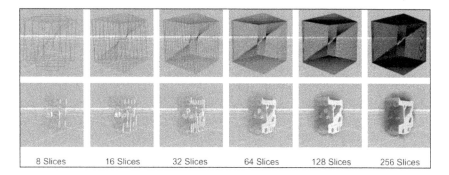

| 8 Slices | 16 Slices | 32 Slices | 64 Slices | 128 Slices | 256 Slices |

As can be seen, increasing the number of slices improves the volume rendering result. When the total number of slices goes beyond 256 slices, we do not see a significant difference in the rendering result. However, we begin to see a sharp decrease in performance as we increase the total number of slices beyond 350. This is because more geometry is transferred to the GPU and that reduces performance.

Note that we can see the black halo around the volume dataset. This is due to acquisition artifacts, for example, noise or air that was stored during scanning of the engine dataset. These kinds of artifacts can be removed by either applying a transfer function to remove the unwanted densities or simply removing the unwanted densities in the fragment shader as we will do in the *Implementing volumetric lighting using half-angle slicing* recipe later.

See also

▸ The *3.5.2 Viewport-Aligned Slices* section in *Chapter 3, GPU-based Volume Rendering, Real-time Volume Graphics, AK Peters/CRC Press*, page numbers 73 to 79

Implementing volume rendering using single-pass GPU ray casting

In this recipe, we will implement volume rendering using single-pass GPU ray casting. There are two basic approaches for doing GPU ray casting: the multi-pass approach and the single-pass approach. Both of these approaches differ in how they estimate the ray marching direction vectors. The single-pass approach uses a single fragment shader. The steps described here can be understood easily from the following diagram:

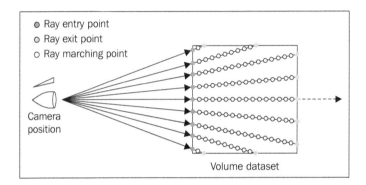

First, the camera ray direction is calculated by subtracting the vertex positions from the camera position. This gives the ray marching direction. The initial ray position (that is, the ray entry position) is the vertex position. Then based on the ray step size, the initial ray position is advanced in the ray direction using a loop. The volume dataset is then sampled at this position to obtain the density value. This process is continued forward advancing the current ray position until either the ray exits the volume dataset or the alpha value of the color is completely saturated.

The obtained samples during the ray traversal are composited using the current ray function. If the average ray function is used, all of the sample densities are added and then divided by the total number of samples. Similarly, in case of front-to-back alpha compositing, the alpha value of the current sample is multiplied by the accumulated color alpha value and the product is subtracted from the current density. This gives the alpha for the previous densities. This alpha value is then added to the accumulated color alpha. In addition, it is multiplied by the current density and then the obtained color is added to the accumulated color. The accumulated color is then returned as the final fragment color.

Getting ready

The code for this recipe is contained in the `Chapter7/GPURaycasting` folder.

How to do it...

The steps required to implement single-pass GPU ray casting are as follows:

1. Load the volume data from the file into a 3D OpenGL texture as in the previous recipe. Refer to the `LoadVolume` function in `Chapter7/GPURaycasting/main.cpp` for details.

2. Set up a vertex array object and a vertex buffer object to render a unit cube as follows:

```
glGenVertexArrays(1, &cubeVAOID);
glGenBuffers(1, &cubeVBOID);
glGenBuffers(1, &cubeIndicesID);
glm::vec3 vertices[8]={   glm::vec3(-0.5f,-0.5f,-0.5f), glm::vec3(
0.5f,-0.5f,-0.5f),glm::vec3( 0.5f, 0.5f,-0.5f), glm::vec3(-0.5f,
0.5f,-0.5f),glm::vec3(-0.5f,-0.5f, 0.5f), glm::vec3( 0.5f,-0.5f,
0.5f),glm::vec3( 0.5f, 0.5f, 0.5f), glm::vec3(-0.5f, 0.5f, 0.5f)};

GLushort cubeIndices[36]={0,5,4,5,0,1,3,7,6,3,6,2,7,4,6,6,4,5,2,1,
3,3,1,0,3,0,7,7,0,4,6,5,2,2,5,1};

glBindVertexArray(cubeVAOID);
glBindBuffer (GL_ARRAY_BUFFER, cubeVBOID);
glBufferData (GL_ARRAY_BUFFER, sizeof(vertices), &(vertices[0].x),
GL_STATIC_DRAW);
glEnableVertexAttribArray(0);
glVertexAttribPointer(0, 3, GL_FLOAT, GL_FALSE,0,0);

glBindBuffer (GL_ELEMENT_ARRAY_BUFFER, cubeIndicesID);
glBufferData (GL_ELEMENT_ARRAY_BUFFER, sizeof(cubeIndices),
&cubeIndices[0], GL_STATIC_DRAW);
glBindVertexArray(0);
```

3. In the render function, set the ray casting vertex and fragment shaders (`Chapter7/GPURaycasting/shaders/raycaster.(vert,frag)`) and then render the unit cube.

```
glEnable(GL_BLEND);
glBindVertexArray(cubeVAOID);
shader.Use();
glUniformMatrix4fv(shader("MVP"), 1, GL_FALSE, glm::value_
ptr(MVP));
```

```
glUniform3fv(shader("camPos"), 1, &(camPos.x));
glDrawElements(GL_TRIANGLES, 36, GL_UNSIGNED_SHORT, 0);
shader.UnUse();
glDisable(GL_BLEND);
```

4. From the vertex shader, in addition to the clip space position, output the 3D texture coordinates for lookup in the fragment shader. We simply offset the object space vertex positions.

```
smooth out vec3 vUV;
void main()
{
  gl_Position = MVP*vec4(vVertex.xyz,1);
    vUV = vVertex + vec3(0.5);
}
```

5. In the fragment shader, use the camera position and the 3D texture coordinates to run a loop in the current viewing direction. Terminate the loop if the current sample position is outside the volume or the alpha value of the accumulated color is saturated.

```
vec3 dataPos = vUV;
vec3 geomDir = normalize((vUV-vec3(0.5)) - camPos);
vec3 dirStep = geomDir * step_size;
bool stop = false;
for (int i = 0; i < MAX_SAMPLES; i++) {
  // advance ray by step
  dataPos = dataPos + dirStep;
  // stop condition
  stop=dot(sign(dataPos-texMin),sign(texMax-dataPos)) < 3.0;
  if (stop)
      break;
```

6. Composite the current sample value obtained from the volume using an appropriate operator and finally return the composited color.

```
float sample = texture(volume, dataPos).r;

float prev_alpha = sample - (sample * vFragColor.a);
vFragColor.rgb = prev_alpha * vec3(sample) + vFragColor.rgb;
vFragColor.a += prev_alpha;
//early ray termination
if( vFragColor.a>0.99)
break;
    }
```

How it works...

There are two parts of this recipe. The first step is the generation and rendering of the cube geometry for invoking the fragment shader. Note that we could also use a full-screen quad for doing this as we did for the GPU ray tracing recipe but for volumetric datasets it is more efficient to just render the unit cube. The second step is carried out in the shaders.

In the vertex shader (`Chapter7/GPURaycasting/shaders/raycast.vert`), the 3D texture coordinates are estimated using the per-vertex position of the unit cube. Since the unit cube is at origin, we add `vec(0.5)` to the position to bring the 3D texture coordinates to the 0 to 1 range.

```
#version 330 core
layout(location = 0) in vec3 vVertex;
uniform mat4 MVP;
smooth out vec3 vUV;
void main() {
    gl_Position = MVP*vec4(vVertex.xyz,1);
    vUV = vVertex + vec3(0.5);
}
```

Next, the fragment shader uses the 3D texture coordinates and the eye position to estimate the ray marching directions. A loop is then run in the fragment shader (as shown in step 5) that marches through the volume dataset and composites the obtained sample values using the current compositing scheme. This process is continued until the ray exits the volume or the alpha value of the accumulated color is fully saturated.

The `texMin` and `texMax` constants have a value of `vec3(-1,-1,-1)` and `vec3(1,1,1)` respectively. To determine if the data value is outside the volume data, we use the sign function. The sign function returns `-1` if the value is less than `0`, `0` if the value is equal to `0`, and `1` if value is greater than `0`. Hence, the sign function for the `(sign(dataPos-texMin)` and `sign (texMax-dataPos))` calculation will give us `vec3(1,1,1)` at the possible minimum and maximum position. When we do a dot product between two `vec3(1,1,1)`, we get the answer `3`. So to be within the dataset limits, the dot product will return a value less than `3`. If it is greater than `3`, we are already out of the volume dataset.

There's more...

The demo application for this demo shows the engine dataset rendered using single-pass GPU ray casting. The camera position can be changed using the left-mouse button and the view can be zoomed in/out by using the middle-mouse button.

See also

▸ *Chapter 7, GPU-based Ray Casting, Real-time Volume Graphics, AK Peters/CRC Press*, page numbers 163 to 184

▸ Single pass Raycasting at The Little Grasshopper, `http://prideout.net/blog/?p=64`

Implementing pseudo-isosurface rendering in single-pass GPU ray casting

We will now implement pseudo-isosurface rendering in single-pass GPU ray casting. While much of the setup is the same as for the single-pass GPU ray casting, the difference will be in the compositing step in the ray casting fragment shader. In this shader, we will try to find the given isosurface. If it is actually found, we estimate the normal at the sampling point to carry out the lighting calculation for the isosurface.

In the pseudocode, the pseudo-isosurface rendering in single-pass ray casting can be elaborated as follows:

```
Get camera ray direction and ray position
Get the ray step amount
For each sample along the ray direction
```

```
        Get sample value at current ray position as sample1
        Get another sample value at (ray position+step) as sample2
        If (sample1-isoValue) < 0 and (sample2-isoValue)>0
            Refine the intersection position using Bisection method
            Get the gradient at the refined position
            Apply Phong illumination at the refined position
            Assign current colour as fragment colour
            Break
        End If
    End For
```

Getting ready

The code for this recipe is in the `Chapter7/GPURaycastingIsosurface` folder. We will be starting from the single-pass GPU ray casting recipe using the exact same application side code.

How to do it...

Let us start the recipe by following these simple steps:

1. Load the volume data from file into a 3D OpenGL texture as in the previous recipe. Refer to the `LoadVolume` function in `Chapter7/GPURaycasting/main.cpp` for details.

2. Set up a vertex array object and a vertex buffer object to render a unit cube as in the previous recipe.

3. In the render function, set the ray casting vertex and fragment shaders (`Chapter7/GPURaycasting/shaders/raycasting` (vert,frag)) and then render the unit cube.

   ```
   glEnable(GL_BLEND);
   glBindVertexArray(cubeVAOID);
   shader.Use();
   glUniformMatrix4fv(shader("MVP"), 1, GL_FALSE, glm::value_
   ptr(MVP));
   glUniform3fv(shader("camPos"), 1, &(camPos.x));
   glDrawElements(GL_TRIANGLES, 36, GL_UNSIGNED_SHORT, 0);
   shader.UnUse();
   glDisable(GL_BLEND);
   ```

4. From the vertex shader, in addition to the clip-space position, output the 3D texture coordinates for lookup in the fragment shader. We simply offset the object space vertex positions as follows:

```
smooth out vec3 vUV;
void main()
{
  gl_Position = MVP*vec4(vVertex.xyz,1);
  vUV = vVertex + vec3(0.5);
}
```

5. In the fragment shader, use the camera position and the 3D texture coordinates to run a loop in the current viewing direction. The loop is terminated if the current sample position is outside the volume or the alpha value of the accumulated color is saturated.

```
vec3 dataPos = vUV;
vec3 geomDir = normalize((vUV-vec3(0.5)) - camPos);
vec3 dirStep = geomDir * step_size;
bool stop = false;
for (int i = 0; i < MAX_SAMPLES; i++) {
  // advance ray by step
  dataPos = dataPos + dirStep;
  // stop condition
  stop=dot(sign(dataPos-texMin),sign(texMax-dataPos)) < 3.0;
  if (stop)
      break;
```

6. For isosurface estimation, we take two sample values to find the zero crossing of the isofunction inside the volume dataset. If there is a zero crossing, we find the exact intersection point using bisection based refinement. Finally, we use the Phong illumination model to shade the isosurface assuming that the light is located at the camera position.

```
float sample=texture(volume, dataPos).r;
float sample2=texture(volume, dataPos+dirStep).r;
if( (sample -isoValue) < 0  && (sample2-isoValue) >= 0.0)
{
vec3 xN = dataPos;
vec3 xF = dataPos+dirStep;
vec3 tc = Bisection(xN, xF, isoValue);
vec3 N = GetGradient(tc);
vec3 V = -geomDir;
vec3 L =  V;
vFragColor =  PhongLighting(L,N,V,250,  vec3(0.5));
break;
}
}
```

The `Bisection` function is defined as follows:

```
vec3 Bisection(vec3 left, vec3 right , float iso) {
    for(int i=0;i<4;i++) {
        vec3 midpoint = (right + left) * 0.5;
        float cM = texture(volume, midpoint).x ;
        if(cM < iso)
          left = midpoint;
        else
          right = midpoint;
    }
    return vec3(right + left) * 0.5;
}
```

The `Bisection` function takes the two samples between which the given sample value lies. It then runs a loop. In each step, it calculates the midpoint of the two sample points and checks the density value at the midpoint to the given isovalue. If it is less, the left sample point is swapped with the mid position otherwise, the right sample point is swapped. This helps to reduce the search space quickly. The process is repeated and finally, the midpoint between the left sample point and right sample point is returned. The `Gradient` function estimates the gradient of the volume density using center finite difference approximation.

```
vec3 GetGradient(vec3 uvw)
{
    vec3 s1, s2;
    //Using center finite difference
    s1.x = texture(volume, uvw-vec3(DELTA,0.0,0.0)).x ;
    s2.x = texture(volume, uvw+vec3(DELTA,0.0,0.0)).x ;

    s1.y = texture(volume, uvw-vec3(0.0,DELTA,0.0)).x ;
    s2.y = texture(volume, uvw+vec3(0.0,DELTA,0.0)).x ;

    s1.z = texture(volume, uvw-vec3(0.0,0.0,DELTA)).x ;
    s2.z = texture(volume, uvw+vec3(0.0,0.0,DELTA)).x ;

    return normalize((s1-s2)/2.0);
}
```

How it works...

While bulk of the code is similar to the single-pass GPU ray casting recipe. There is a major difference in the ray marching loop. In case of isosurface rendering, we do not use compositing. Instead, we find the zero crossing of the volume dataset isofunction by sampling two consecutive samples. This is well illustrated with the following diagram. If there is a zero crossing, we refine the detected isosurface by using bisection-based refinement.

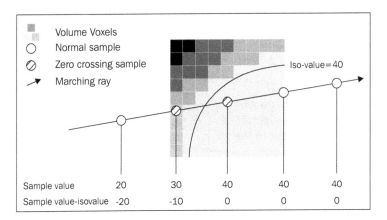

Sample value		20	30	40	40	40
Sample value-isovalue	-20	-10	0	0	0

Next, we use the Phong illumination model to render the shaded isosurface and break out from the ray marching loop. Note that the method shown here renders the nearest isosurface. If we want to render all the surfaces with the given isovalue, we should remove this break statement.

There's more...

The demo application implementing this recipe shows the engine dataset rendered using the pseudo-isosurface rendering mode. When run, the output is as shown in the following screenshot:

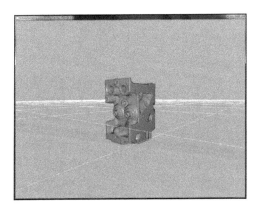

See also

▸ Advanced Illumination Techniques for GPU-based Volume Rendering, SIGGRAPH 2008 course notes, Available online at `http://www.voreen.org/files/sa08-coursenotes_1.pdf`

Implementing volume rendering using splatting

In this recipe, we will implement splatting on the GPU. The splatting algorithm converts the voxel representation into splats by convolving them with a Gaussian kernel. The Gaussian smoothing kernel reduces high frequencies and smoothes out edges giving a smoothed rendered output.

Getting ready

The code for this recipe is in the `Chapter7/Splatting` directory.

How to do it...

Let us start this recipe by following these simple steps:

1. Load the 3D volume data and store it into an array.

```
std::ifstream infile(filename.c_str(), std::ios_base::binary);
if(infile.good()) {
pVolume = new GLubyte[XDIM*YDIM*ZDIM];
infile.read(reinterpret_cast<char*>(pVolume), XDIM*YDIM*ZDIM*sizeo
f(GLubyte));
infile.close();
return true;
} else {
return false;
}
```

2. Depending on the sampling box size, run three loops to iterate through the entire volume voxel by voxel.

```
vertices.clear();
int dx = XDIM/X_SAMPLING_DIST;
int dy = YDIM/Y_SAMPLING_DIST;
int dz = ZDIM/Z_SAMPLING_DIST;
scale = glm::vec3(dx,dy,dz);
for(int z=0;z<ZDIM;z+=dz) {
```

```
for(int y=0;y<YDIM;y+=dy) {
for(int x=0;x<XDIM;x+=dx) {
SampleVoxel(x,y,z);
}
}
}
```

The `SampleVoxel` function is defined in the `VolumeSplatter` class as follows:

```
void VolumeSplatter::SampleVoxel(const int x, const int y,
                                   const int z) {
  GLubyte data = SampleVolume(x, y, z);
  if(data>isoValue) {
    Vertex v;
    v.pos.x = x;
    v.pos.y = y;
    v.pos.z = z;
    v.normal = GetNormal(x, y, z);
    v.pos *= invDim;
    vertices.push_back(v);

  }
}
```

3. In each sampling step, estimate the volume density values at the current voxel. If the value is greater than the given isovalue, store the voxel position and normal into a vertex array.

```
    GLubyte data = SampleVolume(x, y, z);
    if(data>isoValue) {
        Vertex v;
        v.pos.x = x;
        v.pos.y = y;
      v.pos.z = z;
      v.normal = GetNormal(x, y, z);
      v.pos *= invDim;
      vertices.push_back(v);
    }
```

The `SampleVolume` function takes the given sampling point and returns the nearest voxel density. It is defined in the `VolumeSplatter` class as follows:

```
GLubyte VolumeSplatter::SampleVolume(const int x, const int y,
const int z) {
    int index = (x+(y*XDIM)) + z*(XDIM*YDIM);
  if(index<0)
    index = 0;
  if(index >= XDIM*YDIM*ZDIM)
    index = (XDIM*YDIM*ZDIM)-1;
  return pVolume[index];
}
```

4. After the sampling step, pass the generated vertices to a **vertex array object** (**VAO**) containing a **vertex buffer object** (**VBO**).

```
glGenVertexArrays(1, &volumeSplatterVAO);
glGenBuffers(1, &volumeSplatterVBO);
glBindVertexArray(volumeSplatterVAO);
glBindBuffer (GL_ARRAY_BUFFER, volumeSplatterVBO);
glBufferData (GL_ARRAY_BUFFER, splatter->GetTotalVertices()
*sizeof(Vertex), splatter->GetVertexPointer(), GL_STATIC_DRAW);
glEnableVertexAttribArray(0);
glVertexAttribPointer(0, 3, GL_FLOAT, GL_FALSE,sizeof(Vertex),
0);
glEnableVertexAttribArray(1);
glVertexAttribPointer(1, 3, GL_FLOAT, GL_FALSE,sizeof(Vertex),
(const GLvoid*) offsetof(Vertex, normal));
```

5. Set up two FBOs for offscreen rendering. The first FBO (`filterFBOID`) is used for Gaussian smoothing.

```
glGenFramebuffers(1,&filterFBOID);
glBindFramebuffer(GL_FRAMEBUFFER,filterFBOID);
glGenTextures(2, blurTexID);
for(int i=0;i<2;i++) {
  glActiveTexture(GL_TEXTURE1+i);
  glBindTexture(GL_TEXTURE_2D, blurTexID[i]);
    //set texture parameters
    glTexImage2D(GL_TEXTURE_2D,0,GL_RGBA32F,IMAGE_WIDTH,
    IMAGE_HEIGHT,0,GL_RGBA,GL_FLOAT,NULL);
    glFramebufferTexture2D(GL_FRAMEBUFFER,
    GL_COLOR_ATTACHMENT0+i,GL_TEXTURE_2D,blurTexID[i],0);
}
GLenum status = glCheckFramebufferStatus(GL_FRAMEBUFFER);
if(status == GL_FRAMEBUFFER_COMPLETE) {
  cout<<"Filtering FBO setup successful."<<endl;
} else {
  cout<<"Problem in Filtering FBO setup."<<endl;
}
```

6. The second FBO (`fboID`) is used to render the scene so that the smoothing operation can be applied on the rendered output from the first pass. Add a render buffer object to this FBO to enable depth testing.

```
glGenFramebuffers(1,&fboID);
glGenRenderbuffers(1, &rboID);
glGenTextures(1, &texID);
glBindFramebuffer(GL_FRAMEBUFFER,fboID);
glBindRenderbuffer(GL_RENDERBUFFER, rboID);
```

```
glActiveTexture(GL_TEXTURE0);
glBindTexture(GL_TEXTURE_2D, texID);
//set texture parameters
glTexImage2D(GL_TEXTURE_2D,0,GL_RGBA32F,IMAGE_WIDTH,
IMAGE_HEIGHT,0,GL_RGBA,GL_FLOAT,NULL);
glFramebufferTexture2D(GL_FRAMEBUFFER,GL_COLOR_ATTACHMENT0,
GL_TEXTURE_2D, texID, 0);
glFramebufferRenderbuffer(GL_FRAMEBUFFER, GL_DEPTH_ATTACHMENT,
GL_RENDERBUFFER, rboID);
glRenderbufferStorage(GL_RENDERBUFFER, GL_DEPTH_COMPONENT32,
IMAGE_WIDTH, IMAGE_HEIGHT);
status = glCheckFramebufferStatus(GL_FRAMEBUFFER);
if(status == GL_FRAMEBUFFER_COMPLETE) {
    cout<<"Offscreen rendering FBO setup successful."<<endl;
} else {
    cout<<"Problem in offscreen rendering FBO setup."<<endl;
}
```

7. In the render function, first render the point splats to a texture using the first FBO (`fboID`).

```
glBindFramebuffer(GL_FRAMEBUFFER,fboID);
glViewport(0,0, IMAGE_WIDTH, IMAGE_HEIGHT);
glDrawBuffer(GL_COLOR_ATTACHMENT0);
 glClear(GL_COLOR_BUFFER_BIT|GL_DEPTH_BUFFER_BIT);
 glm::mat4 T = glm::translate(glm::mat4(1),
 glm::vec3(-0.5,-0.5,-0.5));
glBindVertexArray(volumeSplatterVAO);
shader.Use();
glUniformMatrix4fv(shader("MV"), 1, GL_FALSE,
 glm::value_ptr(MV*T));
glUniformMatrix3fv(shader("N"), 1, GL_FALSE,
 glm::value_ptr(glm::inverseTranspose(glm::mat3(MV*T))));
glUniformMatrix4fv(shader("P"), 1, GL_FALSE,
 glm::value_ptr(P));
glDrawArrays(GL_POINTS, 0, splatter->GetTotalVertices());
shader.UnUse();
```

The splatting vertex shader (`Chapter7/Splatting/shaders/splatShader.vert`) is defined as follows. It calculates the eye space normal. The splat size is calculated using the volume dimension and the sampling voxel size. This is then written to the `gl_PointSize` variable in the vertex shader.

```
#version 330 core
layout(location = 0) in vec3 vVertex;
```

```
layout(location = 1) in vec3 vNormal;
uniform mat4 MV;
uniform mat3 N;
uniform mat4 P;
smooth out vec3 outNormal;
uniform float splatSize;
void main() {
   vec4 eyeSpaceVertex = MV*vec4(vVertex,1);
   gl_PointSize = 2*splatSize/-eyeSpaceVertex.z;
   gl_Position = P * eyeSpaceVertex;
   outNormal = N*vNormal;
}
```

The splatting fragment shader (`Chapter7/Splatting/shaders/splatShader.frag`) is defined as follows:

```
#version 330 core
layout(location = 0) out vec4 vFragColor;
smooth in vec3 outNormal;
const vec3 L = vec3(0,0,1);
const vec3 V = L;
const vec4 diffuse_color = vec4(0.75,0.5,0.5,1);
const vec4 specular_color = vec4(1);
void main() {
  vec3 N;
  N = normalize(outNormal);
  vec2 P = gl_PointCoord*2.0 - vec2(1.0);
  float mag = dot(P.xy,P.xy);
  if (mag > 1)
    discard;

  float diffuse = max(0, dot(N,L));
   vec3 halfVec = normalize(L+V);
  float specular=pow(max(0, dot(halfVec,N)),400);
   vFragColor = (specular*specular_color) +
                (diffuse*diffuse_color);
   }
```

8. Next, set the filtering FBO and first apply the vertical and then the horizontal Gaussian smoothing pass by drawing a full-screen quad as was done in the Variance shadow mapping recipe in *Chapter 4, Lights and Shadows*.

```
glBindVertexArray(quadVAOID);
glBindFramebuffer(GL_FRAMEBUFFER, filterFBOID);
```

```
glDrawBuffer(GL_COLOR_ATTACHMENT0);
gaussianV_shader.Use();
glDrawElements(GL_TRIANGLES, 6, GL_UNSIGNED_SHORT, 0);
 glDrawBuffer(GL_COLOR_ATTACHMENT1);
gaussianH_shader.Use();
glDrawElements(GL_TRIANGLES, 6, GL_UNSIGNED_SHORT, 0);
```

9. Unbind the filtering FBO, restore the default draw buffer and render the filtered output on the screen.

```
 glBindFramebuffer(GL_FRAMEBUFFER,0);
glDrawBuffer(GL_BACK_LEFT);
glViewport(0,0,WIDTH, HEIGHT);
quadShader.Use();
glDrawElements(GL_TRIANGLES, 6, GL_UNSIGNED_SHORT, 0);
quadShader.UnUse();
glBindVertexArray(0);
```

How it works...

Splatting algorithm works by rendering the voxels of the volume data as Gaussian blobs and projecting them on the screen. To achieve this, we first estimate the candidate voxels from the volume dataset by traversing through the entire volume dataset voxel by voxel for the given isovalue. If we have the appropriate voxel, we store its normal and position into a vertex array. For convenience, we wrap all of this functionality into the VolumeSplatter class.

We first create a new instance of the VolumeSplatter class. Next, we set the volume dimensions and then load the volume data. Next, we specify the target isovalue and the number of sampling voxels to use. Finally, we call the VolumeSplatter::SplatVolume function that traverses the whole volume voxel by voxel.

```
splatter = new VolumeSplatter();
splatter->SetVolumeDimensions(256,256,256);
splatter->LoadVolume(volume_file);
splatter->SetIsosurfaceValue(40);
splatter->SetNumSamplingVoxels(64,64,64);
std::cout<<"Generating point splats ...";
splatter->SplatVolume();
std::cout<<"Done."<<std::endl;
```

The `splatter` stores the vertices and normals into a vertex array. We then generate the vertex buffer object from this array. In the rendering function, we first draw the entire splat dataset in a single-pass into an offscreen render target. This is done so that we can filter it using separable Gaussian convolution filters. Finally, the filtered output is displayed on a full-screen quad.

The splatting vertex shader (`Chapter7/Splatting/shaders/splatShader.vert`) calculates the point size on screen based on the depth of the splat. In order to achieve this in the vertex shader, we have to enable the `GL_VERTEX_PROGRAM_POINT_SIZE` state that is, `glEnable(GL_VERTEX_PROGRAM_POINT_SIZE)`. The vertex shader also outputs the splat normals in eye space.

```
vec4 eyeSpaceVertex = MV*vec4(vVertex,1);
gl_PointSize = 2*splatSize/-eyeSpaceVertex.z;
gl_Position = P * eyeSpaceVertex;
outNormal = N*vNormal;
```

Since the default point sprite renders as a screen-aligned quad, in the fragment shader (`Chapter7/Splatting/shaders/splatShader.frag`), we discard all fragments that are outside the radius of the splat at the current splat position.

```
vec3 N;
N = normalize(outNormal);
vec2 P = gl_PointCoord*2.0 - vec2(1.0);
float mag = dot(P.xy,P.xy);
if (mag > 1) discard;
```

Finally, we estimate the diffuse and specular components and output the current fragment color using the eye space normal of the splat.

```
float diffuse = max(0, dot(N,L));
vec3 halfVec = normalize(L+V);
float specular = pow(max(0, dot(halfVec,N)),400);
vFragColor =  (specular*specular_color) + (diffuse*diffuse_color);
```

There's more...

The demo application implementing this recipe renders the engine dataset as in the previous recipes, as shown in the following screenshot. Note the output appears blurred due to Gaussian smoothing of the splats.

This recipe gave us an overview on the splatting algorithm. Our brute force approach in this recipe was to iterate through all of the voxels. For large datasets, we have to employ an acceleration structure, like an octree, to quickly identify voxels with densities and cull unnecessary voxels.

See also

▶ The Qsplat project: `http://graphics.stanford.edu/software/qsplat/`

▶ Splatting research at ETH Zurich: (`http://graphics.ethz.ch/research/past_projects/surfels/surfacesplatting/`)

Implementing transfer function for volume classification

In this recipe, we will implement classification to the 3D texture slicing presented before. We will generate a lookup table to add specific colors to specific densities. This is accomplished by generating a 1D texture that is looked up in the fragment shader with the current volume density. The returned color is then used as the color of the current fragment. Apart from the setup of the transfer function data, all the other content remains the same as in the 3D texture slicing recipe. Note that the classification method is not limited to 3D texture slicing, it can be applied to any volume rendering algorithm.

Getting ready

The code for this recipe is in the `Chapter7/3DTextureSlicingClassification` directory.

How to do it...

Let us start this recipe by following these simple steps:

1. Load the volume data and setup the texture slicing as in the *Implementing volume rendering using 3D texture slicing* recipe.

2. Create a 1D texture that will be our transfer function texture for color lookup. We create a set of color values and then interpolate them on the fly. Refer to `LoadTransferFunction` in `Chapter7/3DTextureSlicingClassification/main.cpp`.

```
float pData[256][4];
int indices[9];
for(int i=0;i<9;i++) {
int index = i*28;
pData[index][0] = jet_values[i].x;
pData[index][1] = jet_values[i].y;
pData[index][2] = jet_values[i].z;
pData[index][3] = jet_values[i].w;
indices[i] = index;
}
for(int j=0;j<9-1;j++)
{
float dDataR = (pData[indices[j+1]][0] - pData[indices[j]][0]);
float dDataG = (pData[indices[j+1]][1] - pData[indices[j]][1]);
float dDataB = (pData[indices[j+1]][2] - pData[indices[j]][2]);
float dDataA = (pData[indices[j+1]][3] - pData[indices[j]][3]);
int dIndex = indices[j+1]-indices[j];
float dDataIncR = dDataR/float(dIndex);
float dDataIncG = dDataG/float(dIndex);
float dDataIncB = dDataB/float(dIndex);
float dDataIncA = dDataA/float(dIndex);
for(int i=indices[j]+1;i<indices[j+1];i++)
{
    pData[i][0] = (pData[i-1][0] + dDataIncR);
    pData[i][1] = (pData[i-1][1] + dDataIncG);
    pData[i][2] = (pData[i-1][2] + dDataIncB);
    pData[i][3] = (pData[i-1][3] + dDataIncA);
}
}
```

3. Generate a 1D OpenGL texture from the interpolated lookup data from step 1. We bind this texture to texture unit 1 (`GL_TEXTURE1`);

```
glGenTextures(1, &tfTexID);
glActiveTexture(GL_TEXTURE1);
glBindTexture(GL_TEXTURE_1D, tfTexID);
glTexParameteri(GL_TEXTURE_1D, GL_TEXTURE_WRAP_S, GL_REPEAT);
glTexParameteri(GL_TEXTURE_1D, GL_TEXTURE_MAG_FILTER, GL_LINEAR);
glTexParameteri(GL_TEXTURE_1D, GL_TEXTURE_MIN_FILTER, GL_LINEAR);
glTexImage1D(GL_TEXTURE_1D,0,GL_RGBA,256,0,GL_RGBA,GL_
FLOAT,pData);
```

4. In the fragment shader, add a new sampler for the transfer function lookup table. Since we now have two textures, we bind the volume data to texture unit 0 (`GL_TEXTURE0`) and the transfer function texture to texture unit 1 (`GL_TEXTURE1`).

```
shader.LoadFromFile(GL_VERTEX_SHADER, "shaders/textureSlicer.
vert");
shader.LoadFromFile(GL_FRAGMENT_SHADER, "shaders/textureSlicer.
frag");
shader.CreateAndLinkProgram();
shader.Use();
  shader.AddAttribute("vVertex");
  shader.AddUniform("MVP");
  shader.AddUniform("volume");
  shader.AddUniform("lut");
  glUniform1i(shader("volume"),0);
  glUniform1i(shader("lut"),1);
shader.UnUse();
```

5. Finally, in the fragment shader, instead of directly returning the current volume density value, we lookup the density value in the transfer function and return the appropriate color value. Refer to `Chapter7/3DTextureSlicingClassificati on/shaders/textureSlicer.frag` for details.

```
uniform sampler3D volume;
uniform sampler1D lut;
void main(void) {
vFragColor = texture(lut, texture(volume, vUV).r);
}
```

How it works...

There are two parts of this recipe: the generation of the transfer function texture and the lookup of this texture in the fragment shader. Both of these steps are relatively straightforward to understand. For generation of the transfer function texture, we first create a simple array of possible colors called `jet_values`, which is defined globally as follows:

```
const glm::vec4 jet_values[9]={glm::vec4(0,0,0.5,0),
              glm::vec4(0,0,1,0.1),
              glm::vec4(0,0.5,1,0.3),
              glm::vec4(0,1,1,0.5),
              glm::vec4(0.5,1,0.5,0.75),
              glm::vec4(1,1,0,0.8),
              glm::vec4(1,0.5,0,0.6),
              glm::vec4(1,0,0,0.5),
              glm::vec4(0.5,0,0,0.0)};
```

At the time of texture creation, we first reorganize this data into a 256 element array by interpolation. Then, we find the differences among adjacent values and then increment the current value using the difference. This is carried out for all items in the `jet_values` array. Once the data is ready, it is stored in a 1D texture. This is then passed to the fragment shader using another sampler object. In the fragment shader, the density value of the sample that is processed is used as an index into the transfer function texture. Finally, the color obtained from the transfer function texture is stored as the current fragment color.

There's more...

The demo application for this recipe renders the engine dataset as in the 3D texture slicing recipe but now the rendered output is colored using a transfer function. The output from the demo application is displayed in the following screenshot:

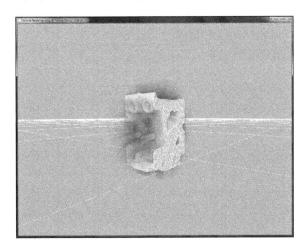

> ▸ *Chapter 4, Transfer Functions*, and *Chapter 10, Transfer Functions Reloaded*, in *Real-time Volume Graphics, AK Peters/CRC Press*.

Implementing polygonal isosurface extraction using the Marching Tetrahedra algorithm

In the *Implementing pseudo-isosurface rendering in single-pass GPU ray casting* recipe, we implemented pseudo-isosurface rendering in single-pass GPU ray casting. However, these isosurfaces are not composed of triangles; so it is not possible for us to uniquely address individual isosurface regions easily to mark different areas in the volume dataset. This can be achieved by doing an isosurface extraction process for a specific isovalue by traversing the entire volume dataset. This method is known as the **Marching Tetrahedra** (**MT**) algorithm. This algorithm traverses the whole volume dataset and tries to fit a specific polygon based on the intersection criterion. This process is repeated for the whole volume and finally, we obtain the polygonal mesh from the volume dataset.

Getting ready

The code for this recipe is in the `Chapter7/MarchingTetrahedra` directory. For convenience, we will wrap the Marching Tetrahedra algorithm in a simple class called `TetrahedraMarcher`.

How to do it...

Let us start this recipe by following these simple steps:

1. Load the 3D volume data and store it into an array:

```
std::ifstream infile(filename.c_str(), std::ios_base::binary);
if(infile.good()) {
pVolume = new GLubyte[XDIM*YDIM*ZDIM];
infile.read(reinterpret_cast<char*>(pVolume), XDIM*YDIM*ZDIM*sizeo
f(GLubyte));
infile.close();
return true;
} else {
return false;
}
```

2. Depending on the sampling box size, run three loops to iterate through the entire volume voxel by voxel:

```
vertices.clear();
int dx = XDIM/X_SAMPLING_DIST;
int dy = YDIM/Y_SAMPLING_DIST;
int dz = ZDIM/Z_SAMPLING_DIST;
glm::vec3 scale = glm::vec3(dx,dy,dz);
for(int z=0;z<ZDIM;z+=dz) {
for(int y=0;y<YDIM;y+=dy) {
for(int x=0;x<XDIM;x+=dx) {
SampleVoxel(x,y,z, scale);
}
}
}
```

3. In each sampling step, estimate the volume density values at the eight corners of the sampling box:

```
GLubyte cubeCornerValues[8];
for( i = 0; i < 8; i++) {
  cubeCornerValues[i] = SampleVolume(
    x + (int)(a2fVertexOffset[i][0] *scale.x),
    y + (int)(a2fVertexOffset[i][1]*scale.y),
    z + (int)(a2fVertexOffset[i][2]*scale.z));
}
```

4. Estimate an edge flag value to identify the matching tetrahedra case based on the given isovalue:

```
int flagIndex = 0;
for( i= 0; i<8; i++) {
  if(cubeCornerValues[i]<= isoValue)
        flagIndex |= 1<<i;
}
    edgeFlags = aiCubeEdgeFlags[flagIndex];
```

5. Use the lookup tables (`a2iEdgeConnection`) to find the correct edges for the case and then use the offset table (`a2fVertexOffset`) to find the edge vertices and normals. These tables are defined in the `Tables.h` header in the `Chapter7/MarchingTetrahedra/` directory.

```
    for(i = 0; i < 12; i++)
    {
      if(edgeFlags & (1<<i))
       {
            float offset = GetOffset(cubeCornerValues[
            a2iEdgeConnection[i][0] ],
```

```
            cubeCornerValues [ a2iEdgeConnection[i][1] ]);
            edgeVertices[i].x = x + (a2fVertexOffset[
            a2iEdgeConnection[i][0] ][0] + offset *
            a2fEdgeDirection[i][0])*scale.x ;
            edgeVertices[i].y = y + (a2fVertexOffset[
            a2iEdgeConnection[i][0] ][1] + offset *
            a2fEdgeDirection[i][1])*scale.y ;
            edgeVertices[i].z = z + (a2fVertexOffset[
            a2iEdgeConnection[i][0] ][2] + offset *
            a2fEdgeDirection[i][2])*scale.z ;
            edgeNormals[i] = GetNormal( (int)edgeVertices[i].x ,
            (int)edgeVertices[i].y ,  (int)edgeVertices[i].z  );
        }
    }
```

6. Finally, loop through the triangle connectivity table to connect the correct vertices and normals for the given case.

```
for(i = 0; i< 5; i++) {
  if(a2iTriangleConnectionTable[flagIndex][3*i] < 0)
    break;
   for(int j= 0; j< 3; j++) {
      int vertex = a2iTriangleConnectionTable
                   [flagIndex][3*i+j];
   Vertex v;
   v.normal = (edgeNormals[vertex]);
   v.pos = (edgeVertices[vertex])*invDim;
   vertices.push_back(v);
  }
 }
```

7. After the marcher is finished, we pass the generated vertices to a vertex array object containing a vertex buffer object:

```
glGenVertexArrays(1, &volumeMarcherVAO);
glGenBuffers(1, &volumeMarcherVBO);
glBindVertexArray(volumeMarcherVAO);
glBindBuffer (GL_ARRAY_BUFFER, volumeMarcherVBO);
glBufferData (GL_ARRAY_BUFFER, marcher-> GetTotalVertices()*sizeof
(Vertex), marcher-> GetVertexPointer(), GL_STATIC_DRAW);
glEnableVertexAttribArray(0);
glVertexAttribPointer(0, 3, GL_FLOAT, GL_FALSE,sizeof(Vertex),0);
glEnableVertexAttribArray(1);
glVertexAttribPointer(1, 3, GL_FLOAT, GL_
FALSE,sizeof(Vertex),(const GLvoid*)offsetof(Vertex, normal)));
```

8. For rendering of the generated geometry, we bind the Marching Tetrahedra VAO, bind our shader and then render the triangles. For this recipe, we output the per-vertex normals as color.

```
glBindVertexArray(volumeMarcherVAO);
shader.Use();
glUniformMatrix4fv(shader("MVP"),1,GL_FALSE,
 glm::value_ptr(MVP*T));
glDrawArrays(GL_TRIANGLES, 0, marcher->GetTotalVertices());
shader.UnUse();
```

How it works...

For convenience, we wrap the entire recipe in a reusable class called `TetrahedraMarcher`. Marching Tetrahedra, as the name suggests, marches a sampling box throughout the whole volume dataset. To give a bird's eye view there are several cases to consider based on the distribution of density values at the vertices of the sampling cube. Based on the sampling values at the eight corners and the given isovalue, a flag index is generated. This flag index gives us the edge flag by a lookup in a table. This edge flag is then used in an edge lookup table, which is predefined for all possible edge configurations of the marching tetrahedron. The edge connection table is then used to find the appropriate offset for the corner values of the sampling box. These offsets are then used to obtain the edge vertices and normals for the given tetrahedral case. Once the list of edge vertices and normals are estimated, the triangle connectivity is obtained based on the given flag index.

Now we will detail the steps in the Marching Tetrahedra algorithm. First, the flag index is obtained by iterating through all eight sampling cube vertices and comparing the density value at the vertex location with the given isovalue as shown in the following code. The flag index is then used to retrieve the edge flags from the looktup table (`aiCubeEdgeFlags`).

```
flagIndex = 0;
for( i= 0; i<8; i++)  {
    if(cubeCornerValues[i]  <= isoValue)
        flagIndex |= 1<<i;
}
edgeFlags = aiCubeEdgeFlags[flagIndex];
```

The vertices and normals for the given index are stored in a local array by looking up the edge connection table (`a2iEdgeConnection`).

```
for(i = 0; i < 12; i++) {
   if(edgeFlags & (1<<i)) {
        float offset = GetOffset(cubeCornerValues[
                    a2iEdgeConnection[i][0] ], cubeCornerValues[
                    a2iEdgeConnection[i][1] ]);
        edgeVertices[i].x = x + (a2fVertexOffset[
                    a2iEdgeConnection[i][0] ][0]  + offset *
```

```
                           a2fEdgeDirection[i][0])*scale.x ;

        edgeVertices[i].y = y + (a2fVertexOffset[
                    a2iEdgeConnection[i][0] ][1] + offset *
                    a2fEdgeDirection[i][1])*scale.y ;
        edgeVertices[i].z = z + (a2fVertexOffset[
                        a2iEdgeConnection[i][0] ][2]  +  offset *
                        a2fEdgeDirection[i][2])*scale.z ;
    edgeNormals[i] = GetNormal( (int)edgeVertices[i].x ,
                                (int)edgeVertices[i].y ,
                                (int)edgeVertices[i].z  );

    }
}
```

Finally, the triangle connectivity table (`a2iTriangleConnectionTable`) is used to obtain the proper vertex and normal ordering and these attributes are then stored into a vectors.

```
for(i = 0; i< 5; i++) {
    if(a2iTriangleConnectionTable[flagIndex][3*i] < 0)
        break;
    for(int j= 0; j< 3; j++) {
        int vertex = a2iTriangleConnectionTable[flagIndex][3*i+j];
        Vertex v;
        v.normal = (edgeNormals[vertex]);
        v.pos = (edgeVertices[vertex])*invDim;
        vertices.push_back(v);
    }
}
```

After the Marching Tetrahedra code is processed, we store the generated vertices and normals in a buffer object. In the rendering code, we bind the appropriate vertex array object, bind our shader and then draw the triangles. The fragment shader for this recipe outputs the per-vertex normals as colors.

```
#version 330 core
layout(location = 0) out vec4 vFragColor;
smooth in vec3 outNormal;
void main() {
    vFragColor = vec4(outNormal,1);
}
```

There's more...

The demo application for this recipe renders the engine dataset as shown in the following screenshot. The fragment shader renders the isosurface normals as color.

Pressing the *W* key toggles the wireframe display, which shows the underlying isosurface polygons for isovalue of 40 as shown in the following screenshot:

While in this recipe, we focused on the Marching Tetrahedra algorithm. There is another, more robust method of triangulation called **Marching Cubes**, which gives a more robust polygonisation as compared to the Marching Tetrahedra algorithm.

▶ *Polygonising a scalar field*, Paul Bourke: `http://paulbourke.net/geometry/polygonise/`

▶ Volume Rendering: Marching Cubes Algorithm, `http://cns-alumni.bu.edu/~lavanya/Graphics/cs580/p5/web-page/p5.html`

▶ An implementation of Marching Cubes and Marching Tetrahedra Algorithms, `http://www.siafoo.net/snippet/100`

Implementing volumetric lighting using the half-angle slicing

In this recipe, we will implement volumetric lighting using the half-angle slicing technique. Instead of slicing the volume perpendicular to the viewing direction, the slicing direction is set between the light and the view direction vectors. This enables us to simulate light absorption slice by slice.

Getting ready

The code for this recipe is in the `Chapter7/HalfAngleSlicing` directory. As the name suggests, this recipe will build up on the 3D texture slicing code.

How to do it...

Let us start this recipe by following these simple steps:

1. Setup offscreen rendering using one FBO with two attachments: one for offscreen rendering of the light buffer and the other for offscreen rendering of the eye buffer.

```
glGenFramebuffers(1, &lightFBOID);
glGenTextures (1, &lightBufferID);
glGenTextures (1, &eyeBufferID);
glActiveTexture(GL_TEXTURE2);
lightBufferID = CreateTexture(IMAGE_WIDTH, IMAGE_HEIGHT, GL_RGBA16F, GL_RGBA);
eyeBufferID = CreateTexture(IMAGE_WIDTH, IMAGE_HEIGHT, GL_RGBA16F, GL_RGBA);
glBindFramebuffer(GL_FRAMEBUFFER, lightFBOID);
glFramebufferTexture2D(GL_FRAMEBUFFER, GL_COLOR_ATTACHMENT0, GL_TEXTURE_2D, lightBufferID, 0);
glFramebufferTexture2D(GL_FRAMEBUFFER, GL_COLOR_ATTACHMENT1, GL_TEXTURE_2D, eyeBufferID, 0);
```

```
GLenum status = glCheckFramebufferStatus(GL_FRAMEBUFFER);
if(status == GL_FRAMEBUFFER_COMPLETE )
  printf("Light FBO setup successful !!! \n");
else
  printf("Problem with Light FBO setup");
```

The `CreateTexture` function performs the texture creation and texture format specification into a single function for convenience. This function is defined as follows:

```
GLuint CreateTexture(const int w,const int h,
                     GLenum  internalFormat, GLenum format) {
  GLuint texid;
   glGenTextures(1, &texid);
   glBindTexture(GL_TEXTURE_2D, texid);
    glTexParameteri(GL_TEXTURE_2D, GL_TEXTURE_MAG_FILTER,
    GL_LINEAR);
    glTexParameteri(GL_TEXTURE_2D, GL_TEXTURE_MIN_FILTER,
    GL_LINEAR);
    glTexParameteri(GL_TEXTURE_2D, GL_TEXTURE_WRAP_S,
    GL_CLAMP_TO_BORDER);
    glTexParameteri(GL_TEXTURE_2D, GL_TEXTURE_WRAP_T,
    GL_CLAMP_TO_BORDER);
    glTexImage2D(GL_TEXTURE_2D, 0, internalFormat, w, h, 0,
    format, GL_FLOAT, 0);
    return texid;
}
```

2. Load the volume data, as in the 3D texture slicing recipe:

```
    std::ifstream infile(volume_file.c_str(),
    std::ios_base::binary);
  if(infile.good()) {
    GLubyte* pData = new GLubyte[XDIM*YDIM*ZDIM];
    infile.read(reinterpret_cast<char*>(pData),
       XDIM*YDIM*ZDIM*sizeof(GLubyte));
    infile.close();
    glGenTextures(1, &textureID);
    glActiveTexture(GL_TEXTURE0);
    glBindTexture(GL_TEXTURE_3D, textureID);
    // set the texture parameters
    glTexImage3D(GL_TEXTURE_3D,0,GL_RED,XDIM,YDIM,ZDIM,0,
      GL_RED,GL_UNSIGNED_BYTE,pData);
      GL_CHECK_ERRORS
    glGenerateMipmap(GL_TEXTURE_3D);
    return true;
  } else {
```

```
      return false;
   }
```

3. Similar to the shadow mapping technique, calculate the shadow matrix by multiplying the model-view and projection matrices of the light with the bias matrix:

```
MV_L=glm::lookAt(lightPosOS,glm::vec3(0,0,0),
      glm::vec3(0,1,0));
P_L=glm::perspective(45.0f,1.0f,1.0f, 200.0f);
B=glm::scale(glm::translate(glm::mat4(1),
  glm::vec3(0.5,0.5,0.5)), glm::vec3(0.5,0.5,0.5));
BP   = B*P_L;
S    = BP*MV_L;
```

4. In the rendering code, calculate the half vector by using the view direction vector and the light direction vector:

```
viewVec = -glm::vec3(MV[0][2], MV[1][2], MV[2][2]);
lightVec = glm::normalize(lightPosOS);
bIsViewInverted = glm::dot(viewVec, lightVec)<0;
halfVec = glm::normalize( (bIsViewInverted?-viewVec:viewVec) +
lightVec);
```

5. Slice the volume data as in the 3D texture slicing recipe. The only difference here is that instead of slicing the volume data in the direction perpendicular to the view, we slice it in the direction which is halfway between the view and the light vectors.

```
float max_dist = glm::dot(halfVec, vertexList[0]);
float min_dist = max_dist;
int max_index = 0;
int count = 0;
for(int i=1;i<8;i++) {
   float dist = glm::dot(halfVec, vertexList[i]);
   if(dist > max_dist) {
      max_dist = dist;
      max_index = i;
   }
   if(dist<min_dist)
      min_dist = dist;
}
//rest of the SliceVolume function as in 3D texture slicing but
//viewVec is changed to halfVec
```

6. In the rendering code, bind the FBO and then first clear the light buffer with the white color `(1,1,1,1)` and the eye buffer with the `color (0,0,0,0)`:

```
glBindFramebuffer(GL_FRAMEBUFFER, lightFBOID);
glDrawBuffer(attachIDs[0]);
glClearColor(1,1,1,1);
glClear(GL_COLOR_BUFFER_BIT );
```

```
glDrawBuffer(attachIDs[1]);
glClearColor(0,0,0,0);
glClear(GL_COLOR_BUFFER_BIT );
```

7. Bind the volume VAO and then run a loop for the total number of slices. In each iteration, first render the slice in the eye buffer but bind the light buffer as the texture. Next, render the slice in the light buffer:

```
glBindVertexArray(volumeVAO);
for(int i =0;i<num_slices;i++) {
    shaderShadow.Use();
    glUniformMatrix4fv(shaderShadow("MVP"), 1, GL_FALSE,
    glm::value_ptr(MVP));
    glUniformMatrix4fv(shaderShadow("S"), 1, GL_FALSE,
    glm::value_ptr(S));
    glBindTexture(GL_TEXTURE_2D, lightBuffer);
    DrawSliceFromEyePointOfView(i);

    shader.Use();
    glUniformMatrix4fv(shader("MVP"), 1, GL_FALSE,
    glm::value_ptr(P_L*MV_L));
    DrawSliceFromLightPointOfView(i);
}
```

8. For the eye buffer rendering step, swap the blend function based on whether the viewer is viewing in the direction of the light or opposite to it:

```
void DrawSliceFromEyePointOfView(const int i) {
    glDrawBuffer(attachIDs[1]);
    glViewport(0, 0, IMAGE_WIDTH, IMAGE_HEIGHT);
    if(bIsViewInverted) {
        glBlendFunc(GL_ONE_MINUS_DST_ALPHA, GL_ONE);
    } else {
        glBlendFunc(GL_ONE, GL_ONE_MINUS_SRC_ALPHA);
    }
    glDrawArrays(GL_TRIANGLES, 12*i, 12);
}
```

9. For the light buffer, we simply blend the slices using the conventional "over" blending:

```
void DrawSliceFromLightPointOfView(const int i) {
    glDrawBuffer(attachIDs[0]);
    glViewport(0, 0, IMAGE_WIDTH, IMAGE_HEIGHT);
    glBlendFunc(GL_SRC_ALPHA, GL_ONE_MINUS_SRC_ALPHA);
    glDrawArrays(GL_TRIANGLES, 12*i, 12);
}
```

10. Finally, unbind the FBO and restore the default draw buffer. Next, set the viewport to the entire screen and then render the eye buffer on screen using a shader:

```
glBindVertexArray(0);
glBindFramebuffer(GL_FRAMEBUFFER, 0);
glDrawBuffer(GL_BACK_LEFT);
glViewport(0,0,WIDTH, HEIGHT);
glBindTexture(GL_TEXTURE_2D, eyeBufferID);
glBindVertexArray(quadVAOID);
quadShader.Use();
glDrawArrays(GL_TRIANGLES, 0, 6);
quadShader.UnUse();
glBindVertexArray(0);
```

How it works...

As the name suggests, this technique renders the volume by accumulating the intermediate results into two separate buffers by slicing the volume halfway between the light and the view vectors. When the scene is rendered from the point of view of the eye, the light buffer is used as texture to find out whether the current fragment is in shadow or not. This is carried out in the fragment shader by looking up the light buffer by using the shadow matrix as in the shadow mapping algorithm. In this step, the blending equation is swapped based on the direction of view with respect to the light direction vector. If the view is inverted, the blending direction is swapped from front-to-back to back-to-front using `glBlendFunc(GL_ONE_MINUS_DST_ALPHA, GL_ONE)`. On the other hand, if the view direction is not inverted, the blend function is set as `glBlendFunc(GL_ONE, GL_ONE_MINUS_SRC_ALPHA)`. Note that here we have not used the over compositing since we premultiply the color with its alpha in the fragment shader (see `Chapter7/HalfAngleSlicing/shaders/slicerShadow.frag`), as shown in the following code:

```
vec3 lightIntensity =  textureProj(shadowTex, vLightUVW.xyw).xyz;
float density = texture(volume, vUV).r;
if(density > 0.1) {
   float alpha = clamp(density, 0.0, 1.0);
   alpha *= color.a;
   vFragColor = vec4(color.xyz*lightIntensity*alpha, alpha);
}
```

In the next step, the scene is rendered from the point of view of the light. This time, the normal over compositing is used. This ensures that the light contributions accumulate with each other similar to how light behaves in normal circumstances. In this case, we use the same fragment shader as was used in the 3D texture slicing recipe (see `Chapter7/HalgAngleSlicing/shaders/textureSlicer.frag`).

```
vFragColor = texture(volume, vUV).rrrr * color ;
```

There's more...

The demo application implementing this recipe renders the scene, as shown in the following screenshot, similar to the previous recipes. The light source position can be changed using the right mouse button. We can see the shadow changing dynamically for the scene. Attenuation of light is also controlled by setting a shader uniform. This is the reason why we can observe a bluish tinge in the output image.

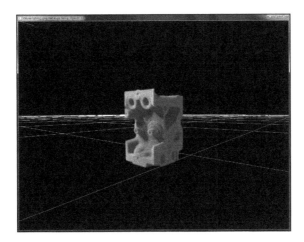

Note that we cannot see the black halo around the volume dataset as was evident in earlier recipes. The reason for this is the if condition used in the fragment shader. We only perform these calculations if the current density value is greater than 0.1. This essentially removed air and other low intensity artifacts, producing a much better result.

See also

- *Chapter 39, Volume Rendering Techniques*, in *GPU Gems 1*. Available online at `http://http.developer.nvidia.com/GPUGems/gpugems_ch39.html`
- *Chapter 6, Global Volume Illumination*, in *Real-time Volume Graphics, AK Peters/ CRC Press*.

8
Skeletal and Physically-based Simulation on the GPU

In this chapter we will focus on the following topics:

- Implementing skeletal animation using matrix palette skinning
- Implementing skeletal animation using dual quaternion skinning
- Modeling cloth using transform feedback
- Implementing collision detection and response on a transform feedback-based cloth model
- Implementing a particle system using transform feedback

Introduction

Most of the real-time graphics applications have interactive elements. We have automated bots that move and animate in an interactive application. These elements include objects that are animated using preset sequences of frames. These are called **frame-by-frame animations**. There are other scene elements that have motion, which is derived using physical simulation. These are called **physically-based animations**. In addition, humanoid or character models have a special category of animations called **skeletal animation**. In this chapter, we will look at recipes for doing skeletal and physically-based simulation on the GPU in modern OpenGL.

Implementing skeletal animation using matrix palette skinning

When working with games and simulation systems, virtual characters are often used to give a detailed depiction of scenarios. Such characters are typically represented using a combination of bones and skin. The vertices of the 3D model are assigned influence weights (called **blend weights**) that control how much a bone influences that vertex. Up to four bones can influence a vertex. The process whereby bone weights are assigned to the vertices of a 3D model is called **skinning**. Each bone stores its transformation. These stored sequences of transformations are applied to every frame and every bone in the model and in the end, we get an animated character on the screen. This representation of animation is called **skeletal animation**. There are several methods for skeletal animation. One popular method is **matrix palette skinning**, which is also known as **linear blend skinning** (**LBS**). This method will be implemented in this recipe.

Getting ready

The code for this recipe is contained in the `Chapter8/MatrixPaletteSkinning` directory. This recipe will be using the *Implementing EZMesh model loading* recipe from *Chapter 5, Mesh Model Formats and Particle Systems* and it will augment it with skeletal animation. The EZMesh format was developed by John Ratcliff and it is an easy-to-understand format for storing skeletal animation. Typical skeletal animation formats like COLLADA and FBX are needlessly complicated, where dozens of segments have to be parsed before the real content can be loaded. On the other hand, the EZMesh format stores all of the information in an XML-based format, which is easier to parse. It is the default skeletal animation format used in the NVIDIA PhysX sdk. More information about the EZMesh model format and loaders can be obtained from the references in the *See also* section of this recipe.

How to do it...

Let us start our recipe by following these simple steps:

1. Load the EZMesh model as we did in the *Implementing EZMesh loader* recipe from *Chapter 5, Mesh Model Formats and Particle System*. In addition to the model submeshes, vertices, normals, texture coordinates, and materials, we also load the skeleton information from the EZMesh file.

```
EzmLoader ezm;
if(!ezm.Load(mesh_filename.c_str(), skeleton, animations,
            submeshes, vertices, indices, material2ImageMap,
            min, max)) {
  cout<<"Cannot load the EZMesh file"<<endl;
  exit(EXIT_FAILURE);
}
```

2. Get the `MeshSystem` object from the `meshImportLibrary` object. Then load the bone transformations contained in the EZMesh file using the `MeshSystem::mSkeletons` array. This is carried out in the `EzmLoader::Load` function. Also generate absolute bone transforms from the relative transforms. This is done so that the transform of the child bone is influenced by the transform of the parent bone. This is continued up the hierarchy until the root bone. If the mesh is modeled in a positive Z axis system, we need to modify the orientation, positions, and scale by swapping Y and Z axes and changing the sign of one of them. This is done because we are using a positive Y axis system in OpenGL; otherwise, our mesh will be lying in the XZ plane rather than the XY plane. We obtain a combined matrix from the position orientation and scale of the bone. This is stored in the `xform` field, which is the relative transform of the bone.

```
if(ms->mSkeletonCount>0) {
  NVSHARE::MeshSkeleton* pSkel = ms->mSkeletons[0];
  Bone b;
  for(int i=0;i<pSkel->GetBoneCount();i++) {
      const NVSHARE::MeshBone pBone = pSkel->mBones[i];
      const int s = strlen(pBone.mName);
      b.name = new char[s+1];
      memset(b.name, 0, sizeof(char)*(s+1));
      strncpy_s(b.name,sizeof(char)*(s+1), pBone.mName, s);
      b.orientation = glm::quat(
      pBone.mOrientation[3],pBone.mOrientation[0],
      pBone.mOrientation[1],pBone.mOrientation[2]);
      b.position = glm::vec3( pBone.mPosition[0],
      pBone.mPosition[1],pBone.mPosition[2]);
      b.scale   = glm::vec3(pBone.mScale[0], pBone.mScale[1],
      pBone.mScale[2]);

      if(!bYup) {
          float tmp = b.position.y;
          b.position.y = b.position.z;
          b.position.z = -tmp;
          tmp = b.orientation.y;
          b.orientation.y = b.orientation.z;
          b.orientation.z = -tmp;
          tmp = b.scale.y;
          b.scale.y = b.scale.z;
          b.scale.z = -tmp;
      }

      glm::mat4 S = glm::scale(glm::mat4(1), b.scale);
      glm::mat4 R = glm::toMat4(b.orientation);
```

```
glm::mat4 T = glm::translate(glm::mat4(1), b.position);

    b.xform = T*R*S;
    b.parent = pBone.mParentIndex;
    skeleton.push_back(b);
}
UpdateCombinedMatrices();
bindPose.resize(skeleton.size());
invBindPose.resize(skeleton.size());
animatedXform.resize(skeleton.size());
```

3. Generate the bind pose and inverse bind pose arrays from the stored bone transformations:

```
for(size_t i=0;i<skeleton.size();i++) {
    bindPose[i] = (skeleton[i].comb);
    invBindPose[i] = glm::inverse(bindPose[i]);
}}
```

4. Store the blend weights and blend indices of each vertex in the mesh:

```
mesh.vertices[j].blendWeights.x = pMesh->mVertices[j].mWeight[0];
mesh.vertices[j].blendWeights.y = pMesh->mVertices[j].mWeight[1];
mesh.vertices[j].blendWeights.z = pMesh->mVertices[j].mWeight[2];
mesh.vertices[j].blendWeights.w = pMesh->mVertices[j].mWeight[3];
mesh.vertices[j].blendIndices[0] = pMesh->mVertices[j].mBone[0];
mesh.vertices[j].blendIndices[1] = pMesh->mVertices[j].mBone[1];
mesh.vertices[j].blendIndices[2] = pMesh->mVertices[j].mBone[2];
mesh.vertices[j].blendIndices[3] = pMesh->mVertices[j].mBone[3];
```

5. In the idle callback function, calculate the amount of time to spend on the current frame. If the amount has elapsed, move to the next frame and reset the time. After this, calculate the new bone transformations as well as new skinning matrices, and pass them to the shader:

```
QueryPerformanceCounter(&current);
dt = (double)(current.QuadPart - last.QuadPart) /
(double)freq.QuadPart;
last = current;
static double t = 0;
t+=dt;
NVSHARE::MeshAnimation* pAnim = &animations[0];
float framesPerSecond = pAnim->GetFrameCount()/
                        pAnim->GetDuration();
if( t > 1.0f/ framesPerSecond) {
    currentFrame++;
```

```
        t=0;
    }
    if(bLoop) {
        currentFrame = currentFrame%pAnim->mFrameCount;
    } else {
        currentFrame=max(-1,min(currentFrame,pAnim->mFrameCount-1));
    }
    if(currentFrame == -1) {
        for(size_t i=0;i<skeleton.size();i++) {
            skeleton[i].comb = bindPose[i];
            animatedXform[i] = skeleton[i].comb*invBindPose[i];
        }
    }
    else {
        for(int j=0;j<pAnim->mTrackCount;j++) {
            NVSHARE::MeshAnimTrack* pTrack = pAnim->mTracks[j];
            NVSHARE::MeshAnimPose* pPose =
            pTrack->GetPose(currentFrame);
            skeleton[j].position.x = pPose->mPos[0];
            skeleton[j].position.y = pPose->mPos[1];
            skeleton[j].position.z = pPose->mPos[2];

            glm::quat q;
            q.x = pPose->mQuat[0];
            q.y = pPose->mQuat[1];
            q.z = pPose->mQuat[2];
            q.w = pPose->mQuat[3];

            skeleton[j].scale  = glm::vec3(pPose->mScale[0],
                                          pPose->mScale[1],
                                          pPose->mScale[2]);
            if(!bYup) {
                skeleton[j].position.y = pPose->mPos[2];
                skeleton[j].position.z = -pPose->mPos[1];
                q.y = pPose->mQuat[2];
                q.z = -pPose->mQuat[1];
                skeleton[j].scale.y = pPose->mScale[2];
                skeleton[j].scale.z = -pPose->mScale[1];
            }

            skeleton[j].orientation = q;

            glm::mat4 S =glm::scale(glm::mat4(1),skeleton[j].scale);
            glm::mat4 R = glm::toMat4(q);
            glm::mat4 T = glm::translate(glm::mat4(1), skeleton[j].
position);
```

```
                    skeleton[j].xform = T*R*S;
                    Bone& b = skeleton[j];

                    if(b.parent==-1)
                        b.comb = b.xform;
                    else
                        b.comb = skeleton[b.parent].comb * b.xform;

                    animatedXform[j] = b.comb * invBindPose[j] ;
                }
            }
            shader.Use();
                glUniformMatrix4fv(shader("Bones"),animatedXform.size(),
                GL_FALSE,glm::value_ptr(animatedXform[0]));
            shader.UnUse();
            shader.UnUse();
```

How it works...

There are two parts of this recipe: generation of skinning matrices and the calculation of GPU skinning in the vertex shader. To understand the first step, we will start with the different transforms that will be used in skinning. Typically, in a simulation or game, a transform is represented as a 4×4 matrix. For skeletal animation, we have a collection of bones. Each bone has a **local transform** (also called **relative transform**), which tells how the bone is positioned and oriented with respect to its parent bone. If the bone's local transform is multiplied to the global transform of its parent, we get the **global transform** (also called **absolute transform**) of the bone. Typically, the animation formats store the local transforms of the bones in the file. The user application uses this information to generate the global transforms.

We define our bone structure as follows:

```
struct Bone {
    glm::quat orientation;
    glm::vec3 position;
    glm::mat4 xform, comb;
    glm::vec3 scale;
    char* name;
    int parent;
};
```

The first field is `orientation`, which is a quaternion storing the orientation of bone in space relative to its parent. The `position` field stores its position relative to its parent. The `xform` field is the local (relative) transform, and the `comb` field is the global (absolute) transform. The `scale` field contains the scaling transformation of the bone. In the big picture, the `scale` field gives the scaling matrix (`S`), the `orientation` field gives the rotation matrix (`R`), and the `position` field gives the translation matrix (`T`). The combined matrix `T*R*S` gives us the relative transform that is calculated when we load the bone information from the EZMesh file in the second step.

The `name` field is the unique name of the bone in the skeleton. Finally, the `parent` field stores the index of the parent of the current bone in the skeleton array. For the root bone, the parent is `-1`. For all of the other bones, it will be a number starting from `0` to `N-1`, where `N` is the total number of bones in the skeleton.

After we have loaded and stored the relative transforms of each bone in the skeleton, we iterate through each bone to obtain its absolute transform. This is carried out in the `UpdateCombinedMatrices` function in `Chapter8/MatrixPaletteSkinning/main.cpp`.

```
for(size_t i=0;i<skeleton.size();i++) {
    Bone& b = skeleton[i];
    if(b.parent==-1)
        b.comb = b.xform;
    else
        b.comb = skeleton[b.parent].comb * b.xform;
}
```

After generating the absolute transforms of each bone, we store the bind pose and inverse bind pose matrices of the skeleton. Simply put, bind pose is the absolute transforms of the bones in the non-animated state (that is, when no animation is applied). This is usually when the skeleton is attached (skinned) to the geometry. In other words, it is the default pose of the skeletal animated mesh. Typically, bones can be in any bind pose (usually, for humanoid characters, the character may be in A pose, T pose, and so on based on the convention used). Typically, the inverse bind pose is stored at the time of initialization. So, continuing to the previous skeleton example, we can get the bind pose and inverse bind pose matrices as follows:

```
for(size_t i=0;i < skeleton.size(); i++) {
    bindPose[i] = skeleton[i].comb;
    invBindPose[i] = glm::inverse(bindPose[i]);
}
```

Note that we do this once at initialization, so that we do not have to calculate the bind pose's inverse every frame, as it is required during animation.

When we apply any new transformation (an animation sequence for example) to the skeleton, we have to first undo the bind pose transformation. This is done by multiplying the animated transformation with the inverse of the bind pose transformation. This is required because the given relative transformations will add to the existing transformations of the bone and, if the bind pose transformation is not undone, the animation output will be wrong.

The final matrix that we get from this process is called the **skinning matrix** (also called the **final bone matrix**). Continuing from the example given in the previous paragraph, let's say we have modified the relative transforms of bone using the animation sequence. We can then generate the skinning matrix as follows:

```
for(size_t i=0;i < skeleton.size(); i++) {
    Bone& b = skeleton[i];
    if(b.parent==-1)
        b.comb = b.xform;
    else
        b.comb = skeleton[b.parent].comb * b.xform;
    animatedXForm[i] = b.comb*invBindPose[i];
}
```

One thing to note here is the order of the different matrices. As you can see, we right multiply the inverse bind pose matrix with the combined bone transform. We put it this way because OpenGL and glm matrices work right to left. So the inverse of bind pose matrix will be multiplied by the given vertex first. Then it will be multiplied with the local transform (`xform`) of the current bone. Finally, it will be multiplied with the global transform (`comb`) of its parent to get the final transformation matrix.

After we have calculated the skinning matrices, we pass these to the GPU in a single call:

```
shader.Use();
    glUniformMatrix4fv(shader("Bones"), animatedXForm.size(),
    GL_FALSE, glm::value_ptr(animatedXForm[0]));
shader.UnUse();
```

To make sure that the size of the bones array is correct in the vertex shader, we append text to the shader dynamically by using the overloaded `GLSLShader::LoadFromFile` function.

```
stringstream str( ios_base::app | ios_base::out);
    str<<"\nconst int NUM_BONES="<<skeleton.size()<<";"<<endl;
    str<<"uniform mat4 Bones[NUM_BONES];"<<endl;
shader.LoadFromFile(GL_VERTEX_SHADER, "shaders/shader.vert", str.
str());
shader.LoadFromFile(GL_FRAGMENT_SHADER, "shaders/shader.frag");
```

This ensures that our vertex shader has the same number of bones as our mesh file.

For this simple recipe we have modified the shader code at loading time before compilation. Such shader modification must not be done at runtime as this will require a recompilation of the shader and will likely hamper application performance.

The `Vertex` struct storing all of our per-vertex attributes is defined as follows:

```
struct Vertex  {
  glm::vec3 pos,
        normal;
  glm::vec2 uv;
  glm::vec4 blendWeights;
  glm::ivec4 blendIndices;
};
```

The vertices array is filled in by the `EzmLoader::Load` function. We generate a vertex array object with a vertex buffer object to store our interleaved per-vertex attributes:

```
glGenVertexArrays(1, &vaoID);
glGenBuffers(1, &vboVerticesID);
glGenBuffers(1, &vboIndicesID);

glBindVertexArray(vaoID);
glBindBuffer (GL_ARRAY_BUFFER, vboVerticesID);
glBufferData (GL_ARRAY_BUFFER, sizeof(Vertex)*vertices.size(),
&(vertices[0].pos.x), GL_DYNAMIC_DRAW);

glEnableVertexAttribArray(shader["vVertex"]);
glVertexAttribPointer(shader["vVertex"], 3, GL_FLOAT, GL_
FALSE,sizeof(Vertex),0);

glEnableVertexAttribArray(shader["vNormal"]);
glVertexAttribPointer(shader["vNormal"], 3, GL_FLOAT, GL_FALSE,
sizeof(Vertex), (const GLvoid*)(offsetof(Vertex, normal)) );

glEnableVertexAttribArray(shader["vUV"]);
glVertexAttribPointer(shader["vUV"], 2, GL_FLOAT, GL_FALSE,
sizeof(Vertex), (const GLvoid*)(offsetof(Vertex, uv)) );

glEnableVertexAttribArray(shader["vBlendWeights"]);
glVertexAttribPointer(shader["vBlendWeights"], 4, GL_FLOAT,
GL_FALSE, sizeof(Vertex), (const GLvoid*)(offsetof(Vertex,
blendWeights)) );

glEnableVertexAttribArray(shader["viBlendIndices"]);
glVertexAttribIPointer(shader["viBlendIndices"], 4, GL_INT,
sizeof(Vertex), (const GLvoid*)(offsetof(Vertex, blendIndices)) );
```

Note that for blend indices we use the `glVertexAttribIPointer` function, as the attribute (`viBlendIndices`) is defined as ivec4 in the vertex shader.

Finally, in the rendering code, we set the vertex array object and use the shader program. Then we iterate through all of the submeshes. We then set the material texture for the current submesh and set the shader uniforms. Finally, we issue a `glDrawElements` call:

```
glBindVertexArray(vaoID); {
shader.Use();
glUniformMatrix4fv(shader("MV"), 1, GL_FALSE, glm::value_ptr(MV));
glUniformMatrix3fv(shader("N"), 1, GL_FALSE, glm::value_ptr(glm::inver
seTranspose(glm::mat3(MV))));
glUniformMatrix4fv(shader("P"), 1, GL_FALSE, glm::value_ptr(P));
glUniform3fv(shader("light_position"),1, &(lightPosOS.x));
   for(size_t i=0;i<submeshes.size();i++) {
   if(strlen(submeshes[i].materialName)>0) {
        GLuint id = materialMap[ material2ImageMap[
                 submeshes[i].materialName]];
    GLint whichID[1];
    glGetIntegerv(GL_TEXTURE_BINDING_2D, whichID);
    if(whichID[0] != id)
      glBindTexture(GL_TEXTURE_2D, id);
    glUniform1f(shader("useDefault"), 0.0);
   } else {
    glUniform1f(shader("useDefault"), 1.0);
   }
    glDrawElements(GL_TRIANGLES, submeshes[i].indices.size(),
                GL_UNSIGNED_INT, &submeshes[i].indices[0]);
  }//end for
shader.UnUse();
}
```

The matrix palette skinning is carried out on the GPU using the vertex shader (`Chapter8/ MatrixPaletteSkinning/shaders/shader.vert`). We simply use the blend indices and blend weights to calculate the correct vertex position and normal based on the combined influence of all of the effecting bones. The `Bones` array contains the skinning matrices that we generated earlier. The complete vertex shader is as follows:

Note that the `Bones` uniform array is not declared in the shader, as it is filled in the shader code dynamically as was shown earlier.

```
#version 330 core
layout(location = 0) in vec3 vVertex;
layout(location = 1) in vec3 vNormal;
layout(location = 2) in vec2 vUV;
layout(location = 3) in vec4 vBlendWeights;
layout(location = 4) in ivec4 viBlendIndices;
smooth out vec2 vUVout;
uniform mat4 P;
uniform mat4 MV;
uniform mat3 N;
smooth out vec3 vEyeSpaceNormal;
smooth out vec3 vEyeSpacePosition;
void main() {
  vec4 blendVertex=vec4(0);
  vec3 blendNormal=vec3(0);
  vec4 vVertex4 = vec4(vVertex,1);

  int index = viBlendIndices.x;
  blendVertex = (Bones[index] * vVertex4) *  vBlendWeights.x;
  blendNormal = (Bones[index] * vec4(vNormal, 0.0)).xyz *
              vBlendWeights.x;

  index = viBlendIndices.y;
  blendVertex = ((Bones[index] * vVertex4) * vBlendWeights.y) +
              blendVertex;
  blendNormal = (Bones[index] * vec4(vNormal, 0.0)).xyz *
              vBlendWeights.y  + blendNormal;

    index = viBlendIndices.z;
    blendVertex = ((Bones[index] * vVertex4) *  vBlendWeights.z)
               + blendVertex;
  blendNormal = (Bones[index] * vec4(vNormal, 0.0)).xyz *
              vBlendWeights.z  + blendNormal;

  index = viBlendIndices.w;
  blendVertex = ((Bones[index] * vVertex4) *  vBlendWeights.w)
              + blendVertex;
  blendNormal = (Bones[index] * vec4(vNormal, 0.0)).xyz *
              vBlendWeights.w  + blendNormal;

    vEyeSpacePosition = (MV*blendVertex).xyz;
    vEyeSpaceNormal   = normalize(N*blendNormal);
    vUVout=vUV;
  gl_Position = P*vec4(vEyeSpacePosition,1);
}
```

The fragment shader uses the attenuated point light source for illumination as we have seen in the *Implementing per-fragment point light with attenuation* recipe in *Chapter 4, Lights and Shadows*.

There's more...

The output from the demo application for this recipe shows the dude.ezm model animating using the matrix palette skinning technique as shown in the following figure. The light source can be rotated by right-clicking on it and dragging. Pressing the *l* key stops the loop playback.

See also

▶ NVIDIA DirectX SDK 9.0 Matrix Palette Skinning demo at http://http.download.nvidia.com/developer/SDK/Individual_Samples/DEMOS/Direct3D9/src/HLSL_PaletteSkin/docs/HLSL_PaletteSkin.pdf

▶ John Ratcliff code suppository containing a lot of useful tools, including the EZMesh format specifications and loaders available online at http://codesuppository.blogspot.sg/2009/11/test-application-for-meshimport-library.html

▶ Improved Skinning demo in the NVIDIA sdk at http://http.download.nvidia.com/developer/SDK/Individual_Samples/samples.html

Implementing skeletal animation using dual quaternion skinning

Matrix palette skinning suffers from candy wrapping artefacts, especially in regions like shoulder and elbow, where there are several rotations across various axes. If dual quaternion skinning is employed, these artefacts are minimized. In this recipe we will implement skeletal animation using dual quaternion skinning.

Before understanding dual quaternions, let us first see what quaternions are. **Quaternions** are a mathematical entity containing three imaginary dimensions (which specify the axis of rotation) and a real dimension (which specifies the angle of rotation). Quaternions are used in 3D graphics to represent rotation, since they do not suffer from gimbal lock, as Euler angles do. In order to store translation with rotation simultaneously, dual quaternions are used to store dual number coefficients instead of real ones. Instead of four components, as in a quaternion, dual quaternions have eight components.

Even in dual quaternion skinning, the linear blend method is used. However, due to the nature of transformation in dual quaternion, spherical blending is preferred. After linear blending, the resulting dual quaternion is renormalized, which generates a spherical blending result, which is a better approximation as compared to the linear blend skinning. This whole process is illustrated by the following figure:

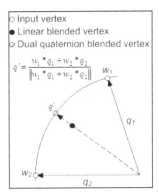

Getting ready

The code for this recipe is contained in the `Chapter8/DualQuaternionSkinning` folder. We will be building on top of the previous recipe and replace the skinning matrices with dual quaternions.

How to do it...

Converting linear blend skinning to dual quaternion skinning requires the following steps:

1. Load the EZMesh model as we did in the *Implementing EZMesh loader* recipe from *Chapter 5, Mesh Model Formats and Particle System*:

```
if(!ezm.Load(mesh_filename.c_str(), skeleton, animations,
submeshes, vertices, indices, material2ImageMap, min, max))   {
    cout<<"Cannot load the EZMesh file"<<endl;
    exit(EXIT_FAILURE); }
```

2. After loading up the mesh, materials, and textures, load the bone transformations contained in the EZMesh file using the `MeshSystem::mSkeletons` array as we did in the previous recipe. In addition to the bone matrices, also store the bind pose and inverse bind pose matrices as we did in the previous recipe. Instead of storing the skinning matrices, we initialize a vector of dual quaternions. Dual quaternions are a different representation of the skinning matrices.

```
UpdateCombinedMatrices();
bindPose.resize(skeleton.size());
invBindPose.resize(skeleton.size());
animatedXform.resize(skeleton.size());
dualQuaternions.resize(skeleton.size());
for(size_t i=0;i<skeleton.size();i++) {
    bindPose[i] = (skeleton[i].comb);
    invBindPose[i] = glm::inverse(bindPose[i]);
}
```

3. Implement the idle callback function as in the previous recipe. Here, in addition to calculating the skinning matrix, also calculate the dual quaternion for the given skinning matrix. After all of the joints are done, pass the dual quaternion to the shader:

```
glm::mat4 S = glm::scale(glm::mat4(1),skeleton[j].scale);
glm::mat4 R = glm::toMat4(q);
glm::mat4 T = glm::translate(glm::mat4(1),
skeleton[j].position);
skeleton[j].xform = T*R*S;
Bone& b = skeleton[j];
if(b.parent==-1)
    b.comb = b.xform;
else
    b.comb = skeleton[b.parent].comb * b.xform;
animatedXform[j] = b.comb * invBindPose[j];
glm::vec3 t = glm::vec3( animatedXform[j][3][0],
animatedXform[j][3][1], animatedXform[j][3][2]);
dualQuaternions[j].QuatTrans2UDQ(
```

```
   glm::toQuat(animatedXform[j]),  t);
   …
   shader.Use();
   glUniform4fv(shader("Bones"), skeleton.size()*2,
   &(dualQuaternions[0].ordinary.x));
   shader.UnUse();
```

4. In the vertex shader (Chapter8/DualQuaternionSkinning/shaders/shader. vert), calculate the skinning matrix from the passed dual quaternion and blend weights of the given vertices. Then proceed with the skinning matrix as we did in the previous recipe:

```
#version 330 core
layout(location = 0) in vec3 vVertex;
layout(location = 1) in vec3 vNormal;
layout(location = 2) in vec2 vUV;
layout(location = 3) in vec4 vBlendWeights;
layout(location = 4) in ivec4 viBlendIndices;
smooth out vec2 vUVout;
uniform mat4 P;
uniform mat4 MV;
uniform mat3 N;
smooth out vec3 vEyeSpaceNormal;
smooth out vec3 vEyeSpacePosition;

 void main() {
   vec4 blendVertex=vec4(0);
   vec3 blendNormal=vec3(0);
   vec4 blendDQ[2];
   float yc = 1.0, zc = 1.0, wc = 1.0;
   if (dot(Bones[viBlendIndices.x * 2],
           Bones[viBlendIndices.y * 2]) < 0.0)
           yc = -1.0;
   if (dot(Bones[viBlendIndices.x * 2],
           Bones[viBlendIndices.z * 2]) < 0.0)
           zc = -1.0;
   if (dot(Bones[viBlendIndices.x * 2],
           Bones[viBlendIndices.w * 2]) < 0.0)
           wc = -1.0;
   blendDQ[0] = Bones[viBlendIndices.x * 2] * vBlendWeights.x;
   blendDQ[1] = Bones[viBlendIndices.x * 2 + 1] *
               vBlendWeights.x;
   blendDQ[0] += yc*Bones[viBlendIndices.y * 2] *
               vBlendWeights.y;
```

```
        blendDQ[1] += yc*Bones[viBlendIndices.y * 2 + 1] *
                      vBlendWeights.y;
        blendDQ[0] += zc*Bones[viBlendIndices.z * 2] *
                      vBlendWeights.z;
        blendDQ[1] += zc*Bones[viBlendIndices.z * 2 + 1] *
                      vBlendWeights.z;
        blendDQ[0] += wc*Bones[viBlendIndices.w * 2] *
                      vBlendWeights.w;
        blendDQ[1] += wc*Bones[viBlendIndices.w * 2 + 1] *
                      vBlendWeights.w;
        mat4 skinTransform = dualQuatToMatrix(blendDQ[0],
                             blendDQ[1]);
        blendVertex = skinTransform*vec4(vVertex,1);
        blendNormal = (skinTransform*vec4(vNormal,0)).xyz;
        vEyeSpacePosition = (MV*blendVertex).xyz;
        vEyeSpaceNormal   = N*blendNormal;
        vUVout=vUV;
        gl_Position = P*vec4(vEyeSpacePosition,1);
    }
```

To convert the given dual quaternion to a matrix, we define a function `dualQuatToMatrix`. This gives us a matrix, which we can then multiply with the vertex to obtain the transformed result.

How it works...

The only difference in this recipe and the previous recipe is the creation of a dual quaternion from the skinning matrix on the CPU, and its conversion back to a matrix in the vertex shader. After we have obtained the skinning matrices, we convert them into a dual quaternion array by using the `dual_quat::QuatTrans2UDQ` function that gets a dual quaternion from a rotation quaternion and a translation vector. This function is defined as follows in the `dual_quat` class (in `Chapter8/DualQuaternionSkinning/main.cpp`):

```
    void QuatTrans2UDQ(const glm::quat& q0, const glm::vec3& t) {
      ordinary = q0;
      dual.w = -0.5f * ( t.x * q0.x + t.y * q0.y + t.z * q0.z);
      dual.x =  0.5f * ( t.x * q0.w + t.y * q0.z - t.z * q0.y);
      dual.y =  0.5f * (-t.x * q0.z + t.y * q0.w + t.z * q0.x);
      dual.z =  0.5f * ( t.x * q0.y - t.y * q0.x + t.z * q0.w);
    }
```

The dual quaternion array is then passed to the shader instead of the bone matrices. In the vertex shader, we first do a dot product of the ordinary quaternion with the dual quaternion. If the dot product of the two quaternions is less than zero, it means they are both facing in opposite direction. We thus subtract the quaternion from the blended dual quaternion, otherwise we add it to the blended dual quaternion:

```
float yc = 1.0, zc = 1.0, wc = 1.0;

if (dot(Bones[viBlendIndices.x * 2],
        Bones[viBlendIndices.y * 2]) < 0.0)
   yc = -1.0;

if (dot(Bones[viBlendIndices.x * 2],
        Bones[viBlendIndices.z * 2]) < 0.0)
   zc = -1.0;

if (dot(Bones[viBlendIndices.x * 2],
        Bones[viBlendIndices.w * 2]) < 0.0)
   wc = -1.0;

blendDQ[0] = Bones[viBlendIndices.x * 2] * vBlendWeights.x;
blendDQ[1] = Bones[viBlendIndices.x * 2 + 1] * vBlendWeights.x;

blendDQ[0] += yc*Bones[viBlendIndices.y * 2] * vBlendWeights.y;
blendDQ[1] += yc*Bones[viBlendIndices.y * 2 +1] * vBlendWeights.y;

blendDQ[0] += zc*Bones[viBlendIndices.z * 2] * vBlendWeights.z;
blendDQ[1] += zc*Bones[viBlendIndices.z * 2 +1] * vBlendWeights.z;

blendDQ[0] += wc*Bones[viBlendIndices.w * 2] * vBlendWeights.w;
blendDQ[1] += wc*Bones[viBlendIndices.w * 2 +1] * vBlendWeights.w;
```

The blended dual quaternion (blendDQ) is then converted to a matrix by the dualQuatToMatrix function, which is defined as follows:

```
mat4 dualQuatToMatrix(vec4 Qn, vec4 Qd) {
  mat4 M;
  float len2 = dot(Qn, Qn);
  float w = Qn.w, x = Qn.x, y = Qn.y, z = Qn.z;
  float t0 = Qd.w, t1 = Qd.x, t2 = Qd.y, t3 = Qd.z;

  M[0][0] = w*w + x*x - y*y - z*z;
  M[0][1] = 2 * x * y + 2 * w * z;
  M[0][2] = 2 * x * z - 2 * w * y;
  M[0][3] = 0;

  M[1][0] = 2 * x * y - 2 * w * z;
  M[1][1] = w * w + y * y - x * x - z * z;
  M[1][2] = 2 * y * z + 2 * w * x;
  M[1][3] = 0;
```

```
M[2][0] = 2 * x * z + 2 * w * y;
M[2][1] = 2 * y * z - 2 * w * x;
M[2][2] = w * w + z * z - x * x - y * y;
M[2][3] = 0;

M[3][0] = -2 * t0 * x + 2 * w * t1 - 2 * t2 * z + 2 * y * t3;
M[3][1] = -2 * t0 * y + 2 * t1 * z - 2 * x * t3 + 2 * w * t2;
M[3][2] = -2 * t0 * z + 2 * x * t2 + 2 * w * t3 - 2 * t1 * y;
M[3][3] = len2;

M /= len2;

return M;
}
```

The returned matrix is then multiplied with the given vertex/normal, and then the eye space position/normal and texture coordinates are obtained. Finally, the clip space position is calculated:

```
mat4 skinTransform = dualQuatToMatrix(blendDQ[0], blendDQ[1]);
blendVertex = skinTransform*vec4(vVertex,1);
blendNormal = (skinTransform*vec4(vNormal,0)).xyz;
vEyeSpacePosition = (MV*blendVertex).xyz;
vEyeSpaceNormal    = N*blendNormal;
vUVout=vUV;
gl_Position = P*vec4(vEyeSpacePosition,1);
```

The fragment shader follows the similar steps as it did in the previous recipe to output the lit textured fragments.

There's more...

The demo application for this recipe renders the dwarf_anim.ezm skeletal model. Even with extreme rotation at the shoulder joint, the output does not suffer from candy wrapper artefacts as shown in the following figure:

On the other hand, if we use the matrix palette skinning, we get the following output, which clearly shows the candy wrapper artefacts:

See also

▶ Skinning with Dual Quaternions at `http://isg.cs.tcd.ie/projects/DualQuaternions/`

▶ Skinning with Dual Quaternions demo in NVIDIA DirectX sdk 10.5 at `http://developer.download.nvidia.com/SDK/10.5/direct3d/samples.html`

▶ Dual Quaternion Google Summer of Code 2011 implementation in OGRE at `http://www.ogre3d.org/tikiwiki/tiki-index.php?page=SoC2011%20Dual%20Quaternion%20Skinning`

Modeling cloth using transform feedback

In this recipe we will use the transform feedback mechanism of the modern GPU to model cloth. **Transform feedback** is a special mode of modern GPU in which the vertex shader can directly output to a buffer object. This allows developers to do complex computations without affecting the rest of the rendering pipeline. We will elaborate how to use this mechanism to simulate cloth entirely on the GPU.

From the implementation point of view in modern OpenGL, transform feedback exists as an OpenGL object similar to textures. Working with transform feedback object requires two steps: first, generation of transform feedback with specification of shader outputs, and second, usage of the transform feedback for simulation and rendering. We generate it by calling the `glGetTransformFeedbacks` function and passing it the number of objects and the variable to store the returned IDs. After the object is created, it is bound to the current OpenGL context by calling `glBindTransformFeedback`, and its only parameter is the ID of the transform feedback object we are interested to bind.

Next, we need to register the vertex attributes that we want to record in a transform feedback buffer. This is done through the `glTransformFeedbackVaryings` function. The parameters this function requires are in the following order: the shader program object, the number of outputs from the shader, the names of the attributes, and the recording mode. Recording mode can be either `GL_INTERLEAVED_ATTRIBS` (which means that the attributes will all be stored in a single interleaved buffer object) or `GL_SEPARATE_ATTRIBS` (which means each attribute will be stored in its own buffer object). Note that the shader program has to be relinked after the shader output varyings are specified.

We also have to set up our buffer objects that are going to store the attributes' output through transform feedback. At the rendering stage, we first set up our shader and the required uniforms. Then, we bind out vertex array objects storing out buffer object binding. Next, we bind the buffer object for transform feedback by calling the `glBindBufferBase` function. The first parameter is the index and the second parameter is the buffer object ID, which will store the shader output attribute. We can bind as many objects as we need, but the total calls to this function must be at least equal to the total output attributes from the vertex shader. Once the buffers are bound, we can initiate transform feedback by issuing a call to `glBeginTransformFeedback` and the parameter to this function is the output primitive type. We then issue our `glDraw*` call and then call `glEndTransformFeedback`.

OpenGL 4.0 and above provide a very convenient function, `glDrawTransformFeedback`. We just give it out primitive type and it automatically renders our primitives based on the total number of outputs from the vertex shader. In addition, OpenGL 4.0 provides the ability to pause/resume the transform feedback object as well as outputting to multiple transform feedback streams.

For the cloth simulation implementation using transform feedback, this is how we proceed. We store the current and previous position of the cloth vertices into a pair of buffer objects. To have convenient access to the buffer objects, we store these into a pair of vertex array objects. Then in order to deform the cloth, we run a vertex shader that inputs the current and previous positions from the buffer objects. In the vertex shader, the internal and external forces are calculated for each pair of cloth vertices and then acceleration is calculated. Using Verlet integration, the new vertex position is obtained. The new and previous positions are output from the vertex shader, so they are written out to the attached transform feedback buffers. Since we have a pair of vertex array objects, we ping pong between the two. This process is continued and the simulation proceeds forward.

The whole process is well summarized by the following figure:

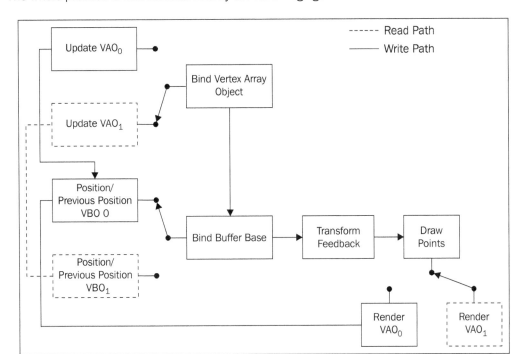

More details of the inner workings of this method are detailed in the reference in the *See also* section.

Getting ready

The code for this recipe is contained in the `Chapter8/TransformfeedbackCloth` folder.

How to do it...

Let us start the recipe by following these simple steps:

1. Generate the geometry and topology for a piece of cloth by creating a set of points and their connectivity. Bind this data to a buffer object. The vectors X and X_last store the current and last position respectively, and the vector F stores the force for each vertex:

```
vector<GLushort> indices;
vector<glm::vec4> X;
vector<glm::vec4> X_last;
vector<glm::vec3> F;
```

```cpp
indices.resize( numX*numY*2*3);
    X.resize(total_points);
    X_last.resize(total_points);
    F.resize(total_points);
    for(int j=0;j<=numY;j++) {
        for(int i=0;i<=numX;i++) {
            X[count] = glm::vec4( ((float(i)/(u-1)) *2-1)* hsize,
            sizeX+1, ((float(j)/(v-1) )* sizeY),1);
            X_last[count] = X[count];
        count++;
        }
    }
    GLushort* id=&indices[0];
    for (int i = 0; i < numY; i++) {
        for (int j = 0; j < numX; j++) {
            int i0 = i * (numX+1) + j;
            int i1 = i0 + 1;
            int i2 = i0 + (numX+1);
            int i3 = i2 + 1;
            if ((j+i)%2) {
                *id++ = i0; *id++ = i2; *id++ = i1;
                *id++ = i1; *id++ = i2; *id++ = i3;
            } else {
                *id++ = i0; *id++ = i2; *id++ = i3;
                *id++ = i0; *id++ = i3; *id++ = i1;
            }
        }
    }
    glGenVertexArrays(1, &clothVAOID);
    glGenBuffers (1, &clothVBOVerticesID);
    glGenBuffers (1, &clothVBOIndicesID);
    glBindVertexArray(clothVAOID);
    glBindBuffer (GL_ARRAY_BUFFER, clothVBOVerticesID);
    glBufferData (GL_ARRAY_BUFFER, sizeof(float)*4*X.size(),
    &X[0].x, GL_STATIC_DRAW);
    glEnableVertexAttribArray(0);
    glVertexAttribPointer (0, 4, GL_FLOAT, GL_FALSE,0,0);
    glBindBuffer(GL_ELEMENT_ARRAY_BUFFER, clothVBOIndicesID);
    glBufferData(GL_ELEMENT_ARRAY_BUFFER,
    sizeof(GLushort)*indices.size(), &indices[0], GL_STATIC_DRAW);
    glBindVertexArray(0);
```

2. Create two pairs of **vertex array objects** (**VAO**), one pair for rendering and another pair for update of points. Bind two buffer objects (containing current positions and previous positions) to the update VAO, and one buffer object (containing current positions) to the render VAO. Also attach an element array buffer for geometry indices. Set the buffer object usage parameter as GL_DYNAMIC_COPY). This usage parameter hints to the GPU that the contents of the buffer object will be frequently changed, and it will be read in OpenGL or used as a source for GL commands:

```
glGenVertexArrays(2, vaoUpdateID);
glGenVertexArrays(2, vaoRenderID);
glGenBuffers( 2, vboID_Pos);
glGenBuffers( 2, vboID_PrePos);
for(int i=0;i<2;i++) {
  glBindVertexArray(vaoUpdateID[i]);
  glBindBuffer( GL_ARRAY_BUFFER, vboID_Pos[i]);
  glBufferData( GL_ARRAY_BUFFER, X.size()* sizeof(glm::vec4),
      &(X[0].x), GL_DYNAMIC_COPY);
  glEnableVertexAttribArray(0);
  glVertexAttribPointer(0, 4, GL_FLOAT, GL_FALSE, 0, 0);
   glBindBuffer( GL_ARRAY_BUFFER, vboID_PrePos[i]);
  glBufferData( GL_ARRAY_BUFFER,
    X_last.size()*sizeof(glm::vec4), &(X_last[0].x),
    GL_DYNAMIC_COPY);
  glEnableVertexAttribArray(1);
  glVertexAttribPointer(1,  4, GL_FLOAT, GL_FALSE, 0,0);
}
 //set render vao
for(int i=0;i<2;i++) {
  glBindVertexArray(vaoRenderID[i]);
  glBindBuffer( GL_ARRAY_BUFFER, vboID_Pos[i]);
  glEnableVertexAttribArray(0);
  glVertexAttribPointer(0,  4, GL_FLOAT, GL_FALSE, 0, 0);
  glBindBuffer(GL_ELEMENT_ARRAY_BUFFER, vboIndices);
  if(i==0)
    glBufferData(GL_ELEMENT_ARRAY_BUFFER,
    indices.size()*sizeof(GLushort), &indices[0],
    GL_STATIC_DRAW);
}
```

3. For ease of access in the vertex shader, bind the current and previous position buffer objects to a set of buffer textures. The buffer textures are one dimensional textures that are created like normal OpenGL textures using the `glGenTextures` call, but they are bound to the `GL_TEXTURE_BUFFER` target. They provide read access to the entire buffer object memory in the vertex shader. The data is accessed in the vertex shader using the `texelFetchBuffer` function:

```
for(int i=0;i<2;i++) {
    glBindTexture( GL_TEXTURE_BUFFER, texPosID[i]);
    glTexBuffer( GL_TEXTURE_BUFFER, GL_RGBA32F, vboID_Pos[i]);
    glBindTexture( GL_TEXTURE_BUFFER, texPrePosID[i]);
    glTexBuffer(GL_TEXTURE_BUFFER, GL_RGBA32F, vboID_PrePos[i]);
}
```

4. Generate a transform feedback object and pass the attribute names that will be output from our deformation vertex shader. Make sure to relink the program.

```
glGenTransformFeedbacks(1, &tfID);
glBindTransformFeedback(GL_TRANSFORM_FEEDBACK, tfID);
const char* varying_names[]={"out_position_mass",
 "out_prev_position"};
glTransformFeedbackVaryings(massSpringShader.GetProgram(), 2,
 varying_names, GL_SEPARATE_ATTRIBS);
glLinkProgram(massSpringShader.GetProgram());
```

5. In the rendering function, bind the cloth deformation shader (`Chapter8/ TransformFeedbackCloth/shaders/Spring.vert`) and then run a loop. In each loop iteration, bind the texture buffers, and then bind the update vertex array object. At the same time, bind the previous buffer objects as the transform feedback buffers. These will store the output from the vertex shader. Disable the rasterizer, begin the transform feedback mode, and then draw the entire set of cloth vertices. Use the ping pong approach to swap the read/write pathways:

```
massSpringShader.Use();
glUniformMatrix4fv(massSpringShader("MVP"), 1, GL_FALSE,
glm::value_ptr(mMVP));
for(int i=0;i<NUM_ITER;i++) {
    glActiveTexture( GL_TEXTURE0);
    glBindTexture( GL_TEXTURE_BUFFER, texPosID[writeID]);
    glActiveTexture( GL_TEXTURE1);
    glBindTexture( GL_TEXTURE_BUFFER, texPrePosID[writeID]);
    glBindVertexArray( vaoUpdateID[writeID]);
    glBindBufferBase(GL_TRANSFORM_FEEDBACK_BUFFER, 0,
    vboID_Pos[readID]);
    glBindBufferBase(GL_TRANSFORM_FEEDBACK_BUFFER, 1,
    vboID_PrePos[readID]);
    glEnable(GL_RASTERIZER_DISCARD);    // disable rasrization
```

```
        glBeginQuery(GL_TIME_ELAPSED,t_query);
        glBeginTransformFeedback(GL_POINTS);
        glDrawArrays(GL_POINTS, 0, total_points);
        glEndTransformFeedback();
        glEndQuery(GL_TIME_ELAPSED);
        glFlush();
        glDisable(GL_RASTERIZER_DISCARD);
        int tmp = readID;
        readID=writeID;
        writeID = tmp;
    }
    glGetQueryObjectui64v(t_query, GL_QUERY_RESULT,
        &elapsed_time);
    delta_time = elapsed_time / 1000000.0f;
    massSpringShader.UnUse();
```

6. After the loop is terminated, bind the render VAO that renders the cloth geometry and vertices:

```
    glBindVertexArray(vaoRenderID[writeID]);
    glDisable(GL_DEPTH_TEST);
    renderShader.Use();
    glUniformMatrix4fv(renderShader("MVP"), 1, GL_FALSE,
    glm::value_ptr(mMVP));
    glDrawElements(GL_TRIANGLES, indices.size(),
    GL_UNSIGNED_SHORT,0);
    renderShader.UnUse();
    glEnable(GL_DEPTH_TEST);
    if(bDisplayMasses) {
       particleShader.Use();
       glUniform1i(particleShader("selected_index"),
       selected_index);
       glUniformMatrix4fv(particleShader("MV"), 1, GL_FALSE,
       glm::value_ptr(mMV));
       glUniformMatrix4fv(particleShader("MVP"), 1, GL_FALSE,
       glm::value_ptr(mMVP));
       glDrawArrays(GL_POINTS, 0, total_points);
       particleShader.UnUse();
    }
    glBindVertexArray( 0);
```

7. In the vertex shader, obtain the current and previous position of the cloth vertex. If the vertex is a pinned vertex, set its mass to 0 so it would not be simulated; otherwise, add an external force based on gravity. Next loop through all neighbors of the current vertex by looking up the texture buffer and estimate the internal force:

```
float m = position_mass.w;
vec3 pos = position_mass.xyz;
vec3 pos_old = prev_position.xyz;
vec3 vel = (pos - pos_old) / dt;
float ks=0, kd=0;
int index = gl_VertexID;
int ix = index % texsize_x;
int iy = index / texsize_x;
if(index ==0 || index == (texsize_x-1))
    m = 0;
vec3 F = gravity*m + (DEFAULT_DAMPING*vel);
for(int k=0;k<12;k++) {
    ivec2 coord = getNextNeighbor(k, ks, kd);
    int j = coord.x;
    int i = coord.y;
    if (((iy + i) < 0) || ((iy + i) > (texsize_y-1)))
        continue;
    if (((ix + j) < 0) || ((ix + j) > (texsize_x-1)))
        continue;
    int index_neigh = (iy + i) * texsize_x + ix + j;
    vec3 p2 = texelFetchBuffer(tex_position_mass,
    index_neigh).xyz;
    vec3 p2_last = texelFetchBuffer(tex_prev_position_mass,
    index_neigh).xyz;
    vec2 coord_neigh = vec2(ix + j, iy + i)*step;
    float rest_length = length(coord*inv_cloth_size);
    vec3 v2 = (p2- p2_last)/dt;
    vec3 deltaP = pos - p2;
    vec3 deltaV = vel - v2;
    float dist = length(deltaP);
    float    leftTerm = -ks * (dist-rest_length);
    float    rightTerm = kd * (dot(deltaV, deltaP)/dist);
    vec3 springForce = (leftTerm + rightTerm)*
    normalize(deltaP);
    F +=  springForce;
}
```

8. Using the combined force, calculate the acceleration and then estimate the new position using Verlet integration. Output the appropriate attribute from the shader:

```
vec3 acc = vec3(0);
if(m!=0)
    acc = F/m;
vec3 tmp = pos;
pos = pos * 2.0 - pos_old + acc* dt * dt;
pos_old = tmp;
pos.y=max(0, pos.y);
out_position_mass = vec4(pos, m);
out_prev_position = vec4(pos_old,m);
gl_Position = MVP*vec4(pos, 1);
```

How it works...

There are two parts of this recipe, the generation of geometry and identifying output attributes for transform feedback buffers. We first generate the cloth geometry and then associate our buffer objects. To enable easier access of current and previous positions, we bind the position buffer objects as texture buffers.

To enable deformation, we first bind our deformation shader and the update VAO. Next, we specify the transform feedback buffers that receive the output from the vertex shader. We disable the rasterizer to prevent the execution of the rest of the pipeline. Next, we begin the transform feedback mode, render our vertices, and then end the transform feedback mode. This invokes one step of the integration. To enable more steps, we use a ping pong strategy by binding the currently written buffer object as the read point for the next iteration.

The actual deformation is carried out in the vertex shader (`Chapter8/TransformFeedbackCloth/shaders/Spring.vert`). We first determine the current and previous positions. The velocity is then determined. The current vertex ID (`gl_VertexID`) is used to determine the linear index of the current vertex. This is a unique index of each vertex and can be used by a vertex shader. We use it here to determine if the current vertex is a pinned vertex. If so, the mass of 0 is assigned to it which makes this vertex immovable:

```
float m = position_mass.w;
vec3 pos = position_mass.xyz;
vec3 pos_old = prev_position.xyz;
vec3 vel = (pos - pos_old) / dt;
float ks=0, kd=0;
int index = gl_VertexID;
int ix = index % texsize_x;
int iy = index / texsize_x;
if(index ==0 || index == (texsize_x-1))
    m = 0;
```

Next, the acceleration due to gravity and velocity damping force is applied. After this, a loop is run which basically loops through all of the neighbors of the current vertex and estimates the net internal (spring) force. This force is then added to the combined force for the current vertex:

```
vec3 F = gravity*m + (DEFAULT_DAMPING*vel);

for(int k=0;k<12;k++) {
  ivec2 coord = getNextNeighbor(k, ks, kd);
  int j = coord.x;
  int i = coord.y;
  if (((iy + i) < 0) || ((iy + i) > (texsize_y-1)))
    continue;
  if (((ix + j) < 0) || ((ix + j) > (texsize_x-1)))
    continue;
  int index_neigh = (iy + i) * texsize_x + ix + j;
  vec3 p2 = texelFetchBuffer(tex_position_mass,
  index_neigh).xyz;
  vec3 p2_last = texelFetchBuffer(tex_prev_position_mass,
  index_neigh).xyz;
  vec2 coord_neigh = vec2(ix + j, iy + i)*step;
  float rest_length = length(coord*inv_cloth_size);
  vec3 v2 = (p2- p2_last)/dt;
  vec3 deltaP = pos - p2;
  vec3 deltaV = vel - v2;
  float dist = length(deltaP);
  float   leftTerm = -ks * (dist-rest_length);
  float   rightTerm = kd * (dot(deltaV, deltaP)/dist);
  vec3 springForce = (leftTerm + rightTerm)* normalize(deltaP);
  F +=  springForce;
}
```

From the net force, the acceleration is first obtained and then the new position is obtained using Verlet integration. Finally, the collision with the ground plane is determined by looking at the Y value. We end the shader by outputting the output attributes (`out_position` and `out_prev_position`), which are then stored into the buffer objects bound as the transform feedback buffers:

```
vec3 acc = vec3(0);
if(m!=0)
    acc = F/m;
vec3 tmp = pos;
pos = pos * 2.0 - pos_old + acc* dt * dt;
pos_old = tmp;
pos.y=max(0, pos.y);
```

```
out_position_mass = vec4(pos, m);
out_prev_position = vec4(pos_old,m);
gl_Position = MVP*vec4(pos, 1);
```

The shader, along with the transform feedback mechanism, proceeds to deform all of the cloth vertices and in the end, we get the cloth vertices deformed.

There's more...

The demo application implementing this recipe shows the piece of cloth falling under gravity. Several frames from the deformation are shown in the following figure. Using the left mouse button, we can pick the cloth vertices and move them around.

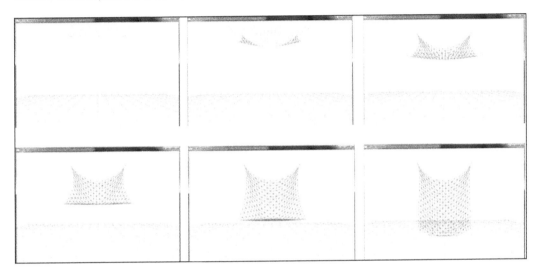

In this recipe we only output to a single stream. We can attach more than one stream and store results in separate buffer objects. In addition, we can have several transform feedback objects and we can pause/resume them as required.

See also

▶ Chapter 17, *Real-Time Physically Based Deformation Using Transform Feedback*, in *OpenGL Insights, AK Peters CRC press*

Implementing collision detection and response on a transform feedback-based cloth model

In this recipe, we will build on top of the previous recipe and add collision detection and response to the cloth model.

Getting ready

The code for this recipe is contained in the `Chapter8/ TransformFeedbackClothCollision` directory. For this recipe, the setup code and rendering code remains the same as in the previous recipe. The only change is the addition of the ellipsoid/sphere collision code.

How to do it...

Let us start this recipe by following these simple steps:

1. Generate the geometry and topology for a piece of cloth by creating a set of points and their connectivity. Bind this data to a buffer object as in the previous recipe.

2. Set up a pair of vertex array objects and buffer objects as in the previous recipe. Also attach buffer textures for easier access to the buffer object memory in the vertex shader.

3. Generate a transform feedback object and pass the attribute names that will be output from our deformation vertex shader. Make sure to relink the program again:

   ```
   glGenTransformFeedbacks(1, &tfID);
   glBindTransformFeedback(GL_TRANSFORM_FEEDBACK, tfID);
   const char* varying_names[]={"out_position_mass", "out_prev_
   position"};
   glTransformFeedbackVaryings(massSpringShader.GetProgram(), 2,
   varying_names, GL_SEPARATE_ATTRIBS);
   glLinkProgram(massSpringShader.GetProgram());
   ```

4. Generate an ellipsoid object by using a simple 4×4 matrix. Also store the inverse of the ellipsoid's transform. The location of the ellipsoid is stored by the translate matrix, the orientation by the rotate matrix, and the non-uniform scaling by the scale matrix as follows. When applied, the matrices work in the opposite order. The non-uniform scaling causes the sphere to compress in the Z direction first. Then, the rotation orients the ellipsoid such that it is rotated by 45 degrees on the X axis. Finally, the ellipsoid is shifted by 2 units on the Y axis:

   ```
   ellipsoid = glm::translate(glm::mat4(1),glm::vec3(0,2,0));
   ellipsoid = glm::rotate(ellipsoid, 45.0f ,glm::vec3(1,0,0));
   ```

```
ellipsoid = glm::scale(ellipsoid,
  glm::vec3(fRadius,fRadius,fRadius/2));
inverse_ellipsoid = glm::inverse(ellipsoid);
```

5. In the rendering function, bind the cloth deformation shader (`Chapter8/ TransformFeedbackClothCollision/shaders/Spring.vert`) and then run a loop. In each iteration, bind the texture buffers, and then bind the update vertex array object. At the same time, bind the previous buffer objects as the transform feedback buffers. Do the ping pong strategy as in the previous recipe.

6. After the loop is terminated, bind the render VAO and render the cloth:

```
glBindVertexArray(vaoRenderID[writeID]);
glDisable(GL_DEPTH_TEST);
renderShader.Use();
glUniformMatrix4fv(renderShader("MVP"), 1, GL_FALSE,
glm::value_ptr(mMVP));
glDrawElements(GL_TRIANGLES, indices.size(),
GL_UNSIGNED_SHORT,0);
renderShader.UnUse();
glEnable(GL_DEPTH_TEST);
if(bDisplayMasses) {
    particleShader.Use();
    glUniform1i(particleShader("selected_index"),
    selected_index);
    glUniformMatrix4fv(particleShader("MV"), 1, GL_FALSE,
    glm::value_ptr(mMV));
    glUniformMatrix4fv(particleShader("MVP"), 1, GL_FALSE,
    glm::value_ptr(mMVP));
    glDrawArrays(GL_POINTS, 0, total_points);
    particleShader.UnUse(); }
glBindVertexArray( 0);
```

7. In the vertex shader, obtain the current and previous position of the cloth vertex. If the vertex is a pinned vertex, set its mass to 0 so it would not be simulated, otherwise, add an external force based on gravity. Next, loop through all neighbors of the current vertex by looking up the texture buffer and estimate the internal force:

```
float m = position_mass.w;
vec3 pos = position_mass.xyz;
vec3 pos_old = prev_position.xyz;
vec3 vel = (pos - pos_old) / dt;
float ks=0, kd=0;
int index = gl_VertexID;
int ix = index % texsize_x;
int iy = index / texsize_x;
```

```
if(index ==0 || index == (texsize_x-1))
   m = 0;
vec3 F = gravity*m + (DEFAULT_DAMPING*vel);
for(int k=0;k<12;k++) {
    ivec2 coord = getNextNeighbor(k, ks, kd);
    int j = coord.x;
    int i = coord.y;
    if (((iy + i) < 0) || ((iy + i) > (texsize_y-1)))
        continue;
    if (((ix + j) < 0) || ((ix + j) > (texsize_x-1)))
        continue;
    int index_neigh = (iy + i) * texsize_x + ix + j;
    vec3 p2 = texelFetchBuffer(tex_position_mass,
    index_neigh).xyz;
    vec3 p2_last = texelFetchBuffer(tex_prev_position_mass,
    index_neigh).xyz;
    vec2 coord_neigh = vec2(ix + j, iy + i)*step;
    float rest_length = length(coord*inv_cloth_size);
    vec3 v2 = (p2- p2_last)/dt;
    vec3 deltaP = pos - p2;
    vec3 deltaV = vel - v2;
    float dist = length(deltaP);
    float   leftTerm = -ks * (dist-rest_length);
    float   rightTerm = kd * (dot(deltaV, deltaP)/dist);
    vec3 springForce = (leftTerm + rightTerm)*
    normalize(deltaP);
    F +=  springForce;
}
```

8. Using the combined force, calculate the acceleration and then estimate the new position using Verlet integration. Output the appropriate attribute from the shader:

```
vec3 acc = vec3(0);
if(m!=0)
    acc = F/m;
vec3 tmp = pos;
pos = pos * 2.0 - pos_old + acc* dt * dt;
pos_old = tmp;
pos.y=max(0, pos.y);
```

9. After applying the floor collision, check for collision with an ellipsoid. If there is a collision, modify the position such that the collision is resolved. Finally, output the appropriate attributes from the vertex shader.

```
vec4 x0 = inv_ellipsoid*vec4(pos,1);
vec3 delta0 = x0.xyz-ellipsoid.xyz;
float dist2 = dot(delta0, delta0);
if(dist2<1) {
   delta0 = (ellipsoid.w - dist2) * delta0 / dist2;
   vec3 delta;
   vec3 transformInv = vec3(ellipsoid_xform[0].x,
   ellipsoid_xform[1].x,
   ellipsoid_xform[2].x);
   transformInv /= dot(transformInv, transformInv);
   delta.x = dot(delta0, transformInv);
   transformInv = vec3(ellipsoid_xform[0].y,
   ellipsoid_xform[1].y,
   ellipsoid_xform[2].y);
   transformInv /= dot(transformInv, transformInv);
   delta.y = dot(delta0, transformInv);
   transformInv = vec3(ellipsoid_xform[0].z,
   ellipsoid_xform[1].z,
   ellipsoid_xform[2].z);
   transformInv /= dot(transformInv, transformInv);
   delta.z = dot(delta0, transformInv);
   pos +=  delta ;
   pos_old = pos;
}
out_position_mass = vec4(pos, m);
out_prev_position = vec4(pos_old,m);
gl_Position = MVP*vec4(pos, 1);
```

How it works...

The cloth deformation vertex shader has some additional lines of code to enable collision detection and response. For detection of collision with a plane, we can simply put the current position in the plane equation to find the distance of the current vertex from the plane. If it is less than 0, we have passed through the plane, in which case, we can move the vertex back in the plane's normal direction.

```
void planeCollision(inout vec3 x,  vec4 plane) {
   float dist = dot(plane.xyz,x)+ plane.w;
   if(dist<0) {
     x += plane.xyz*-dist;
   }
}
```

Simple geometric primitive, like spheres and ellipsoids, are trivial to handle. In case of collision with the sphere, we check the distance of the current position from the center of the sphere. If this distance is less than the sphere's radius, we have a collision. Once we have a collision, we push the position in the normal direction based on the amount of penetration.

```
void sphereCollision(inout vec3 x, vec4 sphere)
{
   vec3 delta = x - sphere.xyz;
   float dist = length(delta);
   if (dist < sphere.w) {
       x = sphere.xyz + delta*(sphere.w / dist);
   }
}
```

 Note that in the preceding calculation, we can avoid the square root altogether by comparing against the squared distance. This can provide significant performance gain when a large number of vertices are there.

For an arbitrarily oriented ellipsoid, we first move the point into the ellipsoid's object space by multiplying with the inverse of the ellipsoid's transform. In this space, the ellipsoid is a unit sphere, hence we can then determine collision by simply looking at the distance between the current vertex and the ellipsoid. If it is less than 1, we have a collision. In this case, we then transform the point to the ellipsoids world space to find the penetration depth. This is then used to displace the current position out in the normal direction.

```
vec4 x0 = inv_ellipsoid*vec4(pos,1);
vec3 delta0 = x0.xyz-ellipsoid.xyz;
float dist2 = dot(delta0, delta0);
if(dist2<1) {
delta0 = (ellipsoid.w - dist2) * delta0 / dist2;
vec3 delta;
vec3 transformInv = vec3(ellipsoid_xform[0].x, ellipsoid_xform[1].x,
ellipsoid_xform[2].x);
transformInv /= dot(transformInv, transformInv);
delta.x = dot(delta0, transformInv);
transformInv = vec3(ellipsoid_xform[0].y, ellipsoid_xform[1].y,
ellipsoid_xform[2].y);
transformInv /= dot(transformInv, transformInv);
delta.y = dot(delta0, transformInv);
transformInv = vec3(ellipsoid_xform[0].z, ellipsoid_xform[1].z,
ellipsoid_xform[2].z);
transformInv /= dot(transformInv, transformInv);
delta.z = dot(delta0, transformInv);
pos +=  delta ;
pos_old = pos;
}
```

There's more...

The demo application implementing this recipe renders a piece of cloth fixed at two points and is allowed to fall under gravity. In addition, there is an oriented ellipsoid with which the cloth collides as shown in the following figure:

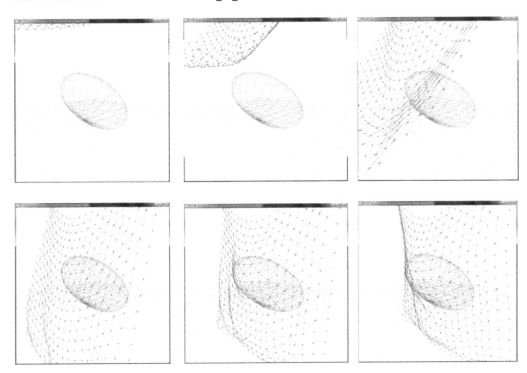

Although we have touched upon basic collision primitives, like spheres, oriented ellipsoids, and plane, more complex primitives can be implemented with the combination of these basic primitives. In addition, polygonal primitives can also be implemented. We leave that as an exercise for the reader.

See also

► MOVANIA Muhammad Mobeen and Lin Feng, "A Novel GPU-based Deformation Pipeline" in ISRN Computer Graphics, Volume 2012(2012), Article ID 936315, available online at http://downloads.hindawi.com/isrn/cg/2012/936315.pdf

Implementing a particle system using transform feedback

In this recipe, we will implement a simple particle system using the transform feedback mechanism. In this mode, the GPU bypasses the rasterizer and, later, the programmable graphics pipeline stages to feedback result to the vertex shader. The benefit from this mode is that using this feature, we can implement a physically-based simulation entirely on the GPU.

Getting ready

The code for this recipe is contained in the `Chapter8/TransformFeedbackParticles` directory.

How to do it...

Let us start this recipe by following these simple steps:

1. Set up two vertex array pairs: one for update and another for rendering. Bind two vertex buffer objects to each of the pairs, as was done in the previous two recipes. Here, the buffer objects will store the per-particle properties. Also, enable the corresponding vertex attributes:

```
glGenVertexArrays(2, vaoUpdateID);
glGenVertexArrays(2, vaoRenderID);
glGenBuffers( 2, vboID_Pos);
glGenBuffers( 2, vboID_PrePos);
glGenBuffers( 2, vboID_Direction);
for(int i=0;i<2;i++) {
  glBindVertexArray(vaoUpdateID[i]);
  glBindBuffer( GL_ARRAY_BUFFER, vboID_Pos[i]);
  glBufferData( GL_ARRAY_BUFFER, TOTAL_PARTICLES*
    sizeof(glm::vec4), 0, GL_DYNAMIC_COPY);
  glEnableVertexAttribArray(0);
  glVertexAttribPointer(0,  4, GL_FLOAT, GL_FALSE, 0, 0);
  glBindBuffer( GL_ARRAY_BUFFER, vboID_PrePos[i]);
  glBufferData( GL_ARRAY_BUFFER, TOTAL_PARTICLES*
  sizeof(glm::vec4), 0, GL_DYNAMIC_COPY);
  glEnableVertexAttribArray(1);
  glVertexAttribPointer(1,  4, GL_FLOAT, GL_FALSE, 0,0);
  glBindBuffer( GL_ARRAY_BUFFER, vboID_Direction[i]);
  glBufferData( GL_ARRAY_BUFFER, TOTAL_PARTICLES*
  sizeof(glm::vec4), 0, GL_DYNAMIC_COPY);
  glEnableVertexAttribArray(2);
```

```
glVertexAttribPointer(2,  4, GL_FLOAT, GL_FALSE, 0,0);
}
for(int i=0;i<2;i++) {
   glBindVertexArray(vaoRenderID[i]);
   glBindBuffer( GL_ARRAY_BUFFER, vboID_Pos[i]);
   glEnableVertexAttribArray(0);
   glVertexAttribPointer(0,  4, GL_FLOAT, GL_FALSE, 0, 0);
}
```

2. Generate a transform feedback object and bind it. Next, specify the output attributes from the shader that would be stored in the transform feedback buffer. After this step, relink the shader program:

```
glGenTransformFeedbacks(1, &tfID);
glBindTransformFeedback(GL_TRANSFORM_FEEDBACK, tfID);
const char* varying_names[]={"out_position",
"out_prev_position", "out_direction"};
glTransformFeedbackVaryings(particleShader.GetProgram(), 3,
varying_names, GL_SEPARATE_ATTRIBS);
glLinkProgram(particleShader.GetProgram());
```

3. In the update function, bind the particle vertex shader that will output to the transform feedback buffer and set the appropriate uniforms and update vertex array object. Note that to enable read/write access, we use a pair of vertex array objects such that we can read from one and write to another:

```
particleShader.Use();
glUniformMatrix4fv(particleShader("MVP"), 1, GL_FALSE,
glm::value_ptr(mMVP));
glUniform1f(particleShader("time"), t);
for(int i=0;i<NUM_ITER;i++) {
   glBindVertexArray( vaoUpdateID[readID]);
```

4. Bind the vertex buffer objects that will store the outputs from the transform feedback step using the output attributes from the vertex shader:

```
glBindBufferBase(GL_TRANSFORM_FEEDBACK_BUFFER, 0, vboID_
Pos[writeID]);
glBindBufferBase(GL_TRANSFORM_FEEDBACK_BUFFER, 1, vboID_
PrePos[writeID]);
glBindBufferBase(GL_TRANSFORM_FEEDBACK_BUFFER, 2, vboID_
Direction[writeID]);
```

5. Disable the rasterizer to prevent the execution of the later stages of the pipeline and then begin the transform feedback. Next, issue a call to the `glDrawArrays` function to allow the vertices to be passed to the graphics pipeline. After this step, end the transform feedback and then enable the rasterizer. Note that to correctly determine the amount of execution time needed, we issue a hardware query. Next, we alternate the read/write paths by swapping the read and write IDs:

```
glEnable(GL_RASTERIZER_DISCARD);
glBeginQuery(GL_TIME_ELAPSED,t_query);
glBeginTransformFeedback(GL_POINTS);
glDrawArrays(GL_POINTS, 0, TOTAL_PARTICLES);
glEndTransformFeedback();
glEndQuery(GL_TIME_ELAPSED);
glFlush();
glDisable(GL_RASTERIZER_DISCARD);
int tmp = readID;
readID=writeID;
writeID = tmp;
```

6. Render the particles using the render shader. First, bind the render vertex array object and then draw the points using the `glDrawArrays` function:

```
glBindVertexArray(vaoRenderID[readID]);
renderShader.Use();
glUniformMatrix4fv(renderShader("MVP"), 1, GL_FALSE,
glm::value_ptr(mMVP));
glDrawArrays(GL_POINTS, 0, TOTAL_PARTICLES);
renderShader.UnUse();
glBindVertexArray(0);
```

7. In the particle vertex shader, check if the particle's life is greater than 0. If so, move the particle and reduce the life. Otherwise, calculate a new random direction and reset the life to spawn the particle from the origin. Refer to `Chapter8/TransformFeedbackParticles/shaders/Particle.vert` for details. After this step, output the appropriate values to the output attributes. The particle vertex shader is defined as follows:

```
#version 330 core
precision highp float;
#extension EXT_gpu_shader4 : require
layout( location = 0 )  in vec4 position;
layout( location = 1 )  in vec4 prev_position;
layout( location = 2 )  in vec4 direction;
uniform mat4 MVP;
uniform float time;
const float PI = 3.14159;
```

```
const float TWO_PI = 2*PI;
const float PI_BY_2 = PI*0.5;
const float PI_BY_4 = PI_BY_2*0.5;


//shader outputs
out vec4 out_position;
out  vec4 out_prev_position;
out vec4 out_direction;


const float DAMPING_COEFFICIENT =  0.9995;
const vec3 emitterForce = vec3(0.0f,-0.001f, 0.0f);
const vec4 collidor = vec4(0,1,0,0);
const vec3 emitterPos = vec3(0);


float emitterYaw = (0.0f);
float emitterYawVar  = TWO_PI;
float emitterPitch  = PI_BY_2;
float emitterPitchVar = PI_BY_4;
float emitterSpeed = 0.05f;
float emitterSpeedVar = 0.01f;


int    emitterLife = 60;
int    emitterLifeVar = 15;


const float UINT_MAX = 4294967295.0;

void main() {
      vec3 prevPos = prev_position.xyz;
      int life = int(prev_position.w);
      vec3 pos  = position.xyz;
      float speed = position.w;
      vec3 dir = direction.xyz;
      if(life > 0) {
         prevPos = pos;
         pos += dir*speed;
         if(dot(pos+emitterPos, collidor.xyz)+ collidor.w <0) {
         dir = reflect(dir, collidor.xyz);
          speed *= DAMPING_COEFFICIENT;
         }
      dir += emitterForce;
      life--;
} else {
uint seed =   uint(time + gl_VertexID);
```

```
life = emitterLife + int(randhashf(seed++,
emitterLifeVar));
float yaw = emitterYaw + (randhashf(seed++,
emitterYawVar ));
float pitch = emitterPitch + randhashf(seed++,
emitterPitchVar);
RotationToDirection(pitch, yaw, dir);
float nspeed = emitterSpeed + (randhashf(seed++,
emitterSpeedVar ));
dir *= nspeed;
pos = emitterPos;
prevPos = emitterPos;
speed = 1;
}
out_position = vec4(pos, speed);
out_prev_position = vec4(prevPos, life);
out_direction = vec4(dir, 0);
gl_Position = MVP*vec4(pos, 1);
}
```

The three helper functions randhash, randhashf, and RotationToDirection are defined as follows:

```
uint randhash(uint seed) {
    uint i=(seed^12345391u)*2654435769u;
    i^=(i<<6u)^(i>>26u);
    i*=2654435769u;
    i+=(i<<5u)^(i>>12u);
    return i;
}

float randhashf(uint seed, float b) {
    return float(b * randhash(seed)) / UINT_MAX;
}

void RotationToDirection(float pitch, float yaw,
                         out vec3 direction) {
  direction.x = -sin(yaw) * cos(pitch);
  direction.y = sin(pitch);
  direction.z = cos(pitch) * cos(yaw);
}
```

How it works...

The transform feedback mechanism allows us to feedback one or more attributes from the vertex shader or geometry shader back to a buffer object. This feedback path could be used for implementing a physically-based simulation. This recipe uses this mechanism to output the particle position after each iteration. After each step, the buffers are swapped and, therefore, it can simulate the particle motion.

To make the particle system, we first set up three pairs of vertex buffer objects that store the per-particle attributes that we input to the vertex shader. These include the particle's position, previous position, life, direction, and speed. These are stored into separate buffer objects for convenience. We could have stored all of these attributes into a single interleaved buffer object. Since we output to the buffer object from our shader, we specify the buffer object usage as GL_DYNAMIC_COPY. Similarly, we set up a separate vertex array object for rendering the particles:

```
for(int i=0;i<2;i++) {
    glBindVertexArray(vaoUpdateID[i]);
    glBindBuffer( GL_ARRAY_BUFFER, vboID_Pos[i]);
    glBufferData( GL_ARRAY_BUFFER, TOTAL_PARTICLES*
    sizeof(glm::vec4), 0, GL_DYNAMIC_COPY);
    glEnableVertexAttribArray(0);
    glVertexAttribPointer(0,  4, GL_FLOAT, GL_FALSE, 0, 0);
    glBindBuffer( GL_ARRAY_BUFFER, vboID_PrePos[i]);
    glBufferData( GL_ARRAY_BUFFER,
    TOTAL_PARTICLES*sizeof(glm::vec4), 0, GL_DYNAMIC_COPY);
    glEnableVertexAttribArray(1);
    glVertexAttribPointer(1,  4, GL_FLOAT, GL_FALSE, 0,0);
    glBindBuffer( GL_ARRAY_BUFFER, vboID_Direction[i]);
    glBufferData( GL_ARRAY_BUFFER,
    TOTAL_PARTICLES*sizeof(glm::vec4), 0, GL_DYNAMIC_COPY);
    glEnableVertexAttribArray(2);
    glVertexAttribPointer(2,  4, GL_FLOAT, GL_FALSE, 0,0);
}
for(int i=0;i<2;i++) {
    glBindVertexArray(vaoRenderID[i]);
    glBindBuffer( GL_ARRAY_BUFFER, vboID_Pos[i]);
    glEnableVertexAttribArray(0);
    glVertexAttribPointer(0,  4, GL_FLOAT, GL_FALSE, 0, 0);
}
```

Next, we specify the shader output attributes that we would like to connect to the transform feedback buffers. We use three outputs, namely `out_position`, `out_prev_position`, and `out_direction`, which output the particle's current position, particle's previous position, and the particle's direction along with the particle's speed, current, and initial life, respectively. We specify that we would connect these to separate buffer objects:

```
glGenTransformFeedbacks(1, &tfID);
glBindTransformFeedback(GL_TRANSFORM_FEEDBACK, tfID);
const char* varying_names[]={"out_position", "out_prev_position",
"out_direction"};
glTransformFeedbackVaryings(particleShader.GetProgram(), 3, varying_
names, GL_SEPARATE_ATTRIBS);
glLinkProgram(particleShader.GetProgram());
```

One last step is the actual initialization of the transform feedback. We do so by first binding the particle vertex shader. Then, we pass the appropriate uniforms to the shader, which includes the combined modelview projection (MVP) matrix and the time (t):

```
particleShader.Use();
    glUniformMatrix4fv(particleShader("MVP"),1,GL_FALSE,
                    glm::value_ptr(mMVP));
    glUniform1f(particleShader("time"), t);
```

We then run a loop for the number of iterations desired. In the loop, we first bind the update vertex array object and assign the appropriate transform feedback buffer base indices:

```
for(int i=0;i<NUM_ITER;i++) {
    glBindVertexArray( vaoUpdateID[readID]);
    glBindBufferBase(GL_TRANSFORM_FEEDBACK_BUFFER, 0,
    vboID_Pos[writeID]);
    glBindBufferBase(GL_TRANSFORM_FEEDBACK_BUFFER, 1,
    vboID_PrePos[writeID]);
    glBindBufferBase(GL_TRANSFORM_FEEDBACK_BUFFER, 2,
    vboID_Direction[writeID]);
```

We then disable the rasterizer and begin the transform feedback. During this, we issue a `glDrawArrays` call to pass the vertices to the vertex shader. Next, we end the transform feedback and then restore the rasterizer. Finally, we swap the read/write pathways. In between, to estimate the amount of time needed for this process, we issue an OpenGL hardware timer query (`GL_TIME_ELAPSED`). This returns the total time in nanoseconds:

```
glEnable(GL_RASTERIZER_DISCARD);    // disable rasterization
  glBeginQuery(GL_TIME_ELAPSED,t_query);
    glBeginTransformFeedback(GL_POINTS);
      glDrawArrays(GL_POINTS, 0, TOTAL_PARTICLES);
    glEndTransformFeedback();
  glEndQuery(GL_TIME_ELAPSED);
```

```
    glFlush();
    glDisable(GL_RASTERIZER_DISCARD);
    int tmp = readID;
    readID=writeID;
    writeID = tmp;
}
// get the query result
glGetQueryObjectui64v(t_query, GL_QUERY_RESULT, &elapsed_time);
delta_time = elapsed_time / 1000000.0f;
particleShader.UnUse();
```

The main work of particle simulation takes place in the vertex shader (`Chapter8/TransformFeedbackParticles/shaders/Particle.vert`). After storing the initial attributes, the particle's life is checked. If the value is greater than 0, we update the position of the particle using the current direction of the particle and its speed. Next, we then check the particle for collision with the colliding plane. If there is a collision, we deflect the particle using the reflect GLSL function, passing it the particle's current direction of motion and the normal of the collidor. We also reduce the speed on collision. We then increase the direction of the particle using the emitter's force. We then reduce the life of the particle:

```
if(life > 0) {
    prevPos = pos;
    pos += dir*speed;
    if(dot(pos+emitterPos, collidor.xyz)+ collidor.w <0) {
        dir = reflect(dir, collidor.xyz);
        speed *= DAMPING_COEFFICIENT;
    }
    dir += emitterForce;
    life--;
}
```

If the life is less than 0, we reset the particle's direction of motion to a new random direction. We reset the life to a random value based on the maximum allowed value. The current and previous positions of the particle are reset to the emitter origin and finally, the speed is reset to the default value. We then output the output attributes:

```
else {
    uint seed =   uint(time + gl_VertexID);
    life = emitterLife + int(randhashf(seed++, emitterLifeVar));
    float yaw = emitterYaw + (randhashf(seed++, emitterYawVar ));
    float pitch=emitterPitch+randhashf(seed++,   emitterPitchVar);
    RotationToDirection(pitch, yaw, dir);
    float nspeed = emitterSpeed + (randhashf(seed++,
    emitterSpeedVar ));
    dir *= nspeed;
```

```
        pos = emitterPos;
        prevPos = emitterPos;
        speed = 1;
    }
    out_position = vec4(pos, speed);
    out_prev_position = vec4(prevPos, life);
    out_direction = vec4(dir, 0);
    gl_Position = MVP*vec4(pos, 1);
```

There's more...

The demo application for this recipe generates a simple particle system running entirely on the GPU using the transform feedback mechanism coupled with a vertex shader that writes to output attributes bound as transform feedback buffers. Running the demo application gives us the output as shown in the following figure:

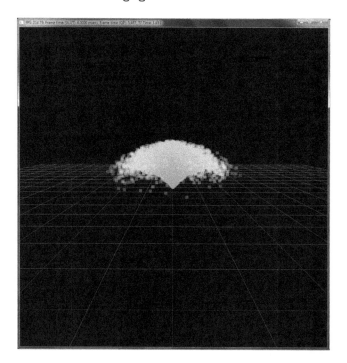

Note that for this demo, we render the particles as points of size 10 units. We could easily change the rendering mode to point sprites with size modified in the vertex shader to give the particles a different look. Also, we can also change the colors and blending modes to achieve various effects. In addition, we could achieve the same result by using one vertex buffer pair with interleaved attributes or two separate transform feedback objects. All of these variants should be straightforward to implement by following the guidelines laid out in this recipe.

We had already looked at a simple approach of simulating GPU-based particle systems using vertex shader in *Chapter 5, Mesh Model Formats and Particle Systems*, we will now detail pros and cons of each. In *Chapter 5* we presented a stateless particle system since all of the attributes (that is, position and velocity) were generated on the fly using the vertex ID, time, and basic kinematic equations on each particle vertex.

As the state of the particle is not stored, we cannot reproduce the same simulation every frame. Hence, collision detection and response are problematic, as we do not have any information of the previous state of the particle, which is often required for collision response. On the contrary, the particle simulation technique presented in this recipe uses a state-preserving particle system. We stored current and previous positions of each particle in buffer objects. In addition, we used transform feedback and a vertex shader for particle simulation on the GPU. As the state of the particle is stored, we can carry out collision detection and response easily.

See also

- OGLDev Tutorial on particle system using transform feedback at `http://ogldev.atspace.co.uk/www/tutorial28/tutorial28.html`

- *OpenGL 4.0 Shading Language Cookbook, Chapter 9, Animation and Particles*, the *Creating a particle system using transform feedback* section, *Packt Publishing*, 2011.

- *Noise based Particles, Part II* at *The Little Grasshopper*, `http://prideout.net/blog/?p=67`

Index

Gouraud shading 108
GPU-based path tracing
   implementing 213-217
GPU-based ray tracing
   implementing 207-211

H

half angle slicing
   used, for implementing volumetric lighting
      254-259
height map
   used, for implementing terrains 142-145

I

image
   area filtering, applying on 98-100
interleaved buffers
   used, for implementing Wavefront ® Obj
      model 157-161
intersectBox function 78

L

level of detail (LOD) 222
Lib3ds
   URL 156
Lift function 62
Lighthouse 3D view frustum culling
   URL, for tutorial 72
linear blend skinning (LBS) 262
local transform 266

M

main() function 12
Marching Cubes 253
Marching Tetrahedra (MT) algorithm
   about 248
   used, for implementing polygonal isosurface
      extraction 248-253
matrix palette skinning
   about 262
   used, for implementing skeletal animation
      262-271
Maya 141

MeshImport library
   URL 170
MeshSystem::mSkeletons array 263
mirror, with render-to-texture
   implementing, FBO used 89-92
modelview projection (MVP) 143
Move function 65

N

NVIDIA PhysX sdk 262

O

object picking
   implementing, color used 74, 75
   implementing, depth buffer used 72, 73
   implementing, scene intersection queries
      used 76-78
OBJ file specification
   URL 162
ObjLoader::Load function 157
ObjLoader object 157
offscreen rendering functionality 81
OnInit() function 12
OnMouseMove function 36
OnRender() function 12, 15
OnResize() function 12
OnShutdown() function 12, 26, 35, 54
OpenGL 4.3 8
OpenGL API 7
OpenGL shading language (GLSL) 7
OpenGL v2.0 7
OpenGL v3.0 8
OpenGL v3.3 55, 141
OpenGL v3.3 core profile
   setting up, on Visual Studio 2010 8-14
order independent transparency
   implementing, dual depth peeling used
      189-193
   implementing, front-to-back peeling used
      182-188

P

Pan function 65
particle system
   about 171

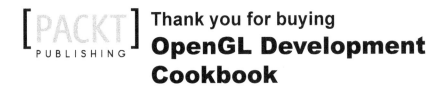

Thank you for buying
OpenGL Development Cookbook

About Packt Publishing

Packt, pronounced 'packed', published its first book "*Mastering phpMyAdmin for Effective MySQL Management*" in April 2004 and subsequently continued to specialize in publishing highly focused books on specific technologies and solutions.

Our books and publications share the experiences of your fellow IT professionals in adapting and customizing today's systems, applications, and frameworks. Our solution based books give you the knowledge and power to customize the software and technologies you're using to get the job done. Packt books are more specific and less general than the IT books you have seen in the past. Our unique business model allows us to bring you more focused information, giving you more of what you need to know, and less of what you don't.

Packt is a modern, yet unique publishing company, which focuses on producing quality, cutting-edge books for communities of developers, administrators, and newbies alike. For more information, please visit our website: www.packtpub.com.

Writing for Packt

We welcome all inquiries from people who are interested in authoring. Book proposals should be sent to author@packtpub.com. If your book idea is still at an early stage and you would like to discuss it first before writing a formal book proposal, contact us; one of our commissioning editors will get in touch with you.

We're not just looking for published authors; if you have strong technical skills but no writing experience, our experienced editors can help you develop a writing career, or simply get some additional reward for your expertise.

OpenGL 4.0 Shading Language Cookbook

ISBN: 978-1-84951-476-7   Paperback: 340 pages

Over 60 highly focused, practical recipes to maximize your use of the OpenGL Shading Language

1. A full set of recipes demonstrating simple and advanced techniques for producing high-quality, real-time 3D graphics using GLSL 4.0

2. How to use the OpenGL Shading Language to implement lighting and shading techniques

3. Use the new features of GLSL 4.0 including tessellation and geometry shaders

OpenCV 2 Computer Vision Application Programming Cookbook

ISBN: 978-1-84951-324-1   Paperback: 304 pages

Over 50 recipes to master this library of programming functions for real-time computer vision

1. Teaches you how to program computer vision applications in C++ using the different features of the OpenCV library

2. Demonstrates the important structures and functions of OpenCV in detail with complete working examples

3. Describes fundamental concepts in computer vision and image processing

4. Gives you advice and tips to create more effective object-oriented computer vision programs

Please check **www.PacktPub.com** for information on our titles

Thank you for buying
OpenGL Development Cookbook

About Packt Publishing

Packt, pronounced 'packed', published its first book "*Mastering phpMyAdmin for Effective MySQL Management*" in April 2004 and subsequently continued to specialize in publishing highly focused books on specific technologies and solutions.

Our books and publications share the experiences of your fellow IT professionals in adapting and customizing today's systems, applications, and frameworks. Our solution based books give you the knowledge and power to customize the software and technologies you're using to get the job done. Packt books are more specific and less general than the IT books you have seen in the past. Our unique business model allows us to bring you more focused information, giving you more of what you need to know, and less of what you don't.

Packt is a modern, yet unique publishing company, which focuses on producing quality, cutting-edge books for communities of developers, administrators, and newbies alike. For more information, please visit our website: www.packtpub.com.

Writing for Packt

We welcome all inquiries from people who are interested in authoring. Book proposals should be sent to author@packtpub.com. If your book idea is still at an early stage and you would like to discuss it first before writing a formal book proposal, contact us; one of our commissioning editors will get in touch with you.

We're not just looking for published authors; if you have strong technical skills but no writing experience, our experienced editors can help you develop a writing career, or simply get some additional reward for your expertise.

OpenGL 4.0 Shading Language Cookbook

ISBN: 978-1-84951-476-7   Paperback: 340 pages

Over 60 highly focused, practical recipes to maximize your use of the OpenGL Shading Language

1. A full set of recipes demonstrating simple and advanced techniques for producing high-quality, real-time 3D graphics using GLSL 4.0

2. How to use the OpenGL Shading Language to implement lighting and shading techniques

3. Use the new features of GLSL 4.0 including tessellation and geometry shaders

OpenCV 2 Computer Vision Application Programming Cookbook

ISBN: 978-1-84951-324-1   Paperback: 304 pages

Over 50 recipes to master this library of programming functions for real-time computer vision

1. Teaches you how to program computer vision applications in C++ using the different features of the OpenCV library

2. Demonstrates the important structures and functions of OpenCV in detail with complete working examples

3. Describes fundamental concepts in computer vision and image processing

4. Gives you advice and tips to create more effective object-oriented computer vision programs

Please check **www.PacktPub.com** for information on our titles

OpenSceneGraph 3 Cookbook

ISBN: 978-1-84951-688-4   Paperback: 426 pages

Over 80 recipes to show advanced 3D programming techniques with the OpenSceneGraph API

1. Introduce the latest OpenSceneGraph features to create stunning graphics, as well as integration with other famous libraries

2. Produce high-quality programs with short and familiar code

3. Enriched with a lot of code and the necessary screenshots

Unity Game Development Essentials

ISBN: 978-1-84719-818-1   Paperback: 316 pages

Build fully functional, professional 3D games with realistic environments, sound, dynamic effects, and more!

1. Kick start game development, and build ready-to-play 3D games with ease

2. Understand key concepts in game design including scripting, physics, instantiation, particle effects, and more

3. Test & optimize your game to perfection with essential tips-and-tricks

4. Written in clear, plain English, this book is packed with working examples and innovative ideas

Please check **www.PacktPub.com** for information on our titles